Praise for *The Over-[Scheduled Child]:*
Avoiding the Hyper-[Parenting Trap]

"In schools that are academically excellent but a Titanic of human values…the parents only contact with their children seems to be in the push, and they push them in every respect, not least into disastrous, premature sexuality. A large percentage of even the little ones are drugged (by prescription), and the parents are never at home but, rather, advancing their 'careers.' Let us hope that [*The Over-Scheduled Child*] slows some of these people down on their sprint to nowhere.…Thanks to the authors for reminding us about what really matters."
—Mark Helprin, author of *A Soldier of the Great War*

"[This] is an excellent book which should be read by every thinking parent. It raises awkward questions for all those who want the world for their children. Thoughtful and funny, it avoids the hectoring tone so many parenting books adopt while offering an unsparing look at the materialistic and often unhappy Me Me Me culture in which we now raise our children. But it also offers hope. We don't have to over-schedule our children to help them succeed. Ironically, they are probably better off if we don't."
—Joanna Coles, coauthor of *The Three of Us*

"Hyper-parents are born from the best intentions: They want their children to be above average. Or better. But too many of us are going overboard, as Alvin Rosenfeld and Nicole Wise document in this perceptive, well-researched book. If you want to truly help your children become the best they can be, it's crucial to establish a healthy balance between activities and family time. This book provides a template for creating and sustaining a happy, fulfilled family."
—Claire Martin, author of *The Nursing Mother's Problem Solver*

"[The book is] now the talk of the Manhattan playground."
—*The Times* (London)

"In our society, where parents feel pressured to enroll children in preschool while they are still in utero, this book is a refreshing splash of cool water.… A wake-up call to parents everywhere; recommended without reservation for public libraries."
—*Library Journal*

"Hyper-parenting is the hot new phrase.… [This book is] a well-timed call to examine parenting choices."
—*The Toronto Star*

"Rosenfeld and Wise understand a central truth about contemporary parenting: We feel so hounded by our fears of letting our children down, we overdo the 'to-do' of parenting at the great expense of the how 'to be' with our children. They have embraced the complexity of this widely-felt tension with a wisdom and affection that leaves the reader feeling more relieved than guilty, and in love again with the child, not the parenting. A wonderfully informative and restorative read for all parents."

—Kyle Pruett, M.D., author of *Fatherneed: Why Father Care Is as Essential as Mother Care for Your Child*

"Bruno Bettelheim, Dr. Rosenfeld's mentor, once said that the worst scars we inflict on our children are the ones on their backs from pushing them too hard. In this wise and clearly written book, Dr. Rosenfeld, a distinguished child psychiatrist, and Nicole Wise, an accomplished writer, examine the current parenting push. They expertly dissect our contemporary preoccupation with power parenting. They show us what is wrong with the 'isms': consumerism, perfectionism, protectionism. Our success as a technological and commercial culture has led us astray—we no longer trust our instincts, emotions, and relationships. We feel we have to plan, organize, and purchase the successful development of our children rather than enjoy its unfolding. In our desire to provide the best for our children, we manage rather than love them. This book provides both critique and guidance. Don't stay home without it."

—David Spiegel, M.D., Professor and Associate Chair, Department of Psychiatry and Behavioral Sciences, Stanford University School of Medicine, and coauthor of *Group Therapy for Cancer Patients*

"They offer the best perspective I've seen on the Potty Wars that rage between pediatrician T. Berry Brazelton ('wait until the child is ready') and parenting columnist John Rosemond ('train them before three')."

—*The Charlotte Observer*

"One of the most important parenting books I have seen in a decade! It provides an up-to-date and balanced review of developmental research and, more important, insight into how parents should interpret and use information about child-rearing. A must-read for all parents."

—Matia Finn-Stevenson, Ph.D., Research Scientist and Associate Director, Bush Center in Child Development and Social Policy, Yale University

"This is an important book that should be read by every parent. If people heed the wise approach contained here, they will regain the joy and satisfaction that should be at the heart of the parent/child relationship."

—Mira Kirshenbaum, author of *Parent-Teen Breakthrough: The Relationship Approach*

"[*The Over-Scheduled Child*] sends an urgently needed message to today's parents, who [themselves] are constantly feeling pressured to achieve, and who are, in turn, constantly pressuring their children to reach for more. It is a plea that parents everywhere should heed. Rosenfeld and Wise persuasively call for a return to authenticity, thoughtfulness, and wisdom in the day-to-day domain of child-rearing during these difficult times. It is meaningful reading for contemporary parents."

> —Lawrence Balter, Ph.D., Professor of Applied Psychology, New York University, and the author of *Who's in Control?: Dr. Balter's Guide to Discipline Without Combat*

"Thanks to [this book], parents can find relief from parent-pressure—the kind of pressure that is leading reasonable adults down irrational paths marked 'more is better.' As children become stress-dependent, so do their parents, leaving families with the expectation that misery equals success. To create a culture of positive, relaxed, caring relationships in families, thoughtful reflection about the ideas in [*The Over-Scheduled Child*] should be a daily habit for all parents."

> —Barbara C. Unell, coauthor, *20 Teachable Virtues*

"A soothing voice for the over-extended parents...Rosenfeld and Wise are right on target as they encourage parents to stop fretting, trust themselves, and enjoy their children."

> —Ann F. Caron, Ed.D., author of *Don't Stop Loving Me: A Reassuring Guide for Mothers of Adolescent Daughters; Strong Mothers, Strong Sons: Raising the Next Generation of Men;* and *Mothers and Daughters: Searching for New Connections*

"Dr. Alvin Rosenfeld, a highly respected, experienced, knowledgeable, empathetic psychiatrist, and Nicole Wise, an insightful journalist, have an important message in their new book—helping parents to restore confidence and re-learn to trust themselves. They remind us eloquently that knowledge and science can undermine parents' innate good will when they rely too much on child-rearing 'experts' to solve their problems. This book will convince today's overly stressed, harried parents—working too diligently but without joy or spontaneity—to stop striving for perfection and renew their faith in their own loving instincts."

> —Nancy Samalin, M.S., author of *Loving Your Child Is Not Enough* and director and parent educator of Parent Guidance Workshops in New York City

"This compelling, well-written book is a cautionary tale for parents who think that signing their children up for after-school activities and lessons is always in their best interest."

> —Susan Gilbert, contributor, *The New York Times* science section

The Over-Scheduled Child

Previous Publications by Alvin Rosenfeld, M.D.

The Art of the Obvious
(with Bruno Bettelheim)

*Healing the Heart: A Therapeutic Approach to
Disturbed Children in Group Care*
(with Saul Wasserman)

*The Somatizing Child: Diagnosis and Treatment of
Conversion and Somatization Disorders*
(with Elsa G. Shapiro)

A Dissenter in the House of God
(fiction)

The Over-Scheduled Child

Avoiding the Hyper-Parenting Trap

Alvin Rosenfeld, M.D.,
and Nicole Wise

Foreword by
Dr. Robert Coles

St. Martin's Griffin New York

www.stmartins.com

Library of Congress Cataloging-in-Publication Data

Rosenfeld, M.D., Alvin A.
    The over-scheduled child : avoiding the hyper-parenting trap /
Alvin Rosenfeld, M.D., and Nicole Wise ; foreword by Robert Coles.
        p.   cm.
    Includes bibliographical references and index.
    ISBN 0-312-20315-2 (hc)
    ISBN 0-312-26339-2 (pbk)
    1. Parenting—United States   2. Child rearing—United States.   3. Success in
    children.   1. Title: The over-scheduled child.   II. Wise, Nicole. III. Title.
HQ755.8.R672 2000
649'.1—dc21
                                                                          99-056670
                                                                          CIP

Originally published under the title *Hyper-Parenting: Are You Hurting Your Child by Trying Too Hard?*

10 9 8 7 6 5 4 3 2

To my beloved wife, Dorothy, who has made my life so rich, full, and very worthwhile, and my dear children, Lisa, Sam, and Mike, who have taught me far more about love, parenting, children, and myself than any textbook ever could.

—Alvin Rosenfeld, M.D.

To Ian, Devin, Bradley, and Holly Sloss, with all my love.

—Nicole Wise

Contents

Acknowledgments

Thanking all the relatives, friends, and patients who helped inspire this book and who encouraged me to finish it would take far too much space. However, I would like to single out a few people who were particularly helpful. I want to give posthumous thanks to my friend Bruno Bettelheim, whose thinking about children and what they need to grow well has become so interwoven with my own ideas that I can not say exactly where one ends and the other begins. I know that his ideas suffuse this book and also remember that he said that ideas belong to everyone, so I need not footnote every place where I draw from him. Friends read every part of it and made numerous helpful suggestions that have improved this book immeasurably. Debbie Cohen, Jeff DeTeso, Rabbi Joshua Hammerman, Robert Kavet, Drs. Arnie and Gail Korval, Lisa Lee Morgan, Patty Nizlik, Dr. Beth Sackler, Margie Smith, Bill and Elissa Tinsman, and Peter Winn all made wonderful comments along the way. I also want to thank my patients, who are an endless source of inspiration, ideas, and a sense of wonder about courage, hard work, and the human spirit and tenacity. Steve Cohen and our editor, Jennifer Weis, of St. Martin's have been our friends and advocates, for which I am deeply grateful. And without the support, love, and understanding of my beloved wife Dorothy and my wonderful children Lisa, Sam, and Mike, this book could never have been conceptualized, let alone finished.

—Alvin Rosenfeld, M.D.

I owe thanks to many more people than I can list, but I'd like to acknowledge by name those whose help has been especially meaningful. First and foremost, that would be my husband, Bob Sloss, not only for his support but also for the many ways he helped to make this a better book. My son Ian and daughter Devin provided invaluable tech support; they and their younger siblings, Brad and Holly, deserve my gratitude for understanding the odd paradox of having an all-too-often unavailable mom, distracted by writing a book that was, in every way, inspired by my deep love for them

I'd like to express sincere appreciation to Marie Faust Evitt and Maxene Mulford, not only for their astute editing but also their unflagging encouragement. Ed Barbieri, Sue Stoga, and Leona Lobell Torkelson each contributed a professional perspective I value. Maida Webster deserves credit for some ideas that have been central to this book (and more). My sisters, Valerie McDonald and Clair Wise, helped in more ways than they know; my parents, Jake and Linda Wise, have always encouraged me. I would also like to thank my good friends—Valerie Law, Mary March, Kiki Cook, Bess Wareing, and Vicki Harris—for reading various portions and versions, and for interest and support that have seemed boundless to me.

—Nicole Wise

Foreword

What follows is an important, forthright, engaging, and inviting book, lucidly written by two parents, Alvin Rosenfeld and Nicole Wise. They lend to the rest of us their considerable knowledge and psychological intelligence. They want to encourage us, who are bringing up children, to stop and think about what we want for our sons and daughters, not to mention ourselves, as their mothers and fathers. The authors are earnest and thoughtful, but wary as well; they know how eager some of us are for "advice," the more, the better, from our various "experts" and how much we crave tips, suggestions, recommendations, and authoritative remarks from on high, to the point that there is scarcely an aspect of family life today that has not been turned into an excuse for counsel, if not outright insistence, often offered in the name of science or medicine. Yet thankfully, here are two authors who refrain from glib pronouncements, who even embrace irony—in the sure knowledge that each of us, as adults or as children, deserve an overall and sustained acknowledgment of the psychological complexity of things, the puzzles and paradoxes, the surprises and disappointments that surely come our way, even as we try with all our might to get control of our lives, to anticipate the troubles ahead, to figure out how we might do better than we seem to be doing.

In a sense, then, this book is meant to be a companion for those of us who heed its call, attend its messages, which in their sum tell us to stop and think, not only of our children and of course ourselves as parents, but of the world in which we live: the social values and cultural customs, the attitudes of mind and heart that constantly exert their daily presence and that persuade us, tempt us, even turn us into people we may not want to be—all done, so often alas, "for the sake of the children," a phrase that haunts so many adults as they regard their youngsters at home or elsewhere. That is why, needless to say, we turn to a volume like this one. We do, indeed, want to do well by our children, to do our best for their sakes. On the other hand, we worry so often that our best, even *the* best, may well not be enough and so we look toward others—our friends and neighbors, the religious figures we know, the schoolteachers, and these days, men and women who put their ideas into books, physicians such as Dr. Rosenfeld, who is a child psychiatrist, or writers such as Nicole Wise, who has spent a lot of time trying to set down, in plain but compelling language, what is known about the young and those who try to rear them. These two contemporaries of ours reach out to us in the pages ahead: tell us what they have learned, what has worked for them, what worries them, as they have gone about fulfilling their parental duties, responsibilities, and, too, done their work observing others, similarly preoccupied.

The result is an extraordinary, compelling encounter that awaits the reader: a meeting between them and us, who are trying to bring up our children successfully but who sense, so often and well, the urgency we feel as we try to do all we can but who sense also the hazards that can bedevil us as we forget what it is we really want for our children when all is said and done. And that is what this book aims to help us do: Stop and think, stop and wonder, so that we, as members of a family and citizens of a nation, have some new ideas about where we hope to head and why.

—Robert Coles

Introduction

Several years ago, we began writing *Hyper-Parenting: Are You Hurting Your Child By Trying Too Hard?*, now being published as, *The Over-Scheduled Child: Avoiding the Hyper-Parenting Trap*. We knew that raising a family could be more pleasurable, and that our children would be better off in every way if parents pulled back a bit, slowed down, and rushed a little less. Our conviction has grown even stronger—and apparently, others agree with us.

Our book has received enormous attention, nationally and internationally. Journalists, educators, and professionals in the fields of child mental health and development almost uniformly applaud our position and support our mission to help families ease up on the intensity of—and turn down the volume on—the frenetic life so many of us had been living. Our term, "hyper-parenting," is now in widespread use in the English lexicon, recently heard even in a British Parliamentary debate!

Formerly frenzied parents have written to thank us, crediting our book with showing them how to be happier with their families and more comfortable with their children. One mom wrote, "Thanks for giving me permission to exhale." Simultaneously and independently, the "Families First" program started by University of Minnesota Professor,

Bill Doherty in Wayzata, Minnesota, has mobilized one community to put these same principles into action, gaining national attention for the effort.

Yet one reaction surprised us. We heard, again and again, from readers who loved our book, believed in its message and suggestions, and wanted to pass it along to friends and family, that they were afraid they might hurt their feelings. It was our title, not our message, that gave pause—but we were dismayed at the idea that any aspect of our book would raise parental guilt and anxiety. More than anything, we want to encourage parents, to help them to relax, trust themselves and their children, and take more enjoyment from everyday life. As parents who have wrestled with these issues ourselves (we call ourselves hyper-parents in partial recovery), we know from personal experience that doing less actually gets us more. It moves us far closer to the goal we all are aiming at in the first place—which is to raise happy, healthy, emotionally sound, and successful children.

Our title has changed but our message remains the same. The phenomenon we identified has two sides, the parents and the children. Since the media has been focusing on over-scheduled children, the ones whose parents are hyper-parents, we decided that a new title would better reflect the book's supportive message in a jargon that was being used with increasing frequency.

Our book addresses a way of life that is undermining contemporary family life, not only here in the United States, but in many other countries. Good, involved parenting has turned into a relentless to-do list. Over-scheduling and hyper-parenting reflect the ways today's parenting magazines, newspapers, Web sites, and news programs urge us to raise our families. The media gives a nod to the need for down time, "letting kids be kids," but the agglomeration of all the articles and news reports we read and hear pressure us in the opposite direction. Barraged with messages from experts who tell us how to raise our children right, we well-meaning mothers and fathers end up worrying about matters big and small, striving to micro-manage every detail of our kids' lives, sometimes starting before birth.

They lead us to wonder whether a child who does not hear Mozart in infancy can still be mathematically astute. They convince us that if our eighteen-month-old is not enrolled in gymnastics, she may not develop grace and comfort with her own body, and will end up tripping and stumbling through life. They make us worry that if we deny our infant swimming lessons, he might drown.

We've heard from many parents who tried to clear their calendars, and were made to feel selfish by families whose kids managed, somehow, to juggle several sports, flute lessons, and advanced French classes in one season. Are they better parents than us? Will their children have an advantage over ours, now and in the future?

As a generation, we contemporary parents desperately want to do right by our kids. We buy into this message for the best reasons. Many adults report that they were raised with benign neglect. They still struggle with pain and insecurity, from feeling that their parents were indifferent to them. Aiming for the opposite, committed to letting their children know how important they are to them, these parents sacrifice adult interests to make their kids' lives central.

But is there any scientific evidence at all that supports this intensive style of parenting?

Should parents really have to agonize over every tiny detail of a child's life, weighing what birth month bodes best for academic success when we bring a child into the world, and fretting about what the teacher will think of our family if a preschooler brings his laser-squirt gun to show-and-tell? Is it really advisable for parents to run drills on afternoons and weekends to make absolutely sure a nine-year-old is a starter on her softball team, or care so much about the outcome of a grade school soccer game that they verbally abuse the teenage ref after a bad call? How did our society get to a place where childhood recreation has become so intense that a Massachusetts father kills another in a fight over an adolescent hockey game? Most important, what will it take to get ourselves back to a balanced, sane position so everyone in the family, parents included, is happier with life? Those questions are what this book is about.

We all want the best for our children. More often than not we put their happiness ahead of our own—way ahead, in fact. We become heavily invested in their childhood at the expense of our own lives—and that isn't healthy, for them *or* us. We adults have done childhood already: We need to let our kids have their own turn, so they can learn and grow from the good and not-so-great experiences in their lives, so they can have the free time to develop their inner lives, to imagine and create new worlds all their own. That is, after all, also an important part of what childhood is about.

As we work so hard to craft for our kids our vision of the perfect childhood, we have lost sight of that essential truth. In *The Over-Scheduled Child: Avoiding the Hyper-Parenting Trap*, we take a hard look at how hyper we, as a generation, are pressed to be about parenting. We identify the external and internal forces that shape our hyper-parenting, and point out some places we can make changes. We show how, surprisingly, spending unproductive time with our kids turns out to be the best, most constructive thing we can do. We provide evidence of how the whole family benefits when parents take back their own lives, and give children a chance to live theirs.

Our hyper-parenting is born of the best intentions. We
contemporary parents are nothing if not committed. Being
good parents is the most important thing in the world to
us: nothing matters more. As this country's most educated
generation ever, we want to be truly well informed about
how to raise children right so that we can do a terrific job.

This is how we have ended up paying such close attention to advice in books, articles, on the radio and television. Some conscientious parents seek out every bit
of information they can find—subscribing to several parenting magazines, investing in a library of books on development, attending workshops, seminars, and lectures.
Uncertain that they have inside themselves the resources
and experience required to raise children right, many are
convinced that all this information is just as crucial to how
families operate as the brochures bundled with an expensive new laptop computer are to its proper setup and use. If
they could just digest it all, they figure, then they would
know exactly how to get their much-loved child to function at his or her maximum performance level.

Despite our own experience as former children, many
parents view childhood as uncharted territory. Children
seem so mysterious; what really makes them tick? It seems
as if good parents should know everything about their children's lives, from conception on. Out of uncertainty and
fear that they might make a terrible mistake, many parents
(and especially first-time ones) carefully scrutinize a child's
every step. They consult child-development books as if
they were technical manuals, gauging developmental

timetables and panicking if a child's progress seems a bit off schedule. Seen through this anxious lens, analyzed in light of our hopeful aspirations for a child's success in life, many milestones come to seem merely like stepping stones to the next: He's crawling! When do you suppose he will begin to walk? We get ambitious. She knows her shapes: Didn't I read somewhere that such early recognition can be a sign of giftedness in the area of visual-spatial relationships? Can we enhance her natural abilities? Maybe it is time to start working to teach her to draw a circle.

Many parents fret when a child's development is not somewhere near the top of the curve. If a child is "average" at, let's say, seventeen months, they feel mortified and worry that he or she is destined to a low-prestige, low-paying career in some line of work they consider undesirable. If, on some particular milestone, a child is nearer the tail end of the development curve, they wonder—and perhaps ask their pediatrician—whether they should get a specialist's evaluation.

Parents often are the first ones to notice when their child is having difficulty, and a pediatrician is certainly the right professional to ask for that sort of advice. For some kids, a little extra help early on can make all the difference. This book is about a different sort of problem. We authors are talking to the vast majority of parents whose children are wonderfully normal and healthy. We hope to bring a different perspective and balance, a new sort of understanding into the lives of the many parents who have become persuaded that (as our generation is fond of saying) parenting is a full-time job. We want to debunk the contemporary myth that the natural sequence of child development represents mediocrity and would benefit, not just from an enriched environment, but from a huge and synthetic boost.

The fact is, parenting should *not* take all our time, money, and energy. Virtually all of us in the American middle class and above are already providing our children with an enriched environment. Compared to us, most of the world's children live in abject poverty. Relatively speaking, our lives are charmed. Yet rather than feeling grateful, many of us feel anxious, precarious, and vulnerable, completely out of touch with the fact that in many ways, we are among the most fortunate people on earth. Somehow, we have come to be afraid of our children, to mistrust their potential and our own instincts. We fear that a misstep in raising them, a momentary lapse of judgment or vigilance, might be traumatic and emotionally scarring—or, worse yet, serve as the trigger that turns a sweet child into a sociopathic monster. Our uncertainty deprives them of the security and confidence they deserve.

American parents have been persuaded that average, typical, or even "normal" is no longer good enough. Every article and news report reinforces that. To prepare children adequately for the impossibly competitive new millennium, parents are exhorted to give them an edge over the competition. The media uses strong, active verbs to convince parents that they not only can but should work hard at helping a child excel: "*Make* Your Baby Smarter," *PARENTING* magazine urges. "*Build* a Better Boy" advises *Newsweek*. It is as though children were born mediocre and by tinkering with their valves and fine-tuning their design to help them function at the optimal level, parents could engineer them into superachievers.

It seems reasonable, given the spectacular scientific and technological progress we hear about on a daily basis. Why not apply science—all those new facts that child and adolescent psychiatrists, developmental psychologists, pediatricians, and academic and medical researchers are learning—to speed up children's development, to accelerate them into more *productive* lives? Distraught at the thought that one ounce of a child's potential might go untapped, many well-meaning parents believe that if a little of something is good, a lot must be great (an approach that gets you into big trouble with, say, vitamins or medications). If a black-and-white mobile focuses an infant's attention, wouldn't an entire high-contrast nursery *really* boost his brainpower?

Insidiously, this attitude leaks into other areas of life. Parents often feel that a child who is not constantly active, whose mind is not challenged 24–7, will become bored and lazy. So out of anxiety and ambition, they push and press on. If a preschooler knows her ABCs, shouldn't we get her to start reading? Once she masters simple words like C-A-T and R-U-N, why not step up to a basic book? And if she can handle that, well, maybe we should find an accelerated school for gifted children that . . .

Although some parents push more and others less, and some children (particularly firstborns) just seem to push themselves from day one, many among us feel uncertain as to what this role of "parent" really means and how to fulfill it responsibly. Most of us planned our children very carefully (the first two, anyway). We spend considerable time fulfilling our obligations to them, often at great personal cost. Not only do we try to help our children grow well physically, which parents have traditionally worked at, but we also try to help them grow well emotionally, something past generations considered at best a lucky by-product of meeting their obligations for food, shelter, and schooling.

But many contemporary parents are tripping over these good intentions. Many sense, on a gut level at least, that something has gone very wrong with the way we are raising kids today, in a life of constant pressure and perpetual motion. Though they acknowledge that something is amiss, they have a hard time taking the idea any further. After all, everyone else is living the same way. And who can hear the soft voice of reason in the midst of a stampede?

We all know there is more to the good life than where we live and what we drive. Yet slowing down to contemplate what is the right path for us might cost us—and worse, our kids—the race (even though we can't really say what we are racing toward, where the finish line is, and what you ultimately get for winning first prize). The very thought of sitting quietly and contemplating the meaning of life fills us with anxiety; it's easier to keep busy. So we keep going. How can you *not* accept that invitation to have your eleven year old dive for the county swim team? What if that one activity turned out to be the place where he or she could really excel—gain confidence, win a few medals, and maybe even someday garner one of those elusive and exclusive athletic scholarships? Despite the fact that the aggressive schedule of weekday practices and weekend meets all over the state and sometimes even farther will stretch the family to near breaking point, we sigh and sign on. When it comes to making life good for our children, we are not quite sure where reasonable ends and ridiculous begins.

No wonder we are all exhausted!

Parents today want to raise "good" kids but are terrified that their children might end up drinking, using drugs, or parading around town with blue hair and tongue rings. Looking at the pressures children face today—sex, drugs, violence—and the values they take in from television, movies, and music, we yearn for a more innocent time, like when we were growing up (though it is a good bet that our own parents didn't see the sex, drugs, and rock 'n' roll of the sixties, seventies, and eighties as particularly innocent). We want reassurance that our earnest, persistent efforts will provide insurance against all potentially bad outcomes. We're willing to work as hard as we have to to get the happy ending.

So it is no wonder we feel annoyed at being mercilessly lampooned in books, magazines, movies, and television programs; at caricatures like the Power Mom tooling around the suburbs in her sport utility vehicle sipping Starbucks, zealously contemplating weighty matters like which local gymnastics programs will give her agile four year old the best edge in future competition. Who wouldn't resent being sneered at as superficial and out of touch, particularly by those who've never walked a mile in our Nikes? Aren't we parents today the ones spending our few free moments working to prevent the century-old children's theater from closing down or inviting an inner-city child to vacation in the country for a few weeks each summer?

But the criticism does hit a nerve. Most of us really do know such people. We talk to "them" as we sit on a playground bench watching the kids play in the sandbox, overhear them in the supermarket. We recognize the many variations on the theme. We find it ridiculous that play dates with the five year old down the block must be booked three weeks in advance because the child's schedule is so full. We mock the guy in the next office who hired a dollar-a-minute "stroke coach" to strengthen his seven year old's freestyle. He says he has no choice or his talented child will fall behind the competition. At *seven?* we joke sarcastically. Then we hate ourselves when we ask him, a bit embarrassed, "Does it work?" We gossip about the couple down the road, so insanely competitive that they've retained an educational consultant to make sure their middle schooler is on track for the Ivy League. And then we sheepishly wonder, "How do they think his chances look? What extracurricular activities do they recommend he take on? How much community service is enough?"

As much as we reject this stereotype, many of us modern parents are horrified to find ourselves wondering, at times, if we really are all that different from those power parents—or would be, if only we could afford it. We may even believe that those parents, the ones willing to do whatever it takes, are doing a better job than we are. If an educational consultant could substantially improve our child's odds of getting into an elite college, how many of us would feel comfortable *not* shelling out the big bucks? Look at the way we react—and we authors have done it too—when our own children underwhelm us, as they inevitably will at times. Say, when we find ourselves fretting because a first grader—above grade level in almost every category in his report card—is only average in "organization" of his written work, whatever that means in first grade. Who is satisfied with an "average" child? Or when we find ourselves recrafting an eighth grader's paragraphs, so an essay will read just a bit more smoothly.

Maybe we can make the case that academic achievement warrants a parent's serious attention. But what's with the activities—the toddler craft classes, the day-long drama camps, the six-day-a-week gymnastics programs? Can't kids just play? Not without structure and supervision, it seems. Today everything is organized, starting at younger and younger ages. Especially sports! It has become unusual to see a child just throwing a baseball with a buddy or actually climbing on one of those expensive wooden swing sets that are planted in backyards in every suburban community. Who has the time?

If a child claims to be tired after school, parents worry about his motivation level and exhort him to find a "passion" so he doesn't end up a dullard at life. Meanwhile, they've overlooked or taken for granted the fact that this child may already be one of the most popular, or creative, or funniest kids in his fifth-grade classroom. Apparently eight hours of work a day is not enough for children.

Of course it is good to broaden kids' perspective and to introduce them to activities they may enjoy. Exercise is essential, for kids and adults. The competitive colleges do seek students who excel at one activity but are somehow, simultaneously, well-rounded. But with college over a decade away, is there any benefit to frustrating four year olds by enrolling them in programs that polish their soccer skills, when anyone can see they lack the developmental skills to master the game? How many of us played team sports before we knew how to read? We were plenty stimulated and motivated kicking a ball, playing catch or hide-and-seek, or just swinging and climbing jungle gyms with the kids in the neighborhood; we didn't have to travel 150 miles to face a group from another state who played "on the same level."

We underestimate the toll this fast-track lifestyle takes on our children, even the ones who really might have a shot at the big-time. If a twelve year old gymnast has Olympic potential, would it really benefit her to move a thousand miles away to live with some master coach and see her family only on occasional weekends? Is a schedule of sixteen hours a week of skating lessons good for *any* adolescent? These frenetic schedules and intense and competitive activities may indeed help our children hone their athletic abilities, but will they help them grow into happy, well-adjusted adults who will have the skills they need to build satisfying lives and families of their own?

Childhood has become a serious business, no question, but grown-up life is not exactly a spa getaway either. The adult world has always had its pressures, but all this rushing around, trying to give the kids everything in addition to doing all the other things adults have to do to keep a home and family afloat is making many parents miserable. When, many wonder, will it be *our* turn? Is a parent's lot all sacrifice till the geriatrician becomes our personal physician? We say we don't mind, but if we really were so sanguine we'd spend less of our social time whining about chauffeuring our children from early morning swim practices to late-night ice time. If we resent this lifestyle so much, it is a good bet that it is also stressful for our children, attuned to our annoyance, yet unquestionably needing our help. They're tuned into how we feel—all kids are. Think how it looks to them, the supposed beneficiaries of all this rushing around: If you were a child watching such stressed-out parents, would this be a lifestyle you'd choose to emulate? Or might you consider dropping out of the rat race, so you can relax? Does any family benefit from a schedule that requires nonstop action from 6:00 A.M. to 8:00 P.M. seven days a week?

This way of life is too costly . . . in financial terms, certainly, but in emotional terms as well.

Few of us hyper-parent in the extreme, in part because it can be an awfully expensive and time-consuming pursuit. But many of us give it our best shot. Without signing on the dotted line or seriously considering the merit of the lifestyle we are subscribing to, we raise our children in an amazingly intense and competitive manner. People who believe in education have always taken an interest in their children's college plans, but the age of intellectual intensity has plummeted. Few of us remain iconoclasts when it comes to our kids: Even Don Imus, cynic of the century, said on-air that he is sending his infant to "school" to learn a foreign language! Preschool curriculums have become a weighty matter. Lots of families are deadly serious about extracurricular activities at the tumblebug stage; most would consider themselves truly negligent if they weren't paying close attention to enrichment by the early elementary years.

Many parents are acting as though life can be planned and children programmed, the ultimate goal being admission to a prestigious college and the supposed success that invariably follows. But let's not forget that Ted Kaczynski, the Unabomber, was a Harvard grad; that an awful lot of top school-cum–Wall Street criminals are currently playing golf behind bars. And that plenty of folks who went to City College or State U moved on to write best-sellers, head up corporations, or make their millions in other ways. Not that making millions makes people happy, or ought to be a child's life goal anyway. Lots of kids dream of growing up to become a police officer, a teacher, or a poet. It is a big world! We needn't all be investment bankers.

It says a lot about our priorities that many parents today put more energy into teaching children how to serve a tennis ball than how to serve humanity. They work harder at making sure children are skilled at public speaking than at teaching them to communicate openly and honestly with one another. Should our goal be preparing our kids to get into the college of their choice or to live the *life* of their choice? They are not necessarily one and the same.

We parents may believe, deep in our hearts, that we understand what is important in life, yet so much of our energy goes toward the things that are not! No question, education is valuable and important. Yet true success in life actually has little to do with the diploma that hangs on your wall. Good connections can certainly help to open doors that may be heavier and stickier for others to push through. In the end, though, what makes a life meaningful grows out of the ability to build a productive and satisfying life, to have friends you feel close to, to forge a marriage and life with someone you cherish. It emerges from doing work that is meaningful to you and creating a family that you love and that loves you back, even when things aren't going that well.

That's true whether you have that very helpful old-boy network to fall back on, or not. We need to get back to the basics in our lives. As one man, a bank president in a large southern city, noted, with some surprise, the greatest moment in his life, his fondest memory thus far, is when his teenage son said, "I love you, Dad," and the father knew that he meant it.

It is scary to look inside our souls, to ask ourselves, "What do I really believe in? What do I really want from this life?" The answers from the past no longer work so well. It is not that we are frivolous. Anything but! If anything, we take life too seriously for our own good. Unsure of what we value personally, we find it easier to follow the herd. We act as though it is our job to script the future. For most families, this deadly earnestness is born of the best intentions . . . but we all know which road is paved with those.

These are the issues we will be discussing in the pages ahead. Our first chapter will give an overview of what hyper-parenting is and the forces that have driven it in our generation. The second discusses how we are deluded into believing we have great control over the children we have and how that leads us to begin working overtime at raising them right even before they are born. Chapters 3 and 4 will demonstrate how the folks with goods and advice to sell get us to believe we need them, their products, and their "wisdom" if we are to be good parents. Subsequent chapters will address such topics as micromanagement, perfectionism, and competition. Chapter 8 looks at the toll hyper-parenting takes on the grown-ups in the house. And our final chapter, "What Really Matters," explores what it is we have actually been looking for all along—and how to get it.

We authors know what this life is like. We, too, are high achievers, working parents, professionals who work long hours at demanding careers. We live in a small city with plenty of upscale neighborhoods in an astonishingly wealthy county. Between our families, we have three religions and are raising seven children. We spend our "off" hours watching these kids perform in plays, gymnastics meets, and at soccer games; we spend our evenings car-pooling and carping about homework. No question, we've been there and done that. We are struggling with the same issues and don't claim to be cured completely—some days it seems like we are hardly cured at all. But we have made some changes in our lives, our schedules, and most particularly in our outlooks that have had a pretty big payoff.

Lately we are hyper-parenting less and enjoying life more, as are our entire families, and that is what this book is really about.

We are also professionals. Alvin Rosenfeld, M.D., is a child, adolescent, and adult psychiatrist practicing in New York City and Greenwich, Connecticut. He was on the medical faculty at Harvard, and headed the Stanford University School of Medicine's child psychiatry training program. He has worked extensively with children, adolescents, and adults, in both affluent and indigent families. Nicole Wise is a freelance journalist who has specialized in writing about family life for more than a decade.

In every chapter of this book, we have tried to illustrate the points we are making with vignettes and anecdotes. Each is drawn from real life, but has been altered to protect confidentiality. These stories of family life today may be interpreted in a variety of ways, in relation to your own experiences, values, aspirations, and lifestyle.

However interesting, it should be noted that these vignettes and anecdotes serve simply to introduce and illustrate ideas. What we authors really hope to do is stimulate a process in which parents will ask themselves what they really want for their families—and then will begin to make the small changes that will help them get there. We want to help parents to look at their family lives in a different way so that they can come to grips with a problem that is impacting the happiness and even health of every family member.

This means we must ask ourselves some difficult questions. To succeed in life, does every child really need the level of intense involvement that has come to characterize family life in America today? Does unquestioning acceptance of this fast-track lifestyle indicate a bankruptcy of common sense? Are all American families so far gone in this madness that, in our blindness, we simply see no alternative? Or is there, perhaps, a better, easier, more balanced and rewarding way for families to live?

We believe there can be. By learning to recognize hyper-parenting for what it is and starting to apply the brakes to our insanely fast-moving lives, we will not only immediately improve the quality of daily life for our families, but we also will improve the odds for happiness in the future. In the meantime, we can probably save time and money as well by becoming both more intelligent consumers of all the kiddy stuff hyped our way and educated assessors of advice and edicts we can't help but absorb as we move around in our media-drenched world. And our kids may get back their childhood, a gift most of them would be extremely grateful for.

By making small but significant changes in the way we live our lives, both parents and children will benefit—not only now, but in the years to come. Our relationship with our children will become more genuine, more connected, and less frantic . . . which is really what most of us have wanted all along.

—Alvin Rosenfeld, M.D., and Nicole Wise
Stamford, Connecticut
October, 1999

1

With the Best Intentions

Kathy and Paul are a little anxious. After three years of try-ing, they are thrilled to finally be parents, and Julia is a de-lightful eight month old with a wonderful disposition. But lately they have noticed that Julia isn't developing at anywhere near the pace of her cousin Andrew who, although a month younger, is already crawling and even saying Ma-Ma and Da-Da. "I'm trying to be calm about all of this," says Kathy. "The pediatri-cian tells me that her development is well within the normal range . . . but I'm worried that maybe Julia is bored and will become lazy. She's home alone with the sitter all day. I really want her to be smart." So she and Paul sit down to order a kit that includes videos, books, and a chart to track a baby's devel-opment. It seems like a good program to ask the sitter to follow since the ad promises it will "nurture and enrich the develop-ment of your child's intellect."

It is Tuesday at 6:45 A.M. Belinda, age seven, is still asleep. School doesn't start until nine and her mother usually lets her sleep until 7:30. But not on Tuesdays. That's the day Belinda has a 7:30 A.M. piano lesson. From it she goes directly to school, which lasts until three. Then the baby-sitter drives Belinda to gymnastics for the 4:00–6:30 class. While Tuesday is the busiest day, the rest of the week is filled up too, with religious school and choir practice, ballet, and (Belinda's favorite) horseback riding. "She's pretty worn out by the end of the day," her mother laments. "But you know, she's much more alert for the morning piano lesson than she was for the Friday afternoon time slot we had before." She pauses for a moment and then says, thoughtfully, "Kids today are so much busier than we used to be. I'm not really sure it is a good thing. But I want to give her the advantages I didn't have." Then she opens the door to Belinda's room and gently pats her daughter's back to awaken her.

———

Tate, age twelve, is one heck of a hockey player. He started skating at two. At first, his father, a former prep school hockey star himself, did the teaching. A few months later, Tate started formal lessons. By age seven, Tate showed real promise and started playing in his New Jersey town's Youth Hockey Program on a demanding schedule. Tate is so good now, he's on the county all-star team and plays aggressive hockey year-round. He has four practices a week, with early morning ice times and Saturday games. For tournaments and championship games he has traveled as far as Virginia and Maine. Next year the coach wants him to practice six days a week. Sure, the time commitment is large—not only for Tate, but also for his parents, who attend every game, and for his younger sister, Morgan, who has to go too. But his mother, Elaine, says, "I really enjoy watching him play. And besides," she adds ruefully, "he still needs me to tie his skates for him. Of course he knows how to tie them, but most kids he plays with are fifteen and can get their laces much tighter. I don't want him to be at a disadvantage just because he's younger."

———

Seeking out a curriculum for an eight month old? Scheduling a seven year old's week so tightly that the grown-up in charge needs a Palm Pilot to keep track? Structuring an adult life around a commitment to tie laces on a twelve year old's hockey skates?

Sure sounds hyper—so long as we are talking about other parents. But when it's our own child's future we are trying to get just right, it's a little different. What good parent would not spend $79.95 for enrichment materials that promise some extra stimulation, especially for a kid we're a little worried might be lagging behind? We may be busy already, but if our child has some particular talent or a hankering to try a new activity, and we can find a tiny window of time through which to squeeze it into our schedule, why *not* give it a go? And what parent wouldn't help his child tighten his skate laces if that small effort turns out to make a big difference to him because hockey is so important in his life? And to be perfectly frank, his prowess with a puck gives us a real charge too.

Meanwhile, though, as we labor ceaselessly, sincerely, and earnestly at doing all the right things to get our children off to a great start in life, many of us moms and dads are feeling overworked, overwhelmed, and underappreciated. Of course we love our kids. We want the world for them and would do just about anything to give them what they need to succeed, first in their little-kid worlds and later in the grown-up game of Life. Yet in trying so hard to do everything we can for them, many of us (including yours truly, the authors) aren't sure when to say when. We sense that our family lives are out of whack, but we aren't sure why. We know we are doing too much for our kids, but don't know where it might be okay to cut back—especially since every time we pick up the paper, turn on the news, or try to lose ourselves in the pages of a magazine, someone else is adding something new to the list of things we are supposed to be doing for our children to make sure they turn out right.

We authors do it too. One of us recalls how, as a young and inexperienced mother, it seemed vitally important to provide only the most natural of diets for her baby daughter—nothing but breast milk and homemade, organically grown baby food, chopped and steamed in large batches, frozen in individual-sized portions. The effort was huge but theoretically worthwhile: All those reports linking pesticides and food additives to allergies and childhood cancers were really scary.

Life so often writes its own ironic endings, however, and as it turned out this same scrupulously fed child turned out to be the *one* of four children who was constantly sick—eventually requiring daily antibiotics to stave off the many infections that plagued her. In time, her health problems were traced to a genetic immune deficiency, which she eventually outgrew—as her mother also outgrew that naive conviction that life could be controlled and shaped by her own intensive efforts. That sincere, well-intentioned belief is the essence of hyper-parenting.

So often we can afford to relax—even in the face of conventional wisdom, let alone the latest scientific advisories! The other of us had a child who loved chocolate, and as a young child begged for some each evening before dinner. Although a little fearful of the nutritional and dietetic implications, her parents nonetheless decided to try it her way. What happened? She remains slender, and ten years later has missed a total of one day of school because of illness.

But it is tough to "try" to be relaxed, especially when we so desperately fear being negligent. What we parents really need as much as, or perhaps even more than, all that important advice about how to raise our children is a reminder that no one ever gets it all just right—and that most children turn out well anyway. Not perfect, but good enough. And, as we will see in chapters to come, that is the best we can hope for anyway.

We authors don't think we are looking at the past through chic pink glasses when we reminisce about how much simpler everyday life used to be—at least for white, middle-class families. Not perfect, mind you, but certainly less complicated. Most of us attended neighborhood public schools, not pricey private ones. We played outside with the kids in the neighborhood; we didn't have private voice lessons or play in organized lacrosse leagues. Our mothers had no need to color code our family calendars to track activities for each family member.

Life seemed reasonably predictable. Our parents had a vision of themselves as a strong generation that had survived the Great Depression, triumphed over evil in World War II, and saved South Korea from the jaws of communism. They had so much to be proud of. Pre-Vietnam America was pretty as a postcard, the best country in the world—at least as far as its white, middle-class citizens were concerned. "We the people" were decent, God-fearing, generous, fair, and law-abiding; our parents found plenty of safe, sunny, sane places to live. Of course there were racism, dysfunctional families, and alcoholic, abusive, and/or depressed parents, then as now, more than anyone then would have guessed. But because problems were kept sealed behind tightly shut doors, they did not disturb our "nice" image of ourselves.

We suffer no such comforting delusions today—in fact, quite the contrary. We get bombarded with news stories that scare the daylights out of us. We authors often find ourselves turning off the news in our own houses—not only is it too scary for our smallest children, but the truth is that it keeps us up at night too. The schoolroom massacres, wartime atrocities, and weather disasters are awful, no question. But it's not only the random horror of the events themselves that raise our blood pressure; humans have always suffered from evil acts and destruction, both natural and man-made.

What's uniquely stressful for today's families is the way that every single report of an awful event is first delivered directly into our living rooms and made up close and personal. The 24-hour news channels give us minute-to-minute coverage, intermittently punctuated by a consultation with an "expert," who does his or her best to provide a tidy explanation of its root causes (though the truth is that some of these events are just plain inexplicable), along with a set of how-to instructions on what you need to do to keep this from happening in your own life. The implication is that with enough effort you *can*.

So, whenever some horrible tragedy befalls a child, we are deluged with a flood of stories that examine why it happened, whatever it was: What oversights led to a toddler's fatal plunge from a skyscraper window, what *didn't* happen to prevent an eight year old from drowning while away at summer camp, which factors may have fueled the transformation of a seemingly normal high school student into a mass murderer. In one way, such stories soothe our angst by providing explanations that serve to make such events seem less arbitrary; in another way, however, they stoke our anxiety by giving us a list of the things we parents can do to keep such tragedies from ruining our own lives. We can invest in swimming lessons, carefully research the safety record of the summer camps we are considering, toss all violent video games in the trash—and lots more. Those of us who aren't taking every conceivable precaution begin to wonder, should we? Ought we change all the rules in our house? We wonder whether our children are in serious danger. Sometimes they might be; usually they are not. Some events are neither predictable nor preventable.

By stoking our insecurities about our children's future and appealing to our anxieties about whether we know how to be good parents, the media is profoundly affecting how we live our lives and raise our families. They are persuading us that just as we have to work far longer and harder at our paying jobs, so too should we work longer and harder at child rearing. There is no time for downtime! In a number of ways, our magazines, newspapers, books, and TV programs are even reshaping our sense of what is real and possible.

It's easy and fashionable to blame the media for every societal problem, from violence and drug abuse to the breakdown of family values. But despite their protestations to the contrary, we don't see them as just convenient scapegoats. The media exposes children, adolescents, and families to unnecessarily violent, ugly, and oversexualized images of life (and others that are ridiculously sugarcoated). That's bad enough. But we authors believe that the information the media transmits *indirectly* may have an even greater impact on the way we parents are raising our children today.

They put before each and every one of us an image of what we have come to accept as the right way to live. These highly contagious and subliminal metamessages about family life and parenting have dramatically altered how we look at the world. In our opinion, it is near impossible to *overestimate* the media's effect on our family lives.

It bears repeating and emphasizing. Directly and indirectly, in ways we are often completely unaware of, the media is poisoning our view of what family life should be like at the dawn of a new millennium. It portrays the world "out there" as brutal and unpredictably dangerous, a malicious maelstrom from which we must provide constant protection. It blurs the lines between fiction and fantasy, encouraging us, and our children, to believe that annihilation lurks everywhere yet that perfection and absolute safety are within our reach.

The "reality" we are presented with is often far more disturbing than even the worst fantasy shows. Nothing on television is scarier than the evening news. Every place is dangerous; no one is ever really safe. As we—parents and children—sit passively taking it all in, we are presented with a ceaseless sense of urgency and immediacy, a constant threat of death lurking just around the next corner or in the next bite of food. The sands shift constantly beneath our feet, leaving us with no place to stand that feels solid. Vigilance is the order of the day; we cannot ever afford to relax ourselves *or* our standards.

We are urged to teach our children to beware of people they don't know, even though the actual number of children harmed or abducted by strangers is minuscule. Scary health reports are sensationalized: "Cafeteria lunches contain flesh-eating bacteria!" Parents are made to feel irresponsible for serving a child a hot dog, which might cause leukemia or harbor listeria. An ice cream sundae is sinful— all that fat and sugar! The facts may change but month to month, the sense of urgency remains a constant. Because with no acknowledgment of the contradiction, a major story the very next month tells viewers definitively that the *absence* of fat in a toddler's diet may impede brain development and that eating chocolate may add years to our life expectancy.

By their very nature, the news programs distort our sense of time and frequency, making disasters seem common, as inevitable as a change in the weather. Seeing these images over and over alters our perceptions of just how safe we are and how unlikely such disasters are to occur in our own lives. Plenty of people believe that cancer is rampant among children, when in reality it is quite rare. The Challenger blew up once, but with our own eyes we saw it explode literally hundreds of times.

Unlike fairy tales, which begin "Beyond the seven mountains and over the three great seas," a brilliant distancing mechanism to keep children from being frightened since these events happened long ago and far away, clips on the local news highlight horrors that happen just around the corner to people who look like you and me. Every day people just like us are gunned down on the streets, or are car jacked, or have scaffolds fall from skyscrapers onto their heads. With our own eyes and the help of a crackerjack cameraman, we listen to the neighbor's surprise, we witness the mother's tears. We see their grief, share their pain. By being exposed in this way, we become unwitting participants in the tragedy, silent victims a continent away. We have imagined how it feels to have a child abducted, a daughter raped and mutilated. And so we react, by finger-printing our families and buying one more bolt for the front door.

Dr. Spock's down-to-earth child-care manual became a bestseller a generation ago. He worked to reassure parents, telling them that they knew more than they thought they did. On the other hand, today's media and some contemporary advertisers work hard to convince us of the opposite. Knowing just how to get our attention, the media use anxiety-provoking techniques so they can tell us how to be better parents. Not only do we know very little, but crucial new information is so complex and is being gathered so quickly that we absolutely must tune in or log on to keep up with the latest developments—or risk being a failure at life's most important job.

The media shows us again and again that perfection is possible: You *can* do this; you *should* do that. Serious advice follows the cue. Inspirational stories recount how, with the right efforts started early enough, each of us can raise a superstar like, say, golf prodigy Tiger Woods. These stories imply that *every* child should be above average, as though this wasn't, by definition, impossible.

Although her son had been accepted for early admission by Boston College, we heard one mother, resident of a Cheeveresque New York City suburb known for having one of the most competitive public high schools in the country, describe her son as "average, not all that bright." It's unrealistic to expect every one of our children (or frankly, even many of them) to earn straight As, captain three varsity teams, and staff the animal shelter on alternate weekends. We aren't all capable of superstardom—but that doesn't mean our lives should be viewed as disappointing.

Even our favorite dramas and sitcoms upgrade our view of reality. It's easy to forget that the only reason TV families can do so much, have such meaningful relationships, and comport themselves with such elegance and charm is that they are make-believe. Many of us feel we know the characters on television more intimately than we know our neighbors, since we see them more regularly and hear them speak more openly. They seem more rounded and substantial than the real folks who people our lives. On television, everything is orderly and coordinated. Even the homes of families of modest means are always well decorated; the furniture is never unmatched, let alone stained with grape juice and threadbare from years of hard use. Although the characters are struggling financially, they lounge around the house in gorgeous pajamas you would never find on the shelves at Wal-Mart.

Maybe sitcoms address real-life problems like drug abuse, teenage sex, and job loss, but they do it with style and a polished tenderness that life as we know it often lacks. Each scene is carefully set and the resolution is beautifully scripted, even if it takes two episodes to get there. In the real world, we may desperately want to offer comfort to a friend who is suffering, but find ourselves tongue-tied and awkward: On television, people always come up with just the right thing to say. They hardly ever fumble awkwardly for the right words, and when they do it's a fumbling that only underscores how sincere, vulnerable, and lovable they are. They don't look like the jackasses we feel we are when *we* say the wrong thing or say nothing at all.

On TV, the downsized and displaced corporate middle manager may be depressed for the first half of the show. But within the twenty-two carefully-crafted minutes he will not only find gainful employment that gets his bills paid;

chances are he will also have long overdue, sensitive, heart-to-heart conversations with family members and, ultimately, discover the true meaning of life. If only real life worked that way. Even in the most affluent neighborhoods, people who lose their jobs suffer, along with their family members, from problems like depression, divorce, and alcoholism. Those of us who've lost jobs remember how hard it was to get out of bed in the morning, let alone follow the well-meaning exhortations of friends who urged us to pick ourselves up, dust ourselves off, and get back into the game.

Try as we will, it is simply not possible for real people in the real world to get all the glitches out of our lives, to get them to work very, very smoothly. Implicitly, in comparison, we feel inadequate. Unlike on TV or at the movies, we have no equipment that allows us to edit out the bad parts of the day. We don't have script consultants and wardrobe specialists and makeup artists and directors in our houses. After behaving in a way we wish we hadn't, we can't roll back the video for another take. Real family life has its awkward moments and regrettable interactions and always will. But many of us find it hard to accept that reality, and maybe we don't really think we should have to. After all, we have seen this distorted image of perfectible reality, how life could be, so often that we have come to believe that it is a goal we should strive for.

Really, as we all sort of know, in one of those corners of our mind that we rarely take the time to look into, objects, achievements, and possessions don't make life meaningful. They never have; they never will. Relationships do. But our lives are so busy, so full of stuff to buy and things to get done, we have precious little time for nurturing those. It's hard to know one another, to attend to our relationships and marriages, when we are always racing around.

. . .

Several other factors have contributed to the particular intensity that infuses today's parenting. For one, time seems to be ticking faster than ever—at least in our own minds. In the olden days, before every household was equipped with electricity, not to mention America Online, dusk marked the end of productivity and the workday. The entire family, including children, worked hard all day, often at a shared enterprise like the family farm. Time moved slowly. Daily life had an organic rhythm tied to the sun, moon, and the seasons. Sundown meant the time for work was over.

Since radio and television didn't exist and the opportunities for entertainment were limited, the family had to spend time together. Parents and children, and often aunts, uncles, and grandparents as well, always dined together. Later, with few other options, they might talk, read (usually the Bible), play a game, or listen to family stories passed down from grandparents or great-grandparents. Family life was neither idyllic nor always peaceful, but family members still had to live together and get along—there were few other options. Most individuals also derived a sense of identity from their faith, which had been the family's religion for centuries, the guidebook that delineated what was important in life and demonstrated how you were supposed to treat your neighbors as you wished to be treated yourself. The Sabbath was sacred whatever your religion, a time to congregate as a community at a place of worship, a day for real rest and contemplation.

Technology has bestowed a mixed blessing indeed. We are deeply grateful for antibiotics that might have saved Todd Lincoln and for the polio vaccine that could have protected Franklin Roosevelt. We cannot imagine life without indoor plumbing or central heating. But electricity and the light bulb—not to mention such further technological refinements as the laptop computer with fax/modem and the pager with its constantly updated ticker of stock prices and news headlines—have turned us inward, away from one another. They have also fueled a rat race that has fundamentally altered our sense of time. Once lives were organized around the changing of the seasons; now they are measured in anxious seconds. Digital clocks make each minute's passing a notable event; microwave ovens work so efficiently that we tap our feet impatiently as we wait the couple of minutes it takes to nuke a weekday family dinner.

We move faster and faster. Everything needs to speed up and work more efficiently: machines, people, children. We race to stay in place. Cell phones and beepers put us on call day and night; we avoid solitude, fearing we might miss something crucial if we tune the world out, even for a little while. After all, no matter what time it is, the market is open *somewhere* in the world. The work-at-home technology that promised to give us more time with our families has actually infringed further. Stressed-out professionals who used to at least have weekends off now feel compelled to "spend a few minutes" on business matters ("Honest, honey, I promise that's all it will take!") even on vacation.

There isn't a person alive who couldn't be more productive. In the midst of astonishing plenty, we somehow feel eternally dissatisfied with who we are, with what we do, and with what we have. If working as hard as we do, we continually feel guilty that we are not doing more, what does that say to our children? Can they ever stop pushing? That dismal view of what they have to look forward to may be a factor behind the fact that in adolescence many kids choose to sign off and drop out, failing in school and turn-ing to drugs and alcohol for escape.

As a culture, we have accepted the idea that work should be continuous, gratification instantaneous. We work constantly, but don't really believe that important things take time. In our E-mail world, where we transmit our words almost as fast as we *think* them, how do we help our children understand that it takes hard work and persis-tence to craft a novel—not to mention to do anything else beautifully? How will they learn that in relationships, the best path often takes time, patience, reflection, and hold-ing your tongue until your anger dissipates, so you can see more clearly what you think and feel, what you should do to preserve a relationship that is really precious to you?

We worship technology. It has become a false idol that gives the illusion of intimacy. It gives our children the er-roneous belief that the good life is the fast, efficiently net-worked life. Our computers can link us via modem, but they prevent us from looking into one another's eyes. Our gadgets and electronic devices can fill and order our time, but they fail to add meaning to our lives—and they distract us from other things that might. They can take away our boredom, but they cannot feed our souls.

How do we teach our children that love really matters, that reflection and careful thought is valuable, that the way we feel and behave toward our family is worth more than the newest Air Jordan basketball sneakers or a faster, more luxurious car? How do we convince *ourselves* that having enough time at home with the people we love en-riches us more than spending another hour at the office or driving a tense, young competitor to a gymnastics meet three states away?

Loving well and working at something you find meaningful are the elements essential to emotional well-being, according to Sigmund Freud. These two are out of whack in our lives. Of course we need to work, not only to achieve our dreams and support our families, but also to support our vision of ourselves. However, we also need to find a way to live that doesn't completely deplete us, that doesn't leave us overworked and stressed out all the time.

It should not require a traumatic event—a brush with death, loss of a loved one, or a threat to our marriage—for us to see how fragile and precious life and relationships are. Those who've lost a loved one would trade a new BMW— or a fleet of them—for an opportunity to just sit by their side and talk about matters both important and inconsequential. So often we hear from those who've looked death in the face that *now* they know what's important in life. In the hours when you realize your child is very sick, and you fear it might be a serious crisis indeed, you are willing to make any sacrifice so it won't be so. Is that the only path to enlightenment? And why do we close our eyes to that insight as soon as the crisis is past?

Maudlin? Maybe. But you hear it again and again from people who have walked life's darkest roads. Sadly, all too often, the new, high-resolution world we live in urges people to invest more of their time in things that lay in the opposite direction. Our days will never be long enough to do all we want or believe we need to. Of course we know what's important in life, really, but we figure we have plenty of time—if we just take the right herbal supplements and follow the right health advice—to catch up on the important stuff at some point in the future. So we direct our immediate energies toward accomplishment and acquisition and figure we can fill in the parts that are missing—as we know, deep inside, they are—later. But will later ever come?

Although we make cocktail party conversation about taking early retirement so we can enjoy our lives more, few of us can spare the time to think seriously about the meaning of life, given the uncertainty of today's job market, let alone take steps toward finding it. A common joke nowadays is that the only thing worse than losing your job is *having* a job, since corporations have downsized to the point where one employee now handles what used to be the province of three. We may be more productive, but there's no mistaking the fact that we're also frazzled from the frenetic pace. The irony is that if we work long, hard, and efficiently enough, we help the lean, mean economic system make us superfluous too.

Sociologist Melvin Kohn long ago demonstrated that based on our own experience, we all prepare our children for the workplace we anticipate they will encounter. In many homes today, both parents tote home briefcases filled with work they didn't get to during the business hours. If Mom and Dad need to work nonstop to get those papers and reports and forms completed, maybe their children should get used to living that way too. It's undoubtedly that worldview that has parents marching into middle and high schools, demanding that their children be given more homework and harder assignments.

The tenor of the times has also changed. Despite enormous prosperity, many of us fear that the years ahead will be difficult. We are parenting in a state of anxiety and pessimism about the future, even if our big-picture angst is obfuscated by high levels of consumer confidence about next week. No one we know feels truly secure. Job security is about as easy to find as a drive-in movie theater; counting on Social Security and a pension plan to support us in our golden years is a little like believing in Santa Claus as a high school senior.

The economy is changing so quickly, and so radically, that even many high achievers have to retool their careers. Professionals who undertook years of training are no longer guaranteed lifetime job security. A once-successful cardiologist, a man in his forties and the father of middle-school-age twins and a younger child, has gone back to school. He studies evenings and weekends to earn an M.B.A. he hopes, without complete certainty, will ensure professional and financial security. With three college-bound children, his wife has returned to work as well. This family's life was already busy and full; now it is stretched to the limit or beyond.

The emphasis on perfection and perpetual motion is destroying family life. The first step toward correcting it is to see it for what it is. For our families to slow down, we need to subscribe—seriously—to the understanding that our feelings make sense, to recognize that they are shorthand messages we receive from ourselves. If we are feeling crazed by the pace of our lives, it's not necessarily because there is something wrong with *us*; it may be because most people cannot handle life at warp speed. Either it exhausts you completely, or it keeps you up all night. Instead of asking ourselves why we feel so rotten, we too often ask our doctors to prescribe Prozac or Xanax—or Ritalin for the kids.

Read on. In subsequent chapters we will provide evidence of how it all starts before we even conceive our children. We will see how our earnest efforts to get it just right get in our way. We will show how we have come to spend so much time "parenting" that we often end up with too little time for being parents, the people who are there when our kids need us, the ones who take time to listen, who will love and protect them, no matter what, and the ones who feel inwardly rich for the connection and opportunity. There is a world of difference between parenting and being a parent. Learning it, and living it, is likely to make life much, much richer.

2

Preconceived Notions

*T*ara and Tom clink goblets at dinner . . . and Tara's is filled with sparkling water. Just yesterday, Tom received the major promotion (to VP!) they'd been hoping for. They're comfortable in their new three-bedroom house in a town known for its great schools. They spent three weeks last summer cycling through France. Finally, the time is right to start a family. Tara knew it would come soon. Just a few months ago, in anticipation, she switched from power aerobics to power walking, and she started popping power vitamins as well. First stop tomorrow morning is the pharmacy, for an ovulation-predictor kit. "Why waste time?" Tara asked Tom, over dessert. "If we conceive right away, we'll have a spring baby. That's so much better when it comes time to start kindergarten."

———

Despite the ten weeks of childbirth classes, the faithful practice of Kegel exercises to strengthen her pelvic muscles, the carefully packed bag of tricks to ease the agony of labor; despite virtually having memorized chapter 14 in What to Expect When You Are Expecting, *and her perseverance in sticking with her determination to take no pain medications, Karen required a caesarean section to deliver her baby girl (8 lb., 6 oz.). And she's disappointed. "Hayley is beautiful," she says on the telephone* to her best friend. "I already love her. I'm so glad she's okay. And I'm okay, too, physically. But I don't understand what went wrong. I tried so hard!"

————

Nell, pregnant with her third child, is puzzled by her obstetrician's assumption that she will undergo genetic testing—for a condition that is neither fixable nor serious enough that she would consider abortion. Her two other sons have a mild bleeding disorder that is not considered all that dangerous now that the family and their doctors know about it. Both boys wear medical alert tags, and Nell makes it a point to tell teachers and coaches all they need to know in the event of an emergency, reassuring them that "it's no big deal." So she is taken aback at the implication that she might want to consider terminating this pregnancy if it turns out this child, too, will have the same problem. "Why would I do that?" she asks. "It hardly affects their lives at all!"

————

Just the *thought* of starting a family today is overwhelming! More than anything we want to be sure our baby is born healthy. We'll do whatever it takes. So at least three months before we start trying to conceive, sincere, well-intentioned mothers-to-be exercise to get their bodies "in shape" for pregnancy (talk about a self-defeating concept!). Even couples with no reason whatsoever to anticipate difficulty conceiving feel they ought to start charting basal temperatures first month out. To give the fetus-to-be the best possible shot at success even before conception, we load up on vitamins and minerals, eliminate known toxins from our diets, and get going on a healthy, low-impact exercise regimen just like the books say we should. There is so much to do when you are expecting to expect!

As is so often the case, our attitude as we embark on this enterprise shapes the entire experience. Even those of us who've tied our tubes and tossed out our cribs and high-chairs can see, when we look back, how the end is (and was) evident from the beginning. We start working over-time to raise our kids right, even before they are born! This chapter will explore how our preconceived notions pre-saged the anxious, hyper-parents many of us are—or, at least, are in some danger of becoming—today.

Many of our problems are rooted in our conviction that we can plan everything about our future, including our children. In figuring out when to "start trying," we weigh every factor—careers, life goals, and finances—trying to pinpoint the exact right time. Sperm and egg have yet to meet, and some of us are already worrying about neighbor-hoods and school calendars. Willing to do whatever it takes to build our baby right, we dramatically alter our eating habits, force down at least three glasses of milk a day even if we hate every drop, and then add a few giant-sized vitamins. A few months later, barely into maternity clothes, we author a birth plan that specifies how the de-livery should go, complete with details like whether or not we want anesthesia during labor. Of course we ought to be responsible and take a long, reasoned view of life as we be-come parents. But as we work so hard trying to make it all happen just right, planning for every little detail of our new family's future, we may end up missing how miraculous the creation of a new life really is.

Becoming a parent can be scarier than getting married, more intimidating than buying a first house. No responsi-bility seems more monumental than bringing a new and utterly dependent human being into the world. If some-thing goes wrong, who can we blame but ourselves? Smart, educated, determined to make no mistakes along the way, we conclude that we must be hypervigilant from the start. Our preparations are serious, rational, and scientific. We pay close attention to countless books and articles on getting, and staying, pregnant. We run ourselves and our partner through a scrupulous medical review: "How's your health? Your parents' health? *Their* parents' health? Are there any genetic conditions for which we ought to screen our embryos?" Then our questions become more personal. "Do you drink more than 1.4 ounces of alcohol a day? Do you smoke—and if so, what exactly? Have you ever been in the same room as a hazardous substance? Did you suck lead paint chips as a child? Did you, in your remote and selfish past, use recreational drugs—understanding, of course, that you have been denying this on a decade's worth of job applications and perhaps that we used to have fun with them together?"

Obsessive? Maybe, if you consider these behaviors in isolation or have an ax to grind with today's parents. But our motivations are sincere, our attitudes and behavior understandable. Prospective parents want to do everything they can to make a healthy baby and a good life for their families-to-be. What responsible adult would just kick back and, like, go with the flow on a matter of such importance? No one *we* know. From our own very personal perspectives as contemporary parents, it may be hard to see how this earnestness about getting it all right gets in our way, especially for the many of us who feel that our parents took far too little interest in us. But, sooner or later, it does.

It's absolutely natural for expectant mothers and fathers to feel some anxiety—and, hopefully, eager anticipation too—at the prospect of what lies ahead. After all, we are embarking on an exciting journey into the unknown. Almost everything about our lives will change when we have kids, even our self-perception. Unless we happen to be pediatricians or preschool teachers, most of us have spent our pre-parental years talking primarily to and about adults on more or less grown-up topics. At work, we may have spent years acting like adults in a responsible job, say a senior engineer at Motorola. But when we got home at night, we could safely regress—pull on our overalls, snack on pizza, Big Macs, and Devil Dogs, and cock a baseball hat backwards so at least we would feel we hadn't sold out; we were still kids at heart. We could go see a movie on the spur of the moment; no need to arrange for a sitter. However, as we think about becoming parents, we realize that becoming someone's mom or dad will make us irrefutably grown up, whether or not we feel ready for it. The life passage is major, as are the responsibilities that go with it.

And yet, does it have to be so intense? Countless prior human beings have made that transition quite well. As one experienced mother told a friend who was expecting her first child, "Listen, childbirth is hard and so is being a mom. But I just told myself, if all those other women I see on the street can give birth, so can I. And if they can raise good kids, well, I can do that too. And so can you." Almost everyone we know ends up meeting the challenges. Not perfectly, but that's okay: Imperfections are *not* the problem for most of us hyper-parents. Perfectionism is!

Which may explain why, as parents-to-be, we are on edge about everything, right from the start. We authors believe that certain aspects of raising children today are getting too much attention, making us even more nervous than we need to be, while others—namely, the natural excitement of creating an entirely new and unique human being—get too little. We're so busy trying to figure out how to make our children's lives perfect, so eager to help them become what we want them to be—smart, successful, sociable men and women, who will enrich our lives and, we hope, someday go on to enrich the world—that we barely acknowledge the most important part of parenting, which is taking the time to get to know who our children actually, and already, *are!*

Contemporary hyper-parenting is a true product of our times—manufactured in a high-tech environment, according to a set of stratospherically high expectations. Our fears get exploited to market advertisers' wares. We read, watch, listen, and become convinced that there is one right way to parent for success—and that a particular book, CD, videotape, or nutritional supplement will make it happen in our homes. Even if we want to choose another path, actually doing so seems irresponsible, maybe even arrogant: How many of us are secure enough to defy the experts? The curriculum seems set; the course load clearly defined (well, maybe that Tuesday evening water aerobics class for pregnant women can be construed as optional).

When we first embark on the journey that parenthood is, most of us have limited personal experience with raising kids, although we are all former children. So while in truth we don't *have to* subscribe to this particular view, in actuality we feel safer taking the practical approach that confident, experienced media voices tell us is right. If doing things the prescribed way is presented as the most certain path to a good outcome, it seems adolescent and irresponsible to insist on taking a more relaxed view of the world, a little like showing up for an important job interview in the droopy, threadbare jeans we live in on weekends. Isn't it more mature to take the advice of those who know more?

We want raising a child to be risk free, as if children came with a set of explicit directions that make it a process so well-conceived, so carefully thought-out, that nothing can go wrong. Everywhere we look, recipes for success are proffered. Read the instructions, add the right ingredients, measured precisely, follow the directions to the letter, and . . . poof! There is your affable, attractive, athletic UCLA grad!

Every generation is committed to their children's success. But lately the parental window of responsibility has been thrown wide open. Past generations tried very hard to assure that their kids turned out to be solid citizens. We feel all that *plus* an obligation to give our baby-to-be an unblemished genetic endowment, perfect soil for the fertilized ovum to grow in, and unlimited opportunities thereafter. Before we even have adjusted to our new identity as parents, we are told that being "responsible" means taking every possible prenatal step to maximize a child's opportunities. Long before our babies can roll over, count to ten, or even slide out of the birth canal, for that matter, we read that there is a scientifically proven way to enrich their environment and optimize their physical and mental capacities. And it means that we must be maximally involved. So of course, as good parents-to-be, we start piping Mozart symphonies into the womb and doing all the other things we are told we should so our children get the best possible start in life.

What a contrast to how the previous generation of parents started out! Whether it actually happened that way or not, many of us envision our own parents as young couples courting on porch swings, sipping lemonade, and listening to Frank Sinatra croon romantic ballads. (It didn't strike us as hyperbole when Gore Vidal said in a radio interview at the time of Sinatra's death that half of Americans over age forty were conceived with his records playing in the background.) Our parents dreamily debated which names (Bobby? Barbara?) they liked best for the children they hoped someday to have. Boys? Girls? How many of each? Of course they worried about nuclear war and wondered what their children's future would hold, but they didn't feel the weight of constructing it, one two-by-four at a time. Like us, they loved to fantasize about what their family would be like; but unlike us, it wouldn't have occurred to them to draw up a blueprint in advance. Children were expected to fit into their lives; they never expected to build their lives around their kids.

It was understood that life might hold some surprises. Many of our parents married early, often right out of high school. Children were simply what they did after they got married. (More accurately, perhaps, they were what they supposedly did *after* what they did when they got married!) Birth control was pretty unreliable, so pregnancies were planned only in the very roughest sense. If not exactly taken in stride, unplanned births were frequent—at least till a couple of kiddies were knocking around the family station wagon, at which point many of our own parents did whatever it took to not have any more.

The reason that stepmothers are common characters in old-fashioned fairy tales is because a couple of hundred years ago many women died in childbirth. Even when our own mothers were carrying us, the experience of pregnancy was enormously different. Careful timing and spacing of children was difficult, if not impossible. A man's contribution to the birthing process was limited to safely delivering his wife to the hospital; once there he could either comically pace around the waiting room or find a nearby bar in which to pass the time till it was time to pass out the cigars.

Most of our mothers were grateful to get through the nine long months of pregnancy with grace, good humor, and not too many extra pounds. Science had certainly made their lives easier and safer—better hygiene and new techniques for emergency intervention had made it an aberration for a woman to die during childbirth. Yet medicine was understood to have limits. The conviction that genetics and human nature were under control and that medical vigilance could, and most certainly would, eradicate all danger and discomfort—be it miscarriage in the third month or misbehavior in the third grade—had yet to become an article of faith. Childbirth was to be gotten through, a means to an end, not an accomplishment to train for, photograph, videotape, and cherish as one of life's top ten experiences. Everyone understood that pregnancy could be dangerous, that sad things could happen without it necessarily being anyone's fault.

We simply do not accept that premise today. A 1993 study by Vern Katz, titled "Two Trends in Middle-Class Births in the United States" reported that American parents look not to some higher being to explain a problem in pregnancy but to their obstetrician:

> Tremendous technological innovations, such as ultrasound, prenatal genetic analysis, and fetal monitoring have promoted the perception that physicians can control the prenatal environment and predict the pregnancy outcome. This expectation may lead to bitterness and anger in the event of an adverse pregnancy outcome.

Not to mention guilt. Given all we now know about what is best for fetal development, many women irrationally heap blame on themselves when something goes wrong in pregnancy or childbirth. Midwestern science professor Alice Dreger, who ironically at the time of her miscarriage was engaged in studying developmental anomalies, published a thoughtful essay in *The New York Times*. Though she certainly knew better, she found herself blaming her loss, bizarrely, on a household accident.

A few days before the miscarriage, I accidentally slammed my fingers in the garage door and a searing pain went through my whole body. That's when it must have happened. . . .

When a friend reassured her that this could not have been the case, Dreger said:

I had to agree with her. After all, I'm a science-minded person . . . if slamming one's finger in a garage door really caused miscarriages, garage door sales would be up and abortion clinic attendance down. So when absolved of the explanations, I felt relief. And then I felt powerless.

Guilt, of course, is the flip side of control. They are a matched set, those two, though we don't always understand that to be so when we buy into the premise that human destiny can be bent completely to our will, when we allow ourselves to be convinced that through careful planning we can avoid all pain and tragedy. Even given our scientific advancements, not every child is born perfect.

Despite improved techniques for open-heart surgery and the development of synthetic lung surfactant, some babies just don't make it.

But who can blame us for wanting the facts and risk/benefit analysis to read differently? Especially when it comes to our children, we desperately want to maintain the delusion that we are absolutely safe and always will be—unless we make a mistake. When it comes to bearing babies, we have come to believe we can have it both ways: An obstetrician who guarantees a good outcome but who lets us control how the delivery will go, a perfect child, and a transcendent birth experience. In the obstetric study mentioned above, Katz also notes that "women and their families have also come to desire more control over the birth experience. If the parents' birth plan is not achieved and their expectations not fulfilled, many parents feel they have not performed well."

The columnist Lillian Bressman, who was born to an immigrant family on New York City's Lower East Side, wrote a lovely piece that captured the difference that just a couple of generations have made. She recounted how her Harvard-trained psychologist daughter Beth discussed with the family matriarch, Lillian's own mother, a book, *Expectant Fathers*, which was described as a "practical guide for the anxious male, so he could share with his wife the incredible miracle *they* are achieving."

The grandmother listened and apologized, saying she didn't want to appear unfeeling. "But in all my years I never heard of a man dying in childbirth." She added that even if the father-to-be got an "A-plus" in the long childbirth course, "let's be practical and realistic—physically speaking, what else can he do except help her moan and groan?" The older woman continued, perhaps with some curmudgeonliness but also with considerable wisdom,

> I bet the couples enrolled in the natural childbirth courses think it is a new invention. Childbirth used to be a natural function—now it has to be practiced, studied, and learned. If you ask me, this makes it "artificial" natural.

As obstetrical care has evolved in just the past few decades, the subjective perception and focus of pregnancy and childbirth have changed dramatically and in ways far beyond being able to find out the gender in advance. Two inventions in the 1960s transformed both the focus of obstetrical care and our approach to pregnancy: The Doppler stethoscope, which enabled both mother and doctor to hear the fetal heartbeat, and the ultrasound, which provided an early peek at the baby-to-be, not only improving the quality of obstetrical care, but, some say, altering its very philosophy. The spotlight shifted from mother to baby. There it stays today, right on "His Majesty, the fetus!"

Now, even before expectant mothers have outgrown their jeans, they are bonding with their in utero "babies" (which makes loss due to miscarriage all the more painful). Our new technologies provide a sneak preview to the life that will soon be, enabling us to hear the baby's heartbeat, to see him or her somersault on an early ultrasound, even to predict with some accuracy the baby's birth weight several months hence. Research has shown that back when a mother's account of how many kicks she felt within the last hour was the best way to gauge fetal well-being, a woman began to consider her fetus a "baby" only in the last weeks before birth. It took fathers even longer. Today a positive home pregnancy test sends couples scuttling to the bank to open a college savings account. As we pore over the intimate photographs in Lennart Nilsson's, *A Child Is Born*, we think in very concrete terms of the process whereby an egg becomes a fertilized ovum becomes a fetus becomes a person. "This is the week my child's heart began to beat." "Now my daughter has eyelashes." We even have custody battles over frozen embryos.

With snapshots and often video footage from the now-requisite twenty-week ultrasound, the baby becomes a member of the family—arguably the center of the family—long before he or she actually makes an appearance in the world. We proudly pass around a snapshot and wonder with coworkers who our tiny fetus looks like. Though many couples opt not to know the child's gender in advance so they can "keep some mystery" in the process, others see no need to put off painting the nursery. The fact of a pregnancy may still be invisible to all but close friends and family, the fetus may weigh only a few ounces, but once a man and woman have seen their unborn child sucking his or her thumb and kicking precious little legs the dream has become reality. The child-to-be may be a scant two inches long, but once you have felt those first stirrings of parental love, there is no turning back.

In our age of information, for most newly expectant mothers the first stop after the doctor's office is the bookstore, for a pregnancy primer. An astonishing 93 percent of all pregnant women now read the reigning classic of the genre, *What to Expect When You're Expecting*. This book, along with other mother-to-be manuals, does a great deal to alleviate the very understandable anxiety of the "just-found-out-I'm-pregnant" woman and her spouse, who both want to know exactly what is happening inside her body. Having this factual knowledge readily available—at 3:00 P.M. or 3:00 A.M.—is very reassuring, particularly when few of us have close relatives and friends to ask. After a quick perusal, reading the book may even allow anxious parents-to-be to get back to sleep.

But we move quickly along the continuum of knowledge. First, we want to understand, just so we can become well-informed. Then we want to know more, so we can do the right thing. And then, almost inevitably, we begin to want some control, attaching great value to how "right" the things we do are and berating ourselves all those times when we can't seem to get it perfect for our cherished and utterly dependent child-to-be.

We should be kinder to ourselves. Selfless sacrifice is no more reasonable during the nine months of pregnancy than for the decades of active parenting that lie ahead—yet somehow that has become the yardstick by which we have come to believe we should measure our lives. In truth, life is not scored on a scale where you either earn a ten or a zero. In the real world, we have plenty of room to relax, to loosen up. Most of us are taking excellent care of our unborn child and ourselves already. Restricting ourselves to a joyless diet of only whole-grain breads and organic fruits and vegetables will not substantially improve our already overwhelming odds of delivering a healthy baby, nor will such measures substantially decrease the already small risk that our child might be born unhealthy. An ice cream sundae alters the odds not a whit. Pregnancy need not be a no-pleasure zone.

It should go without saying that any pregnant woman who willfully flaunts medicine and exposes her unborn child to known dangers and risks should feel remorse.

Some guilt trips take people to the right places: Hang-gliding in Yosemite, smoking two packs of cigarettes a day, or downing an endless stream of beers-and-shots is not responsible behavior for a mother-to-be nor, arguably, for anyone else. Most of us, however, do not flagrantly mis-behave in the face of conventional wisdom. Given the way information is often presented today though, it is as though there were no difference between a glass of wine once a week and a daily bottle of tequila. It's pretty diffi-cult for a normal, mentally healthy human being to be self-sacrificing to the degree we are told is optimal.

This persnickety perfectionistic attitude sets the stage for what comes later, particularly if something goes wrong. If for some unknown reason a child is born with problems, the best-intentioned mother may well conclude it was her fault in some unknown way. Why? Because, as Alice Dreger pointed out, taking the blame preserves the illusion that she has some control. Had she only learned that one other fact earlier, the baby might have been born perfectly well. It is oddly reassuring, even if the guilt feels like hell.

At least it seems that way in the short run. One woman, the mother of two, who has suffered six miscarriages over a period of ten years, says her experience has taught her that control is only an illusion, and that there is plenty to be learned from letting go.

"It hurts to lose a child, even when you've only just found out you were pregnant," she says. "But I've learned to just let myself feel that, so I can move on to what comes next. There's no point in beating myself up, in being angry, in questioning everything I did and everything the doctors didn't do. All that does is make me feel worse, for longer. It does nothing to change the outcome at all. I find a certain peace in accepting that, for whatever reason, a child was not meant to be."

We all need to learn to accept the limits of what we can control. It is the only avenue to serenity. But it is hard to let go that way. We now know a lot about what is good for a baby, what circumstances are optimal for healthy development, but we don't know everything about why things sometimes go awry. Biology has its own wisdom, its own way to protect the human gene pool from many fatal mutations. Miscarriages are often the body's way of solving severe birth defects before the pregnancy gets too far along. Some babies don't get the best start in life; some babies don't even make it to infancy. But because it is so difficult to accept the fact that we have so little control, ultimately, even in our age of science and high-tech medicine, it quite often ends up that, sadly and unfairly, the parents who are most sincere, who try the hardest and make the most earnest efforts, are the ones who feel guiltiest. So many of us who are truly doing our best, who are already better than "good enough," feel inadequate for making choices that, if not exactly optimal, are certainly harmless.

And if we pay close attention to all we read, it is no wonder we feel that way. Consider the "Best Odds Diet" chapter in *What to Expect When You're Expecting*. It starts by citing a Harvard University study that found that 95 percent of women who had diets they described as "good to excellent" had healthy babies. Only 8 percent of those whose self-reported diets were "really awful" had healthy babies. Well, this is not exactly news. What sort of pregnant woman would admit to eating mostly junk food? Is healthy food the only thing lacking in those women's experiences or might they also be, say, cocaine-addicted prostitutes? Who knows? We aren't given that information. Nor are we reminded that people who eat well also tend to take good care of themselves in other ways as well—even if they indulge in an occasional chocolate bar. Scientifically, it would be helpful to know whether the study was retrospective or was a far superior prospective study—though, in truth, even if the fine print with that information were included, few of us would read it. Nonetheless it is likely true that in every way, and not just nutritionally, these babies are given the best odds.

With the stage set thusly, however, we may not be thinking so critically and precisely when we go on to read the admonishment derived from this premise, "Make Every Bite Count."

> Before you close your mouth on a forkful of food, consider, "Is this the best I can give my baby? If it will benefit your baby, chew away. If it will benefit only your sweet tooth, or appease your appetite, put your fork down."

And do what, one wonders? Go outside and pick a handful of organically grown green beans from the garden? What if you are sitting in your office and the only food you can get your hands on is a bag of Doritos, which look pretty good, come to think of it. When women were at the center of pregnancy, it was understood that pregnant women wanted to eat strange things at strange times. The often uncomfortable nine months of pregnancy are the time for coming to terms with becoming a parent. But now the fetus is the focus: In the equation where every bite must count for the baby, precious little wriggle-room remains for the soon-to-be-mom. Surely there's no real harm in indulging herself with the pickles and ice cream she craves—even if they aren't fortified with extra vitamins and folic acid! It must be okay for hungry pregnant women—most of whom would inform you that, far from being optional or a luxury, appeasing the appetite is a necessity second only to frequent emptying of the bladder—to eat what they want, so long as their diets, overall, are reasonably balanced and nutritious. And overall can be over the course of a few days, not in every meal.

By the standards put forth in that paragraph, a fistful of M&M's falls just short of child abuse. True enough that a diet that consists exclusively of Nestlé Crunch, Mars bars, and Baby Ruth's is less than optimal for mother or baby, but there is no basis in fact for the belief that healthy pregnant women risk harm to their babies by eating some foods, including sweets on occasion, for their own pleasure. Mother Nature designed the system well enough that women really don't need an hourly check-in with a nutritionist to assure them that their growing fetus is getting what he or she needs.

A woman who is considering getting pregnant certainly should refrain from gulping down martinis or polishing off a bottle of wine with dinner. Every individual ought to be held responsible, at the very least in their own minds, for their own health habits—particularly when those habits infringe on the health and well-being of the unborn. However, we seem to have lost sight of the line between responsible behavior and fanatical control. Ought waiters or the couple at the next table in an expensive restaurant make a pregnant woman who sips her husband's beer feel like a felon? Might all of France and Italy perform better on IQ tests if their national habits were different? We have a difficult time being intelligent consumers of even good science, and as chapter 4 will discuss, not all science reported in the media or even in the better professional journals has been done in a way that makes the results trustworthy.

When it comes to health, we Americans are extremists. We make the de facto assumption that if too much of something is harmful, total abstinence must be the way to go. It's all, or nothing. Using the rigid interpretation makes us feel safer; relying on common sense, a commodity that is somewhat *un*common today, is downright scary. It implies that if anything goes wrong, we have no one to blame but ourselves.

We are not advocating throwing out the baby with the too-hot and possibly toxic bathwater. Certain health warnings are very important. Every potentially pregnant woman ought to know that modern science has proven that taking folic acid from the very earliest moments of gestation helps reduce the already low incidence of spina bifida. Prenatal multivitamin pills ensure that a growing fetus gets some advantageous nutritional building blocks that may not be abundant in the average woman's diet. But the benefits of those measures are based on statistical findings that evaluate outcomes across an entire population. Any reasonably healthy individual woman who is surprised to find she is pregnant and doesn't start on folic acid until her eighth week has little reason to panic. A mother-to-be who suffers from extreme nausea and cannot keep down a saltine—let alone a powerful prenatal vitamin—can usually put aside the supplements until she feels better, without fretting that she will impair her child's health and well-being. What is optimal, if possible, and what is good enough without really endangering anyone, can be very different.

All the advice about diet and exercise, vitamins and alcohol is part of the illusion modernity has created. It deludes us into believing we have total control over what babies mothers will give birth to. But we can make a "scientific" case for almost anything. If you believe that clapping your hands in downtown Minneapolis will keep away an impending invasion of elephants, you can gather evidence in your mind that it works; because of your clapping hands and the fact that no elephants show up, there is a causal relationship. We look at childbearing the same way. Since most children are thankfully born normal and healthy, our talismanic fantasies may be helpful in reducing anxiety. However, such behaviors will never be a guarantee. And if following these strict guidelines makes a pregnant woman feel anxious and invaded, if she becomes persuaded that her happiness, well-being, and fondness for ice-cream sandwiches no longer matter much at all, maybe some of that advice ends up doing more harm than good.

Scientific and medical research can give us practical advice that can improve the mathematical odds of delivering a healthy baby. In every particular case, clinical judgment, and not simply the latest story in the health segment of the evening news, guides a competent physician's decisions about what is best for a particular pregnant woman, at this point in her pregnancy. Each situation needs to be judged individually.

That's why you need to find a health professional you can trust, so that in the unlikely event that things do go wrong, he or she can make an educated and experienced, individualized decision about what is best for you and your fetus. But trusting a professional seems unenlightened in our age of information. It's hard to know for sure that our very busy OB has time to read every single study, to assimilate the latest, most up-to-the-minute findings. Where we once considered the gift of life to be equal parts miracle, mystery, and medicine, we now want to believe we can make it all happen ourselves, with a little help from our doctors and scientists.

Statistical information about scientific research studies can help boost the odds. But as any mathematician will acknowledge, statistics can never do away with the luck of the draw, which still plays a role in medicine. No precaution or pill can ever guarantee a perfect child. We don't like to acknowledge it, but that remains out of our control.

The end is in the beginning. If we start out on our journey as parents with preconceived notions that we can and should control it all before our child is born, we certainly will behave that way once he or she is really here. We forget that the real wonder is that a child is conceived at all. We know it is scientific, but it's still amazing that sperm meeting egg (and in such a way!) can really end up making a child.

But times have changed. In the past, for example, the single woman who desperately wanted to become a mother could either learn to live with the fact that her lot in life did not include diapers and day care or accept being publicly shunned for having a child out of wedlock. Today, the truly modern single mother is where she is by choice. Women no longer require a relationship, or even a one-night stand, to have a child. They can simply visit a sperm bank and select the superficial traits of the man they choose to donate semen, "knowing" him from his description in the catalog and often indulging in rich fantasies about what his genes will bring to "their" child-to-be.

One highly accomplished single television executive in her late thirties had no desire to marry, ever. She recently visited such a clinic, paid her fee, leafed through the books, and selected as the genetic dad for her child an athletic college kid supposedly with an IQ of 151. She had always wanted a scholar-jock for a child! Recounting her experience to a friend, she waxed rhapsodic about the frat-boy donor—his great personality, his dashing appearance, his intelligence and athletic abilities—all for a human being she had never met and from whom all she had was a simple, straightforward letter of introduction.

Sperm donors selected from a catalog, egg donors recruited on college campuses, companies that enable you to choose the sex of your child—these situations are already a little strange and a lot complex. But compared with the opportunities to plan that they are likely leading us toward, artificial insemination and egg donation are simple. The way things are going, advances in controlling genetics will soon make it possible for a potential parent to select specific traits for a fertilized ovum, sort of like adding options to a luxury car.

The laws of supply and demand impact scientific research as surely as they do what is stocked on the shelves of our supermarkets. Given our cultural predilection for perfection, a great deal of energy is being expended not only toward the devastating diseases but also to the more commercially viable endeavors, like locating genes for baldness and obesity. We may soon become a society in which selecting physical attributes for a child-to-be is treated as matter-of-factly as we've come to view plastic surgery. Because when it becomes possible to do something, it becomes hard to choose not to.

Some wonderful people are allergic to progress, sometimes for good reasons, sometimes just because they hate change. To some people the manual typewriter just "feels right," even though they acknowledge that word processors are superior tools. Maybe there truly will be no down side to using genetics to optimize human potential. It simply is too soon to know. Yet genetic advances, from genetically engineered insulin to cloning mammals, are moving along so fast that we barely have enough time to ask important moral and ethical questions. As our technical expertise increases and we move into more ethically challenging issues, like intelligence or creativity or even, if some current speculation is on-target, homosexuality, mothers and fathers may soon be asked, based on a genetic profile, which of their children should live beyond the first trimester. With technology like in vitro fertilization and artificial insemination that enables a couple to stack the deck for success, by implanting only designer eggs and hunky sperm, anyone who can afford the special services may soon believe in survival of only the truly *perfect*.

Is there anyone among us who is confident of their ability to decide what is "perfect" in human beings? Perhaps we need to be a bit more humble about our wisdom, a bit less certain that it would be a service to humanity to remove "undesirable" genes from the human pool. Might we be creating unforeseen dangers by selecting for certain traits? Some scientists maintain that the same genes that give some people bipolar disorder or even schizophrenia are related to extraordinary musical, mathematical, or creative ability. If the purported gene, or genes, for addiction were eliminated from the human gene pool, might we rid future generations of alcoholic geniuses like Mozart and Hemingway?

Issues like our tendency to do whatever we *technically* can simply because we now know how to post us at the precipice of a very slippery slope. We authors do not pretend to have answers. We just want to remind ourselves, the parents of the children we are working so hard to polish, protect, and perfect, that we ought to carefully consider the direction in which we are hurtling. If society accepts, as it someday might, the premise that parents are responsible for cultivating genetically positive attributes in their unborn children, it quite likely will also change the way we look at the imperfect ones already here. We may begin to act as though it is our responsibility to do whatever we can to perfect them as well. (Chapters 6 and 7 will demonstrate that we are already traveling a good distance down that road.)

Our scientific sophistication and knowledge is amazing. However, the blessing of genetic science, like some others—atomic energy, for instance—challenges us to be uniquely wise in knowing how, when, and where to use it. Just because we think we know something, just because specialists believe they have tools for gazing into the future and knowing what will happen next, just because we *can* do something, does not always mean that we should. Genetic breakthroughs and our ardent desire to give our children every advantage we can, tempt us to act prematurely without completely understanding the implications our actions have. As one mother of three says, "We all start out saying, all I want is a healthy baby. But once we get that healthy baby, we seem to start wanting a whole lot more than that."

Each of us may want a perfect child with a perfect life. But we would do well to reflect on the fact that in Latin, the root of the word "perfect" is *per-ficio*, which means complete, or finished. Life is a journey, with surprises around every corner. We are never perfect, or finished, at least not while we are alive.

. . .

The media and the marketers help us focus our preparations on the physical, the practical, and as we will see in the next chapter, the material. That orientation makes it easy to forget that the truly essential elements in preparing to love a child are our feelings and inner lives, our relationships to our spouse, family, and friends. What many parents-to-be fear deeply is that between our children and us, at least in the early stages, there are no intermediaries. Creating and carrying a baby inside of you is really the closest you can ever be to another person (which some psychologists contend is what men envy most about women).

Many women find that even the very first separation—childbirth—is painful, and not just because those final contractions have them hanging from the ceiling by their fingernails. The child who began life as a part of you must separate and start growing toward independence, one baby step at a time. For a parent—mother *or* father—to first fall passionately in love and then to let go is the greatest challenge, life's deepest sacrifice. Though it can be searingly painful, this separation is utterly essential in every step of successful child rearing. That's why one concentration camp survivor we know said that the hardest day of his life was when he had to take his daughter to college and leave her there.

Raising a child together requires that we connect with our spouse in some ways we may never have done before. We have to be really honest with ourselves about who we are and who we want to be as parents. The two of us must work together to understand what we think is important and what is less so and about the ways we love and work out conflicts. As father and mother, we should be talking about our hopes and dreams, what we consider crucial, and what really doesn't matter very much to either of us. The months before a baby is born are better passed as a time of deep intimacy, fun together, shared pleasure in preparation and exploration, one of communication and connection, rather than in the sort of frantic running here and there, getting this and that done, that serves to excuse us from sincere, and scary, reflection.

Our most elusive personal qualities, the traits and characteristics we need to develop in becoming parents, are not celebrated by society in the same way as, say, cutthroat competitiveness, seductive salesmanship, or Machiavellian management skills. So instead of looking inward, instead of examining their state of mind and emotional preparedness, many mothers-to-be are urged to focus on their bodies and on the physical aspects of preparing to be a parent. All that planning and preparation serves to distract mothers and fathers alike.

Because in becoming someone else's mom or dad, it is very important to also nurture our own emotional health and well-being. Instead of buying more prepregnancy planners that will tell us how to do it all—work, travel, decorate the nursery, exercise, prepare for childbirth, cook nutritious meals, and, oh yes, have mind-blowing sex up to the day the baby is born—as parents-to-be we need to spend more time doing less.

After all, none of us comes from a family that really resembled the "Seventh Heaven" image of vulnerable perfection. That's why we struggle with ourselves in the quiet moments at night, as we lie awake troubled that we can't fall asleep. We, who will soon be parents, can no longer easily evade our real fears. Most of us lived through a childhood that was, in one way or another, less than perfect. Is it our dissatisfaction with the nurturing *we* received that is keeping us awake, wondering if we, too, will yell in the same scary voice, be so insensitive, or make the same mis-guided mistakes? We may remember in vivid detail some hideously painful episode from childhood and wonder will I do something to scar my child as deeply? Do I really have inside me the love I will need to help him or her grow well?

"What do I do about the fact that despite all I believe about motherhood and apple pie, every time I think of Mom, it is with those glazed eyes she had by the time we sat down to dinner every night?"

"Will I also complain and criticize incessantly?"

"And if I believe in the importance of being a good fa-ther, what does that mean? What does it make me think about my dad, who always said the right words but invari-ably never *did* the right thing, or very much at all? Family time on weekends was always family time after eighteen long holes—and usually a visit to the nineteenth."

These are real and legitimate worries. The very act of ac-knowledging and wrestling with feelings like these is part of overcoming them. In the same vein, but later, if we struggle honestly against the impulse to slap our son or daughter the way our own mother slapped us, our child will at least sense that we really try, that we are working to sub-due our less-than-perfect impulses.

What more can our child expect from a parent who hap-pens to also be a real human being? What should we expect from ourselves? The issues we struggle both against and for are as much a part of who we are as our love of the out-doors, classical music, skiing, or reading. Along with the incredible passion and excitement of creating an entirely new person, a biological meshing of ourselves and our part-ner—and some other elements we will never precisely track to their source—comes a certain amount of anxiety about what lies ahead.

One mother says she often recalls the wise advice of her pediatrician when he walked into the hospital room and saw her newborn boy nestled in her arms. Knowing she and her husband to be exacting individuals, high-achieving professionals, graduates of the prestigious Rice University, he said to her, "I'd like you to try to remember this moment forever. Because that perfect little baby sleeping so peacefully in your arms is going to grow into a little boy and eventually a young man who is never, ever going to be this perfect again. And the best and most important thing you can do for him, as his parents, is to always love him as you do right now."

In the process of preparing to be parents, knowing and appreciating ourselves, respecting the good genes and values we will pass on, accepting the bad ones as an unavoidable part of the complete package, celebrating those aspects of ourselves we are proudest of and trying to modulate what about us is unpleasant . . . these are the most important things we can do to prepare ourselves for the birth of a child. Ultimately we are going to raise a person who, like us, will be less than ideal. As the wisdom goes, none of us will be a perfect person or a perfect parent. All we can hope for is the will and stamina to be good enough.

3

The Right Stuff

What a view little Jason has from his crib! The walls of his nursery are papered in a soft blue check; the azure ceiling is painted with puffy white clouds to resemble the Montana sky on a clear summer morning. Fluffy down bumpers cushion him from the cold, hard slats of his brass crib; a matching quilt keeps him toasty warm as he sleeps. Extra electrical outlets have been added to the room to accommodate a vaporizer, video nursery monitor, self-dimming night-light, automatic reverse tape player (for the lullaby tapes), and a diaper-wipe warmer. Jason's parents have invested heavily in transportation: They bought two strollers (a lightweight model to keep in the car and a cushy one for long strolls in the neighborhood); a portable infant car seat; a backpack carrier, and a strap-on Snugli. To keep Jason entertained at home, they have borrowed an infant swing from Aunt Jean, purchased a "crib gym" that dangles farm-animal toys over his head, and bought a brightly colored seat with toys on a tray that will allow him to spin and rock safely in one place. There is also a playpen for indoor use and a portable "baby hut" that can keep Jason bug-free out of doors. His closet and drawers are already overflowing with clothing and toys for the year ahead. "We're ready for anything," Jason's dad says confidently, nestling in his arms his newborn son, just four days old and approximately the size of a loaf of bread.

———

Sally is mightily frustrated. Her two toddlers, Erin and Elizabeth, are so prone to ear infections that she found herself visiting the pediatrician just about weekly. She spent forty dollars on an ear examination kit, thinking she could at least cut down on the number of visits—but it's all to no avail. It's not the device—basically a flashlight that enables her to peer into the ear canal—that is the problem. It lights up just fine. It is just that even after poring over the photographs in the brochure that came with the kit, even though she has begun using the instrument daily so she can acquaint herself with what a healthy ear looks like, Sally cannot tell the difference between a normal ear and one in which an infection is brewing. (No surprise to her pediatrician, who already told her that it took him years of training and an estimated two thousand or more peeks into infected ears to acquire the knowledge base for making what still often amounts to a judgment call.) So when Erin gets a cold, which historically has been followed by an ear infection about half the time, Sally gives up and calls the doctor to schedule an appointment for later in the day. "What a waste," she fumes. "I should never have bought this thing."

———

We parents are an easy mark! In this age of rampant consumerism and information overload, we'll buy just about any product that promises to make our lives easier and/or our child's trip through childhood better.

We've worked hard and have grown to appreciate quality, especially in material goods. So that's what we want for our kids too. Most of us waited long enough to have them, after all. Be prepared! The more the better! Better safe than sorry! Those phrases guide us as we wander the aisles of the vast baby-and-child superstores trying to figure out which of the hundreds of arcane baby-care items for sale are truly child-rearing essentials. In the end, we mechanically toss electronic thermometers, pacifier tethers, and diaper-bag "systems" into our carts, and off we go, outfitting ourselves for life with baby as though we are headed for a two-year safari in the deep wilderness.

In reality, though, kids are pretty low-tech. Almost always, the simpler, less expensive solution is more than sufficient. But every step of the way we are reluctant to settle for anything but the best. We drop big bucks at Baby Gap for fashion accessories, hats, headbands, belts, and other items that can be frankly annoying to any baby so uncomfortably attired. We shell out a few hundred more for a Gymboree tumbling class, then within a year or two, when we feel we can't put it off any longer, we spend thousands on a state-of-the-art computer. This despite the fact that it will be used primarily by our three-year-old for point and label games—and will be completely outdated by the time he or she is ready to use its real capabilities. A few years later, when our kids are ready to start playing team sports, we dig deeply into our wallets to outfit them with the highest quality sporting goods and accessories, so they'll look and hopefully play like the superstar athletes we're secretly hoping they have the talent to be.

Then we gasp in horror and dismay when the media trots out its annual estimate of the exorbitant cost of raising children today!

In virtually every aspect of contemporary American life, including parenting, happiness gets measured materially.

We've allowed ourselves to become convinced that the right possessions will make us safe and happy. Whether we have the means to support it or not, we all feel entitled to live—and raise our families—in an affluent lifestyle. Just like our cars and computers, we want our children, indeed our entire lives, to be shiny, new, and state-of-the-art.

Living above our means and planning to earn enough in the future to afford the excess shapes our parenting. That holds true even if we are financially quite comfortable. As we search for fulfillment in possessions, homes, and ever-larger incomes, we are ignoring life's most precious and only irreplaceable commodity, time. Wanting happiness, always and everywhere, aspiring to see ourselves as good, benevolent parents, we commit our time, energy, and even a good portion of our identity to giving our children a luxurious ride through their already materially privileged lives. And many of us who are struggling financially—and our consumerism means that plenty are, quietly at least—dig deeper to meet the anticipated, unexpressed needs of our precious infant who, if he or she could express an opinion, would likely be satisfied with being kept warm, full, and dry. We are striving to raise our children in the manner of Louis XIV, free from all avoidable discomfort and frustration.

And then, when our kids get to be four or five, we wonder how they got to be so &^$@# spoiled!

Nesting is a natural desire, even a built-in biological one. But for us humans, this planning period really ought to mean more than a shopping spree at the local baby boutique. In part, the process of nesting also means becoming more intimate with yourself and your spouse, thinking through and talking over serious matters relating to beliefs, hopes, and dreams. Nesting is a crucial part of trading in our own previous identity and finding the commitment, pleasure, and deep meaning in the new one.

To be sure, a huge part of the fun of getting ready for our new baby is the physical preparation: Buying the crib and car seat, decorating the nursery, getting the diapers, clothing, and bed linens together. And on a practical level, life is smoother those first few weeks at home with a newborn if we have had the chance to prepare in advance. But it really need not be so expensive or materialistic. We don't need anywhere near as much stuff as we think we do. One of us, expecting a fourth child, was taken aback when, the week before the baby was due, she happened to walk by the nursery, which was stacked literally to the ceiling with boxes of clothing and baby equipment—all for a tiny little baby who, this experienced mom knew full well, really required only some diapers, a couple of snuggly stretchies, and a warm cozy place to sleep!

By offering us products that seem to anticipate our most minute need—read: perceived and often created need—specialty stores and catalogues feed our impulse to prepare. They play to our misperception that as good parents we have an obligation to ensure our children a journey through life as rich and smooth as silk. We want to keep our kids from knowing, for as long as possible, that everyone encounters some bumps and potholes in their life. We may even believe, if we do our job right, they will be the exceptions. So we conclude that to keep our children safe and protected we need those brightly colored, extra-cushy strollers with built-in entertainment systems and refrigeration compartments.

The desire to help our children avoid discomfort is natural and beneficial. But our money would be better spent on things that really matter. All the stuff we buy can put one more layer between us and our children when what they really crave, and what feels so good to us when we have a chance to give it to them, is love, guidance, intimacy, involvement, and approval. What our children really want is to be with us.

But our high-tech world pulls us away from any simple vision. We are offered a truly amazing array of products designed to make life convenient and easy for parents, and that are fun and educational—*always* educational—for children. We can buy a sound system to broadcast classical music to a baby in utero, and another that lets us listen in on him in the months before he is born. We have to choose carefully among the different kinds of baby monitors, so many are available: Should we invest in the superpowered one that lets us, as one copywriter puts it, "listen to every gurgle and coo," or might we safely settle for one that is not quite so sensitive? Maybe though, if we really want to be responsible, we should go for the video version—so we can both see and hear our baby as he sleeps the night away. We want products that will guarantee complete safety so our anxiety about being parents will melt sweetly away, like a snowman in the sun. Carrying that thinking to its logical conclusion, it might make sense, then, to invest in a heart monitor and an ICU suite. Then we could really sleep soundly!

Oh, the stuff you can buy! There are carriers to strap your infant in front, on your hip, in your arms, or on your back. And if you settle on a backpack, check out your options carefully: You can buy anything from a basic cotton model to a Rolls-Royce version which has storage for bottles and toys, reflective piping, and an optional sun/rain shield with clear plastic vinyl for maximum visibility for the tiny passenger, who, if you asked her, might vastly prefer sleeping in her warm crib to hiking in the driving rain. You can pick a diaper bag designed to hold—exactly, in specific pockets and slots—one day's worth of diapers, clothing, baby food, and bottles for day care. You might want a cup holder that clamps onto your grocery cart. And for the truly tidy—you know who you are, so stop lining up the pencils on your desk and pay attention—products like the Popsicle shield are specially designed to keep tiny fingers from getting sticky.

Many of these products are patently absurd, but patented nonetheless. A rubber duck with a built-in thermometer tells you—the grown up—when the water is "TOO HOT" for baby. Pity those poor parents before us, who had to stick their elbows in to test the water. A bralike device can be strapped on by dads who want to experience what it feels like to breast-feed. Please! Listen up, guys: A bra that dangles bottles in terrycloth udders doesn't even come close.

What selling to us parents has come down to is this: If it was a frustration or fantasy for someone, at some time, somewhere, then some marketeer has a pragmatic and, for him, potentially profitable solution to offer. Every tussle, every minor inconvenience, every absurd wish presents an opportunity. And that's why we live in a world where we have specially designed food-and-bottle warming systems, and terrycloth baby-bathing aprons with giant pockets that hold the many products we need to make absolutely certain a two-month-old infant is certifiably sanitary. It is why we can buy pee-on targets for the reluctant potty user, and six-stage training cups to help baby make an effortless transition from bottle to cup.

Who knows how well any of these products actually sell? But we do know that we all have a choice in the matter; we don't have to buy every one of them. Few make us better parents. Most don't help our children in the long run. In fact, some of them could actually inhibit a child's developing autonomy. The infant who smoothly moves from bottle to cup without even noticing he has done so is deprived—yes, deprived—of the satisfaction he'd feel in learning how to handle the cup himself. After all, one of the first ways babies and toddlers feel pride is when they have mastered some new physical skill. Even very young children feel good about themselves when they've accomplished something difficult; we shouldn't take that sense of accomplishment away from them. Life will offer plenty of real paths parents can help pave for the child. No need to smooth out every single bump between now and then.

Doing so can be counterproductive. The conviction that each and every moment in our child's life ought to be joyful, that he ought never to know what it means to "suffer" is misguided. In life, some suffering is inevitable: Freud defined "emotional health" as the ability to tolerate unavoidable human misery and to steer clear of the self-created kind. Nonetheless, in working toward the ill-advised goal of eliminating all discomfort and inconvenience, we well-meaning parents do more and more and more—and end up presenting our dearly beloved baby with an overworked, stressed out, anxious caretaker. Who needs a child-rearing expert to tell us how bad *that* is for a child?

At bottom, this behavior is rooted in our very deep love for our children and having that strong foundation of love makes them fortunate beings indeed. Nothing can substitute for the unshakeable sense we give them that they are treasured, appreciated, and valued. Our sincere efforts and devotion contribute to their sense of security. Some highly acclaimed child-rearing experts, like the legendary English pediatrician and child psychiatrist D. W. Winnicott, have provided a theoretical underpinning for that view of child rearing. Winnicott wrote that in the child's first year of life, the parent should create the illusion that the world is wonderful and bountiful, that needs like being changed and fed are met so easily as to seem almost magical. We know that we are the ones providing those services. But from the infant's naturally egocentric point of view, all he has to do is cry and his problem is solved. He is enormously powerful— look how potent his cries are. It works every time: Wail, and mom or dad appears like magic. Somewhere inside, he begins to believe that he is omnipotent and effective. As he grows older and more able to understand reality, the parents and everyday experience slowly begin to dismantle the illusion. Sometimes he has to wait a few minutes. Winnicott's is a lovely vision, and a beautiful philosophy for child rearing. But we do not need a multimedia David Copperfield magic production to accomplish it, when sleight of hand will do the trick quite well. Are you hungry? I'll feed you. Lonely? Come into my lap.

Yes, it is admirable that we are trying so hard to raise our children well. But all these devices may actually interfere with our ability to form an easy emotional connection, a reciprocal relationship that is mutually gratifying. Our standards need not be so impossibly high. We do not need to completely shield our children from pain, discomfort, and unhappiness. It would be humanly impossible and ultimately counterproductive, since when later life undoes all that hard work, as real life invariably must, our carefully "shielded" children may not have developed the tools they need to cope with adversity.

One mother of two sets of twins reports on an important lesson: "When my first two were young, I bought two of everything: I wanted everything to be fair. But when they were four or five, I realized that they were really bad at sharing: They didn't think they should have to! My younger two are much better at sharing—because they had to be. I didn't make it so easy for them."

We do not need to produce a perfect life for our children. Infants are born resilient, with considerable tolerance for frustration, a strong instinct to survive, and a potent capacity for restoring homeostasis once their very basic needs are met. If they are unhappy and unconsoled (or inconsolable, as babies are known to be on occasion), they fall asleep; it is the same mechanism by which the adult "zones out" after a trying day. An infant's ability to sleep anywhere, under almost any circumstances, is a built-in protective shield. Having escaped successfully from the stressful situation, the baby awakens refreshed and ready to try again. We adults would do well to adopt such a resilient attitude; take a walk, a nap, or a day off—then come back to the problem and try again.

In fact, there is solid evidence that we American middle-class parents really can afford to be much more relaxed with our children, that the simple fact of our secure socioeconomic status gives our babies a boost. Researcher Clyde Hertzman cites a study that "shows that severe pregnancy, and delivery complications did not lead to impairment of the physical and psychological development of children from upper-class families in the way that they did for lower class children. This example suggests that high class status not only protects healthy children from future risks and vulnerabilities, *but can actually help reverse the long-term consequences of birth stresses*" [italics added]. Hertzman reports similar findings even for the connection between mild lead paint exposure and learning and behavior problems.

The picture is less promising for the poor, unfortunately. If they start out at a disadvantage, they are less likely ever to catch up completely. They don't have the resources—financial, educational, medical, or emotional, often—to close the gap. So almost always, the better-off are indeed better off.

One of the reasons we work so hard at trying to keep our kids happy is that we hope they will grow into optimistic individuals who see the world as a kind place. But what really seems to contribute to the child's ultimate optimism—the sense that all will be just fine—is the parent's ability to do a "good enough" job, to use Winnicott's felicitous phrase. However, to parents in our day and age, good enough doesn't seem even adequate. We say we hyper-parent for our children's benefit. But clearly, we also do so to satisfy that big part of our self-image wrapped up in parenthood. We fear that if our children are uncomfortable, unhappy, or frustrated, even for a moment, we may be doing something really wrong. We fret that a tiny distress might make us look bad, not to mention cause irreversible trauma.

If our species were so fragile, we never would have survived this long. In reality, experiencing some tolerable disappointment and frustration—like say, getting through a brief time between starting to cry and being picked up and fed—and learning that such experiences can be lived through, is an aspect of mental health and well-being no matter how old you are. The ability to defer gratification, at whatever developmental level is appropriate, is a sign of maturity. One of the greatest gifts we parents can give our

children is the inner conviction that adversity can be survived and overcome. If we stand by their side, supporting
them through the tough times, letting them know that we
believe in our hearts that they can do it, they will often surprise us with what they can accomplish. Then the triumph
becomes theirs, not ours. That conviction, that sense of
personal competence, can only be acquired through direct
experience.

Not only is frustration unavoidable, but familiarity with
small, manageable doses of it helps a child to develop a realistic view of what he or she can expect from life and the
world. Quite often, life is messy: The Chinese have a saying to the effect of, "No family can hang out a sign saying,
'No Problems here.'" Tension, ambivalence, and difficulty
beset every family, in every culture. Each of us must struggle with our own nature and impulses as we figure out how
to fit ourselves comfortably into our families. It's the reason
contemporary psychologists speak about the emotional significance of a child's struggle with toilet training and sibling rivalry, a teens' difficulty finding an identity and a role
for themselves, or the adult midlife crisis. Identifying and
predicting such normal developmental passages makes
them no less personally painful, nor poignant. When challenged with getting through difficulties, many of us surprise
ourselves with what we can do. And we feel stronger, after-
ward, for having done so.

That's not to say we should manufacture a Spartan regimen or sign our children up for a week at Outward Bound
to build their character. An infant or child who is frustrated intentionally may come to view the world as a cruel,
hostile place and will struggle against it tooth and nail. But
a child who is allowed to experience the average, ex-

pectable frustration that comes from being a member of a family of imperfect mortals who are nonetheless trying to do a good job will develop realistic expectations of people and an optimistic view of the world. The stubborn belief that so many of us have that we can, by doing it all really, really well, avoid adversity altogether, will only lead to disappointment.

We don't advocate going back to swaddling infants in rags—or even using cloth diapers—unless you really want to. Disposables made life easier in our own families. Many other products enhance our lives. Nebulizers improve the quality of life immensely for children with asthma. Colorful bed linens, beautiful toys, and lovely musical tapes add an aesthetic richness to daily life.

But many of the objects parents feel they absolutely must possess are simply a waste of money. It is not only that these products take up too much space, which is true even if you invest in a good closet-organizing system. It is not even a matter of how much of a hassle these supposedly convenient products turn out to be—folding up some of these easy-to-use strollers has reduced many of us to very childish displays of temper, especially when we are trying to rush into a waiting cab. And when we have to bring along a list of eighteen arcane items—hanging cooler and clip-on fan for the stroller, stage-three training cup with lid for juice, antibacterial hand wipes—each time we plan to go out, well, we end up staying home a lot!

No, the real problems with the proliferation of parenting paraphernalia are more subtle and serious. Subliminally, they portray a potentially poisonous and ultimately woefully misleading view of family life. These ads promise—implicitly or explicitly—that if you just buy this little item, your life with children can be convenient and "just right" in some officially approved way. Sort of like a cross between the American Red Cross, and the Good Housekeeping Seal of Approval. You can just picture Betty Crocker and Robert Young, in his famous *Father Knows Best* cardigan, nodding approvingly in your direction. No crumbs, no spills, no messes. No problems!

No dice! Kids are messy and inconvenient, bless their little hearts. It's the way they're built. More frightening yet, they come with no guarantees. Families must work to find the balance between individual desires, different temperaments, and the family's needs as a unit. Each of us needs to learn to live with some frustration, some dissatisfaction, some inconvenience, without losing our tempers too often, our marbles (well, we should admit that a few misplaced marbles go with the territory), or our lust for life. That is just how the world works. We do well to face up to that fact and get on with our lives. We can try our best, hope for the best. And the odds are, our children will turn out just fine. Most do.

But we can't count on bettering the odds simply by buying up. Sure, good medical care is worth paying for and vaccinations do boost considerably the odds of making it to adulthood. But if money, even indirectly, could buy a good family life, the tell-all biographies of the rich and famous would be far less fascinating. All money buys is financial security—and many would argue that, subjectively, cash doesn't even purchase that.

Much of the "stuff" we buy does not improve our lives. In fact, it has a rather insidious effect. In some ways, the assumptions that underlie such purchases may actually increase our angst. Having shelled out hard-earned money in the hope of finding solutions to our problems, we end up even more frustrated with ourselves—because with all this help and expensive equipment, we still can't make the machinery of our lives run as smoothly as we really think it ought to. That elaborate diaper-bag system, fully loaded with bottles and clothes and diapers, is nonetheless an unwieldy piece of luggage that needs to be unpacked and repacked at the end of a long day. A child who isn't ready will resist toilet training, even with that nifty new potty that trills a tune as a reward for every little tinkle deposited therein.

Perfectionism, in the guise of the promise that you, too, can have a perfect life, has a deceptively appealing face—and we buy into it as eagerly in our parenting practices as we do when we slather on our antiaging face creams every morning. The marketers sell a single, shiny vision of American life: easy, happy, clean, convenient, and above all, comfortable. Marketers don't really know more about how we should be living our lives than we do. But they do know exactly how awkward a first-time parent feels changing a diaper or bathing a slippery baby. They know how frustrating it is to try and meet the incessant needs of a newborn, and still have some sort of a life. Have you ever noticed how slim, radiant, and composed those new moms in the ads are—even in the hospital, just after they've delivered that gorgeous, clean, fat, "new" baby who looks to be about four months old? They know just how to use this information to make us feel inadequate, so we'll be sure to buy the product that promises to solve the problem.

However, heaping all the responsibility for our consumerism on the marketing mavens is not unlike the two-pack-a-day smoker who says his habit is really all the fault of the Marlboro man. Ours is the land of opportunity and those who sell to us cannot take all the blame. H. L. Mencken once said no one ever lost money underestimating the intelligence of the American public. We grown-ups need to learn to resist the siren call of salesmen offering materialistic solutions to our problems and most especially the ones who hold out the promise that goods can buy us perfection. We need to recognize that we are the ones responsible for making the decisions—including writing the purchase orders—in our own lives.

Families are idiosyncratic; no two are remotely alike. Our memories and photo albums are not supposed to be interchangeable; we are all different, all awkward at times. Even within families, siblings have very different experiences as they grow up with the same parents in the same home. Real families and real people learn, struggle, and adjust to one another. But *that* view of life, in which you roll with the punches and improvise as you go along, is less compelling. In reality, we all muddle through as best we can, occasionally with some grace, more often just okay, sometimes downright foolishly. We try to assess each new situation in its uniqueness and come to a sensible course of action. For one family, a five hundred dollar English pram may be such an enjoyable luxury that it is well worth the money, even if it will only be used for a few months. (A family we know that did splurge in exactly that way subsequently derived enormous pleasure from lending out their baby buggy to friends and neighbors, whose newborn then also had a luxurious ride for the first few months.) Another family, however, might enjoy using that money for a weekend in the mountains; a family that can't really afford such an indulgence would unquestionably be better off applying that money to next month's rent.

No two situations, no two relationships are identical.

But that individualistic approach doesn't quiet our discomfort at the unpredictable. So, sometimes indirectly and sometimes with all the subtlety of a sledgehammer, the ad guys can hit us right in our hearts. Where we are all very, very vulnerable.

And, in fact, those heart-wrenching ads sometimes pitch important products. Take, for instance, the dramatic advertising campaign intended to get parents to ask their pediatricians for the relatively new chicken pox vaccine. The American Academy of Pediatrics recommends the vaccine because it has been proven effective in helping children avoid suffering, and even forestalls a few fatalities each year. But the fact is, as it has always been, the vast majority of cases of chicken pox resolve without complications more serious than a few missed days of school and perhaps a small scar or two. As many as 10 percent of kids who get the vaccine still get the chicken pox, albeit milder cases. Chicken pox is not, in and of itself, considered a life-threatening illness: Far and away the most common complication is a secondary infection picked up through the skin, which truth be told is as likely to happen with a scabbed toe or a skinned knee. But we don't consider those sorts of injuries so potentially dangerous that we prohibit our children from playing outside. We just urge them to be careful and treat their boo-boos with a kiss, a cleansing, and a cute Band-Aid. What more should a good parent do?

Plenty apparently, at least if you pay heed to the ads on the radio that promote the chicken pox vaccine. The sensationalist scriptwriting goes right for the jugular and sends our anxiety through the roof. In a recent series of radio spots, a young mother's voice is heard leaving messages on her husband's answering machine, informing him that the doctor has diagnosed chicken pox, as they had suspected, but is recommending hospitalization for their sick little boy. The next message reports that the boy is now in intensive care—but "they think Timmy is going to make it." Another scenario has two moms discussing a neighbor's child, also hospitalized with the chicken pox. "I had no idea the chicken pox could be so serious," one says. "Oh yes," the other replies. "Every year a hundred people die of the chicken pox, and forty are children and adolescents." The two women agree that they will immediately get their own children vaccinated.

Talk about a scare tactic. Do we really need to worry that our as yet unvaccinated child might die if, before getting that vaccine, he or she snatches a truck from some other kid in the sandbox who, two weeks from now, conceivably could break out with the chicken pox? The odds are overwhelmingly against such an outcome: More kids die each year of injuries sustained in accidents in the home, yet we let them live there with us anyway and do our level best to keep them out of harm's way.

Good parents take whatever precautions are reasonable. Probably most of us will opt for the vaccine, as we authors have for those of our children who haven't already lived through the chicken pox. Like ads urging parents to give their children vitamins, fruit juices, and fortified breakfast cereals, these commercials promote commendable behavior. But they also create anxiety—actually build it from the ground up. They feed parental fears and uncertainty where little, if any, need exist.

Of course we parents must do what we can to keep our children safe, to protect them from serious illness. But products like one we saw in an infant-product catalogue, a sleeping harness that supposedly protects a child from

SIDS (sudden infant death syndrome) by immobilizing him in his crib so he can't turn over onto his stomach seem to promise an extra edge of protection when, in fact, what they more likely do is add to our list of things to worry about. They imply that a parent not only can but should be able to forestall any risk no matter how small.

It's akin to wearing a surgical mask and gloves to the supermarket. Yes, taking such measures might keep a few people healthier than they otherwise might be and might even save the life of one or two especially vulnerable individuals who conceivably could pick up a dangerous bit of salmonella poisoning from the skin of a tainted cantaloupe. Should we all don scrubs each time we leave the house? Nope. It's not worth it in the big picture. We simply cannot accept as a reasonable charge the responsibility for protecting our children from all conceivable dangers. If we set that as our goal, a vulnerable infant's needs would be unlimited; someone, somewhere has been hurt by everything, even things that under almost every condition are considered safe. Childproofing our homes is a time-tested way to help keep babies safe as they begin to crawl and toddle around. But we can't take the stairs out of our homes because a baby might topple down; we can install gates.

Despite what the ads intimate, parental time, patience, and prescience are not unlimited. Nor should one expect them to be. Most of us have things to do other than watch and play with baby. No parent who lives in the real world can take steps to keep her baby completely safe from every identified risk. It's not possible. Even if we are very careful, no safety is absolute. Bad things do happen to good, careful people, as the popular book by Rabbi Harold Kushner says so eloquently. One adolescent we know spent two days in a coma when the branch of a tree fell onto a car at exactly the spot she was sitting in. Her father was driving, at a safe speed, on a safe road. Her seat belt was buckled. Yet disaster struck, and it was no one's fault. Nothing could have averted that accident. Luckily, she's fine now.

Spinning ourselves into unproductive circles trying to keep a child safe from every remote possibility will put the entire family into a state of perpetual panic and, perhaps, eventually into therapy for agoraphobia. We need to save our energy and money for the things that do matter, that have a far higher probability of making a difference. Strap your baby into a car seat, by all means. Into bed? We think that's way over the top.

Other products, designed to take some of the load off stressed-out parents, actually add to it. And they also detract from the development of a mutually gratifying relationship, based on instinct and intuition. A digital timekeeper and clock promises to "take the guesswork out of caring for your baby." The device keeps close track of feedings (frequency and quantity consumed) so there is no need for you or your baby to work out your own highly individual rhythm. Why would you, when you can measure scientifically, down to the exact minute, the tiniest fraction of an ounce? Now *there's* a tool sure to send an uncertain parent over the edge! Subtly we are urged to feed our babies on a schedule rather than on demand; subtly we're pushed to pay close attention to tiny incremental increases or decreases in intake, as if precision and exact measurement meant something, as if small feeding fluctuations had great significance. This device feeds into obsessionality, persuading a parent, or a caretaker (whose monitoring is probably being closely monitored), into carefully processing concrete data in order to really *know* his or her child. Wouldn't tuning into the body's inner, but far less regular, clock be better? So much for emotional rapport! Maybe this device will help ensure that a child is never, ever underfed. But wouldn't watching the child's face, learning his or her cry, soothing the baby in a rocking chair be more helpful and human, more meaningful, to both mother and child?

But the place we are really sold a bill of goods is when the marketers target education and intellectual achievement, which our generation considers essential to a child's future success. They eagerly offer us a wide range of products to get little Luke and Lucy off to an accelerated intellectual start. Drawing dubious conclusions from scientific studies, stating as fact what the professional research community is still debating actively, they tell us that it is never *too* early to begin formal education.

The tools are there for the buying! Developmental and educational toys, books, tapes, and videos that virtually guarantee ultimate academic success to the toddler who spends enough time working—um, playing—with them. Can't you just hear the singsong, wheedling voice of the loving mom at work on boosting her baby's intellect? "Here, sweetie, let's play some fine motor games! Okey-doke: Now we'll move on to cognition!" Somehow we can imagine that same toddler as a fifteen-year-old, saying, in a less than sweet voice, "The hell with you, Mom!"

We all know that young children will play with any-thing—laundry baskets, pots and pans, dad's shoes. So if they're going to do it anyway, why waste time playing mindless games with spools of yarn when matching squares and circles and triangles is entertaining *and* develops cer-tain core intellectual skills? Developmental psychologists tell us, after all, that play is the work of childhood. So the ads suggest we can direct that work and make it a little more purposeful, a little more productive, by using the tools the "experts" have contrived to fine-tune the process.

It's a good thing to be smart. So why *not* pick up some software (lapware, it has been cutely called) for your infant to poke at on your computer? It is supposed to give your child a "jump start." Why *not* buy videos that develop intellectual skills, CDs that promise Mozart will boost mathematical genius in an infant? The sales copy suggests that parents who really want their children to do well (and who among us doesn't want to be counted in that group) would be wise to take steps toward structuring a program for brain development today. *Before* he or she says that first word.

"Genius in the making?" asks one headline. "University of California infant brain-development researchers have proved that listening to music by Mozart aids in the development of spatial reasoning and other cognitive skills . . ." it states. (Ironically, recent studies dispute this much-touted finding—which is, in fact based on research performed on college students.) A "video-mobile" that features animated geometric shapes in baby-friendly shades of red, black, and white, actually spotlights on its cover a photo of an infant wearing a mortarboard and gripping a diploma. Subtle, huh?

How'd they keep the child from chewing on that diploma, we wonder? *That's* how babies that age, roughly six months, learn about things—by putting them in their mouths. Visual stimulation is just one way of learning and rather a passive one at that, kind of like sitting in lecture hall in college. Not that there is anything inherently wrong with letting a baby sit quietly gazing for a few minutes at an entertaining view of floating shapes with an interesting musical background. It is not, after all, as though you are popping *The Texas Chainsaw Massacre* into the

VCR and handing the little cowboy a shot of tequila. Looking at some floating shapes won't harm him in the least, might even be somewhat interesting for a short period of time.

Such videos are neither offensive nor harmful products. In and of themselves, they are benign at best, visual Muzak for the infant mind. What is inappropriate is the notion behind them, that a parent's job is to properly program the computer, which the child is subliminally analogized to.

Babies don't need to use their time productively. They shouldn't be pushed to perform on any timetable other than their own. These products divert parental attention away from the stuff that is equally—no, way more—important.

It is absolutely true that a healthy, stimulating infancy is crucial to healthy brain development. Read the articles carefully, however, and what you'll discover is that stimulation is built into normal, loving caregiving. Our homes are stimulating. Our hugs are enriching. Making funny faces and saying ridiculous things to babies boosts their self-esteem. And it is so delightfully personal. Watching us cook or clean is "educational." It's not like they've seen it before. Stimulation does not need to be scheduled into an infant's day in thirty-minute increments: Ten minutes staring at a high-contrast mobile (that crib harness might come in handy here), followed by labeling and pointing games with an attentive caregiver, then fifteen minutes in front of a visually stimulating video.

None of this is the least bit necessary! Some might debate this point, but we believe that not a single moment of structured intellectual exercise is required during infancy in an average, and by international standards, exceedingly affluent and enriched American home. The world, as it exists in an apartment in Atlanta or on a farm in Minnesota or in a ranch house in the suburbs of Detroit, is already very stimulating to a small baby if he or she is just given the chance to take it all in at his or her own pace, and most especially if a loving and playful adult is present, attentive, and involved.

Children are very good at constructing visions that interest them, especially if given some opportunities to practice—not that we are in favor of scheduling *that* into a baby's day either! And if they are given the opportunity to find what in their surroundings catches *their* (not the mom's or dad's) fancy. One mother we know used to place her fussy baby in a sunny corner of her living room next to a tall potted tree for brief periods when the child was out of sorts or her mom needed to get something done. The baby would gaze up at the leaves, look at the patterns the sunlight played on the pastel walls, watch the dancing dust motes in the light. "I call it her quieting spot," says her mother. "I want her to learn to calm herself." And she did—as most infants will—when left in peace to learn to do so. The sights, sounds, smells, and feelings of the most mundane of existences are *all* new and exciting, especially after nine months in the darkness of the womb! And out of all those sensations, the child will create his or her own vision of the world, a personally constructed and owned sense of the world all their own.

Brain development is not a simple, easily measurable process. We know when it starts: at conception. We know when it ends: with death. Of course it is important to provide our children with experiences that enrich their lives, and help them to develop intellectually. But a good life is not all about who has the most educational toys. One billionaire we know wrestled with how he could get his grown daughter to have the same philanthropic feelings he did.

To him, what mattered was the quality of the trip, what you did along the path of life; not only what you got, but what you could give back. Another wealthy man, who had a great deal of fun with his money, also worked hard to help his children grow up to be ethical people and to find ways to share with family, friends, and worthy neighbors some of the pleasure his wealth had brought him. Both of these self-made men spoke of an obligation to give something back. These two very wealthy men—in our opinion, rich by every standard—absolutely believed that developing their children's brains was important; but developing their ethics and values and shaping the kind of human beings they turned out to be was at least as important.

Human development isn't finished by the time a child reaches his or her first, seventh, eleventh, or eighteenth birthday; and ethical development likely continues into senescence. Every single hour, thousands of tiny images are processed in the brain: Light filtered through the leaves of a tree, an ant crawling across a countertop, the beep of the microwave oven timer, the smell of soap and the soft comfort of the towel after the bath. The warmth of mother or father or the baby-sitter's arms, the gentle touch of a hand. The intrigue of watching a sparrow outside the window. The bird hopping onto a slender brown branch: This is stimulation! Each experience leads the brain to strengthen some neural connections and likely to deemphasize others.

We don't need to "jump start" our babies: Humans improved biologically through millions of years of evolution. We are naturally designed to maximize our developmental opportunities if given a chance, and we parents can relax and enjoy watching the process as our children strive for safe, new accomplishments. We need to provide safety and security; we don't need to set up a theme park on the family room floor. A child will work hard to crawl to reach and then pick up the red block by the gray chair; he will take delight in discovering what happens when he sticks his fist into the applesauce in the bowl on the tray of his high-chair: This is brain development. Banging a wooden spoon on the kitchen floor. Changing the rhythm and intensity: This is enrichment! And they all are in the child's control and add to the child's sense of being in charge of his or her personal universe. How wonderful is that for self-esteem?

All these are the daily experiences that help a brain develop. A child's curiosity is a better guide than a parent-planned curriculum. Mozart (or Bach or Chopin or Haydn) may indeed help enrich the atmosphere—for everyone in the family, not just the developing genius in the highchair. So, too, do the Beatles, Louis Armstrong, and Willy Nelson. Heck, even alternative groups like Smashmouth can be fun to bang a spoon to. It is good to enjoy music in our homes. A parent needn't purchase a special set of CDs and a sound system to blare the music into the nursery for thirty-minute increments twice daily. A baby does not need to concentrate on taking in classical music on a schedule, to sit through a season's subscription to the symphony, especially if her parents prefer jazz or rock. Sharing your particular passion with your child will enrich him or her forever. Forcing something upon a child that the experts recommend but you find dull runs directly contrary to this impulse; it is imposing an outer standard on your child, rather than freely sharing what you love.

Early stimulation is vital to children's health, well-being, *and* intellectual development. It would be antediluvian to deprive a baby of the warmth and color, the contact and cuddles, that make infancy so enjoyable and stimulating—and, it should be noted, gives a child the inner conviction that life can be rich and meaningful. That is both the product and pleasure of excellent parenting. We do not have to "work" at providing more. A parent who actively loves, plays with, and cherishes baby regularly, at times throughout the day, is providing him or her with all the right stuff already.

4

Listen to the Experts

*S*andy is a down-to-earth midwestern girl, raised in Ohio and bringing up her own sons in a Chicago suburb. She has two active preschool-age boys who, truth be told, are wearing her down. She shares a fantasy with a friend: No, it is not a romantic weekend with her husband (or anyone else); not a decadent week at a spa; not even a two-hour shopping spree at the local mall. No, what Sandy wants most of all is to spend one night in a hotel . . . alone. She aspires to read, uninterrupted, through the stack of parenting books and magazines that have been piling up on her nightstand because by bedtime she is always too tired to read. When she can find the time to concentrate on those materials, she tells her friend, she will know how to get her children to behave and her life to run smoothly.

———

Jack and Nancy know how lucky they are to have found Alita, who has been living with the family as baby Leah's nanny for three months now, since several weeks before Nancy returned to her full-time job. Alita is warm and loving, experienced (though only in her 40s, she is a grandmother to four already), energetic, and flexible; she even has a great sense of humor. What she does not have, however, is the same appreciation for education and intellectual development as Jack and Nancy. In *fact, her two sons are day laborers and her daughter had a baby right out of high school. This worries Jack and Nancy a little. Feeling uneasy about making the request but believing it is important, they have instructed Alita not to use baby talk with Leah. They would like her to speak as much as possible, and always in full sentences. "I've read these are the critical months for brain development," Nancy tells a colleague. "We need to be sure Leah is hearing the things she needs to hear."*

———

No one in the Hennesey household was getting all that much sleep, till Dave and Ellen gave in and started bringing eight-month-old Alex into their bed when he awakens in the wee hours. They actually kind of liked having the baby to cuddle with in the morning . . . until Ellen confessed to the other moms in her play group, that is. They all told Ellen she should "Ferberize" little Alex as soon as possible or he'd be sleeping in her bed till he was a teen. "What the heck does that word mean?" Dave wanted to know. "And who are they to tell us how to raise our child?" On the one hand, Ellen agrees with her husband; on the other, she realizes her friends have done a lot more reading on parenting than Dave has. What should she do? She really doesn't know.

———

In our service-based, technical economy, we Americans have grown accustomed to hiring help when we need it. We believe in education. We believe in science. We believe in specialization. We hire experts to help us with our cars, computers, and careers. It's a good thing we can, because more often than not, we'd be clueless without them. So why not get help when we run into a problem with our kids?

That's why we turn to parenting professionals. Listening to them seems more efficient than the slow, often uncomfortable process of working out how to be good parents on our own or with the help of friends or family. For many parents, experts are the most logical place to turn. American families move often; ages segregate. Families live in homogenous suburban communities, with few wise grandmothers to reassure them that a potty-phobic preschooler will not end up wearing Pampers on junior prom night. Parents who grew up in troubled families but are determined to do better with their own children may lack the confidence that they know how to do the job right, may mistrust their instincts and intuition.

Many of us are just too busy for the sorts of soul-searching conversations with one another that help clarify what we are trying to accomplish with our kids—and to figure out why we feel so darned nervous about it. Being open doesn't always come naturally. It's hard to admit that we have a problem since it might leave us vulnerable to criticism— humble pie is no one's favorite meal! It may seem easier to get advice from perfect strangers than to admit to those we do care about how confused, inept, and angry we feel when we can't get a preschooler to stop soiling himself, or a seven-year-old to sleep at a reasonable hour.

The problem is, in seeking out the experts, in hiring outside help to solve the problems inside our homes, we parents give up important creative control. Of course, some families need help at times. But buying into a set of standard behaviors authored by an expert, a person who doesn't know us, our child, our lives, our aspirations, and our dreams, makes it easy for us to relinquish a sense of unique ownership—and with it full involvement and responsibility. In the short run it may seem like a deal worth doing:

Who wouldn't trade embarrassing scenes in the public restroom for the freedom to leave home without bringing along three changes of clothes and a case of wet wipes? But is it really worth it if, in exchange, you lose the opportunity to feel pride in working it out yourself, to forge your own unique connection based on understanding, and communicating with a child you are passionate about?

Our fear of being who we are and trusting ourselves makes it difficult for us to recognize, let alone to follow, our own instincts. We may feel some anxiety about our less generous, more aggressive, and critical, inner voices. But they too are a part of who we are. We do well to tune in to our own soft voice of reason, the one that has good sense and gives clear directions about what is best for *us*. Ultimately that voice is the only one that will feel right and true.

But it's so enticing to think that some expert has "solutions" to our "problems," that if we can just manage to do things the *right* way, our family life will hum along as sweetly harmonious as the New York Philharmonic. We find it hard to accept that cacophony is inevitable, even *productive,* among people who live together, even those who love one another. Conflict is the unavoidable result of people wanting different things and wanting them badly. On the path toward arriving at a solution everyone can live with comfortably, some struggles inevitably ensue. Unpleasant as they may be, the conflicts are very much a part of the creative process—not only in our families, but at school, in sports, and later on, at work.

Yet many of us consider dissension problematic, perhaps even pathological. So we trust experts who specialize in child development and who've been invited on the morn-

ing news shows to tell us how to get siblings to stop bickering, or to entice a stubborn kindergartner to eat her vegetables. Insecure about ourselves, convinced that family
life really should just roll seamlessly along, we look for direction from mainstream people with better credentials,
more specialized knowledge and training, practical and
professional experience, and obvious self-confidence. It's
comforting to think that someone, somewhere, knows
their stuff and can teach us—that by listening and taking
good notes, we could become far better parents than we
could ever figure out how to be on our own.

And, in fact, sometimes experts do help. Parents can
benefit by using advice selectively and carefully. But problems are likely to arise when they end up trusting the experts more than they trust themselves, when they imbue
these parenting professionals with the authority and confidence Mom and Dad really need to become good parents
themselves.

Let's say parents hear that families should dine together
every night to develop a child's intelligence. Those parents
whose styles and schedules make that particular feat tough
to pull off ought to say, "Okay, good idea. But our way
works too. We do it differently, but well enough." Yet many
who are already uncertain feel queasy, worried that maybe
it's folly to think they can get to the same place in another
way. If a pediatrician-author makes the case that a certain
sort of bedtime routine is critical for a child's sense of security, many parents feel unnerved if they consider an entirely different approach more practical and enjoyable.
Doubting that they know enough to challenge an authority who wrote a book, they grimly and dutifully walk
through that structured routine on a nightly basis, even

though their personal preference would be to read stories at other times of the day (and they never really did see the point of pajamas).

Is there really something magic about sitting down as a family to fork pasta together at 6:00 P.M. every night or to a particular structured schedule of bedtime activities? No. What means so much is the ritual and the family's interaction, mutual concern and interest, and togetherness: Some very close families only eat dinner together on weekends and special occasions. But they find other ways and times to connect—at breakfast, after school, on weekends. One woman we know whose husband is rarely home at dinnertime makes a practice of reading chapter books, like *Winnie the Pooh* and *Charlotte's Web* to her preschoolers as they eat their meal. Not a textbook solution, but it works for her. Another family far from their native country has a special dinner every week on their Sabbath. It makes them feel connected because they know that their sisters, brothers, cousins, aunts, and uncles in the old country are doing exactly the same thing for their Sabbath meal.

Another mother, a teacher, ruefully reports that on many nights, at least a couple of her four kids fall asleep in the family room, sometimes quite late. True enough that in a perfect world, baths would be taken, nighties buttoned up, stories read . . . but the family is a happy one, and the children are delightful, friendly, and doing well in school.

Problems with family relationships are nothing new. Many are timeless and universal. After all, *Romeo and Juliet* and *Hamlet* remain as relevant today as when they were written, and the family life portrayed in the Bible was hardly idyllic: If you think your sons' sibling rivalry is problematic, look at what Joseph's brothers did to him! But we postmodern parents feel that even eternal truths about family relationships can be tweaked. In our contemporary vision, conflict, disagreement, negotiation, and compromise have no place at our tables. All that we define as "dysfunction." We can do better!

Instead of trusting our instincts and accepting the obvious (that interactions between people will always be messy and at least occasionally frustrating), we look to books, TV, magazines, and the Internet for the quick, complete fix. They give us a scripted vision of harmony that transcends friction—and usually has a happy ending. So in much the same way *This Old House* host Bob Vila provides step-by-step instructions on how to install up-to-date electrical circuitry in a vintage Victorian, we want a parenting pro to tell us which wires to connect and which switches to pull to get our children to do what we want when we want it. Yet relationships between people cannot be improved with a set of how-to directions. Humans are not linear; children are not machines. Our relationships are a subtle, shifting, but (one hopes) satisfying process of learning, leaning, bending, and loving as three, four, or more individuals somehow figure out how to live in relative comfort with one another.

Such a process inevitably includes good days and some not-so-good ones. We need to give ourselves space and sympathy when the bad ones occur. Some days we just don't feel like talking to anyone, least of all to our kids. One family of five, with two pediatrician parents, laughingly labels those their "dysfunctional" days: A teen in a sulk over a curfew disagreement becomes not a big crisis, not an issue that weighs down the weekend. It is simply part of life. Rather than beating themselves up for being imperfect, these parents simply go about their business. Now's not a time to talk about it—she'll just blow up—and tomorrow's another day. Their acceptance probably keeps those bad days from multiplying into weeks or months— and no doubt goes a good distance toward cementing this family's solid, connected relationship. The daughter knows that in the end the parents love and accept her and will discuss what really is important to her when the time is right.

Expecting that parenting professionals can help us to get our children to behave the way we want or to grow up to be the adults we want them to be is setting our hopes way too high. But news reports would have us believe otherwise. The entire American middle class now reads articles trumpeting the premise that all children can be smarter, more socially adept, and far superior if we parents take their development very seriously and foster it actively. Child development research findings are presented as if our current state of knowledge were complete and ready for full implementation in every family. Reports pinpoint crucial periods of brain development almost down to the phase of the moon, telling us exactly what is needed (weekly piano lessons) and when (between a child's third and fourth birthday) for superior mathematical prowess to blossom. As for feeding infants, no question can remain; breastfeeding, we are told, boosts IQ by (precisely) eight points.

In fact, many scientists are dismayed at how these sorts of findings are presented. In *The Myth of the First Three Years* (Free Press, Sept. 1999), Dr John Bruer voices real concern. "What science policy should tell you is something about root causes and mechanisms," he told *The New York Times*. He went so far as to say the highly touted research studies based on brain scan and molecular study techniques say "nothing at all" about how we should parent, or even teach our children.

The reports make it seem as though missing the dead-lines means missing the boat. It simply is not so. After all, Leonard Bernstein didn't even start playing piano until the age of ten, when his aunt gave the family a piano and the child developed an instant attachment to the instrument. Just look at the career he built for himself—well after his musical critical period had ended!

What's truly ironic is that the net result of this infor-mation and expert advice, most especially for those of us already doing our very best to raise our children right, leads us to mistrust our own instincts. We begin to believe that there is one right way and lots of wrong ones. Yes, the brain is absolutely more pliable and receptive in the early months and years of life, and a child ought to receive ade-quate stimulation so the brain forms vital connections. That is the scientific underpinning for the current trend. Sure a rich and stimulating environment helps a child to develop well, while neglect and sensory deprivation can lead to lifelong deficiencies that, sadly, is the lot of many of the world's children now living in desperate poverty. But let us not forget that many of the world's babies whose brains develop most poorly are behind because they don't get enough food—not because they are deprived of specially textured blankets, high-tech teething toys, and night-lights that silhouette shapes on the nursery ceiling.

Does that really apply to brain development here in the affluent West? Not really. But we are encouraged to work to make every day of an infant's life a veritable three-ring cir-cus. Has research shown that the child who has never heard a bar of classical music has no hope of conquering calculus? Does the infant who is—dare we even suggest—*bottle-fed* have no prayer of making it into the gifted and talented pool at the local magnet school? Of course not. Yet we've grown accustomed to exactly this kind of literal interpretation of statistical scientific findings.

One mother of a fifteen month old burst into tears when her pediatrician told her that the child needed tubes to treat his chronic ear infections. "But I breast-fed him for a year, made all his baby food from organic fruit and vegetables, and quit my job so I wouldn't have to put him in day care! What did I do wrong?" She'd read the advice and followed it all—to the last letter. She truly believed that her due diligence should have been rewarded with a 100 percent healthy child. In her eyes, the tubes in her son's ears, hardly the end of the world, were a sign of her failure. Were he old enough to understand her words, he might feel that by being ill, he was letting his mother down—an emotional complication no child needs.

But this mother is hardly alone in her way of thinking. Many parents have trouble viewing real scientific information from a reasonable perspective. Another new mom was having difficulty breast-feeding her newborn son, who seemed insatiable. "He's always hungry; I can't seem to feed him enough," she told her obstetrician. She went on, near tears, "I feel like a complete and utter failure!" The experienced doctor, mother to three grown kids who had *not* been breast-feed all that long since she was back to work when they were just eight weeks old, suggested that the new mother start supplementing with an occasional bottle of formula. Her proposal was met with protest. "Isn't breast milk best for his intellectual development?" the distraught new mother asked. "Not if it comes at the expense of his mom's sanity," was the wise doctor's reply.

But such commonsense wisdom is often discounted if it seems to fly in the face of what the most up-to-date article reports. How can you question a "scientific" study? Easily if you have had firsthand experience with scientific research, less easily if you do not. In our opinion, even if studies of breast-feeding turn out to be completely accurate—and we have serious doubts about that—we question whether having an anxious, depressed mother who constantly frets about her inadequacies will help *any* child's IQ, brain development, or emotional well-being.

Yet contemporary American parents are told that every little thing matters. This generation has swallowed—and is choking on—a vision of child rearing as a skill that requires the right equipment, access to the right research, the right books and magazines, and the right pediatrician and psychologist or psychiatrist, to get the right information and advice on everything, from tone of voice to toilet training. Then, and only then, will parents get the right relationships and, most important in this vision, the right results.

It sounds extreme, but many people feel this way. How often have you heard someone shake their head at some news report of a neglectful parent and say, "Amazing. You need a license to drive a car, but not to raise a child." Of course there are parents who need some instruction in the fine art of parenting—and others who shouldn't be allowed near their children, they are so abusive and harmful. But such parents are the exception and, fortunately, not the rule.

Raising a child is not at all like learning to drive a car or working to memorize a complicated set of traffic and safety laws. What most of us need is not a set of books filled with rules to memorize so we can pass a test and become certified parents. Maybe that would be a good program for teenage parents, but what the rest of us need is the very antithesis of that view. When it comes to raising good children, we need to learn to trust who we really are, to enjoy the experience more by restoring our faith in our own loving instincts.

We need to relax, to tune in to our intuition, to know our children and ourselves better. We need to contend with the fears we may feel that we might be destructive to our children and to wrestle with aspects of ourselves that we don't like—like the impulse to tease little Tyler sarcastically when he makes a mistake, the way we may have been teased, belittled, and punished by our own dad for our foibles and failures. We have to accept some sadness about our disappointments in our own parents and face the fact that we too will be less than perfect.

We need to learn to strike a balance between wholehearted involvement and standing back in order that our children, particularly as they mature, have enough space not to feel smothered. We need to guide them, but also to give them the room to make their lives their own, and to slowly learn to stand on their own two feet.

We need to accept our imperfect selves. To love our children, we need first to love ourselves, as we are, not as we will be if we just manage to solve this one little problem (then the next, then the next). Perhaps surprisingly, accepting who we actually are will likely make us much better parents, more fully involved heart and soul.

Dr. Benjamin Spock knew this. "Trust Yourself," were the first two words in his child-rearing book. Penelope Leach, a more contemporary back-to-basics parenting expert, cautions parents against trying to raise children "by the book." Dr. T. Berry Brazelton good-naturedly urges parents to relax and trust their own instincts.

But relaxing can be difficult in our edgy culture, when

such warm, cozy reassurance is about as fashionable as an orange tweed Barcalounger, comfortable maybe, but for sure a decorating don't. Everywhere we turn some supposedly knowledgeable source pelts us with "reliable" information about parenting. These popular approaches insist that we can be better parents if we just read this, watch that, or listen right now. Parenting magazines overflow newsstand racks; child-rearing manuals fill enormous sections at the bookstore, usually adjacent to self-help. Newsletters go out from universities and groups on a vast number of parenting topics: raising gifted kids, traveling with kids, healthy kids, vegetarian kids, safety, psychological and psychiatric research, mental health letters, and more. Television shows and radio broadcasts blare advice from the experts. An armada of parenting professionals sails the national lecture circuit offering seminars and workshops on their particular topic. Not to mention the web sites, local support groups, and parenting classes at schools and hospitals.

Some of this is helpful. It is wonderful that people have places to turn to for information and help. The best advice is presented as a thought-provoking discussion that helps parents clarify how they feel so they can find approaches that work in their own unique situation. But in reality, editors and producers know that their consumers are anxious and pressed for time. Today's parents are insecure about themselves, overscheduled, and in search of efficient and informative advice that will work *now* if not sooner. So most editors frame it all in a clever, concise, "how to" kind of way.

We can try to "Ferberize" the wakeful infant, with the simple steps outlined in the controversial but very popular *Solve Your Child's Sleep Problems* by Richard Ferber, a book offering advice that even the author says today's parents are taking too literally. Toddler tosses the green beans she ate so willingly the week before off the highchair tray? Expert solution: Involve her in meal preparation. Backtalk from a nine year old? Say this, do that, and the whole contretemps will melt away as quickly and sweetly as a mini-marshmallow in a mug of hot cocoa.

Books, articles, and shows make conflict seem undesirable. But it is in that give-and-take of disagreement, in anger, frustration, and learning to hear one another despite it, in the effort to get a resolution that both kids and parents can live with relatively—though not absolutely—comfortably, that lies the real opportunity for important personal and ethical growth. Family life is a child's real-life field course in conflict resolution and learning to live together; only if that learning has been sidestepped do our kids have to study these "skills" in peer-group mediation classes. Those lessons should be lived, not lectured about.

Some of our most important growth can come from painful family situations if we let them play themselves out and work to understand what is happening between us when things go wrong. One mother we know, who grew up in an alcoholic home, wanted more than anything to build a happy home life for her own children. But her eldest child, a girl, was thwarting her efforts at every turn. Practically from infancy, this child seemed to want to define herself as the polar opposite of her mother. Chores, clothing, household rules—every issue became a battle. Predictably, the onset of adolescence propelled the situation from bad to worse.

And then it got better. Why? Because over time the mother began to realize that she had been counting on her daughter to rectify her own childhood wounds, that she was trying to create for her first child, since she was a girl, the life she'd wanted for herself. As the mother learned to appreciate the daughter for *herself*—a young woman who was, in some ways, very different from her mother, and in other ways, amazingly like her—their relationship became transformed. Although they still have the usual arguments of mothers and teenage daughters, the fact is that by learning to let go of her illusion, her inner image of who she wanted her daughter to be, this woman has come much, much closer to realizing her dream of having the kind of mother-daughter relationship she had always craved. It also likely happened in large part because the daughter no longer felt rejected for who she is, a disappointment in not being the child her mother wanted. Feeling fundamentally accepted, she could be freer, more playful, more herself.

No doubt the mother would have loved to bypass those difficult years—but reading a book could not have given her the same insights that arrived so slowly because they took time and emotional struggling to unfold. No prepackaged, shrink-wrapped solution could have helped her resolve a specific, and very personal, dilemma. She had to work it out to make it her own. She and her daughter *created* their relationship. It was theirs alone, an intensely personal production.

But muddling through to find your own individual way is not an appealing concept in our very efficient world. Why waste time? A shortcut through all the hard work is alluring. If we just knew what to do, wouldn't everyone be happy most, if not all of the time? It's that line of reasoning that has elevated to guru status those wise folks who have managed to convince us that raising children doesn't have to be a pain in the backside, ever. Some experts are reasonable, thoughtful, helpful, and rational. But often the ones who stand out as "great" are the ones who, like a new and improved brand of cream rinse, promise to quickly make our typically snarled and frequently unruly family lives flow as easily and attractively as the long, shiny tresses of a homecoming queen riding in a convertible on a breezy autumn afternoon.

It's an illusion. Raising kids can be frustrating as all get out. No book or expert in the world (present company included) can change that. One of the best things we can do for our kids is to get real in our relationships with them, so they can see for themselves how real human beings work out real problems in the real world. More important, it allows us to be among the active creators of our lives with them, messy, sloppy artists slapping paint on a unique canvas all our own.

"Getting real" means getting involved, down and dirty with the mess of everyday existence that no expert is going to eliminate. It means that we stop polishing the surfaces of our lives to such a sheen that no one can see inside to who we really are. It means pointing out the times we adults do things exceptionally well, by working hard at them. It also means that we are willing to talk about mistakes and messes we've made. That we get comfortable with the idea of making an apology to our child when we are wrong. And likely we need to honestly commend ourselves more often for the many times we got it good enough.

One father realized that his relationship with his son had taken a turn for the better when he openly and honestly acknowledged that the solution his son proposed to a problem between them was better than the father's idea. We are being real with our children when we admit to them how much we dread making a condolence call but then go ahead and do it anyway. We get real when we acknowledge that yes, we are being two-faced in our interactions with that guy at work we dislike so much but have to get along with on a day-to-day basis. It is good to let our children witness the realities of adult life: To see us disagree with our spouse, but that it does not end our marriage; to watch us swallow our rage at the ineptitude of the checkout girl in the supermarket line; to be there as we wrestle with the checkbook after neglecting it one month longer than we should have. They also see us as real when we handle a slight well, are kind to a needy neighbor, or even express great glee when we slaughter an opponent in a tennis match.

Being real does not mean never editing yourself. Sometimes keeping quiet until anger has dissipated spares your spouse an unkindness you won't have to regret later. At times, though, you say those things anyway . . . we all do. So we make amends. Being real means that we do not constantly work hard to manicure the small details of our lives so that everyone at the club, office, or school will think that we (and, it goes without saying, our kids, marriages, and homes) are picture-perfect.

Children do well to see that life means doing some things very well, being average at many, and perhaps even poor at more than a few. Being real means making mistakes, accommodations, and compromises in our lives, not because we love to, but because doing so accomplishes the most good for the greatest number of family members. No one gets everything they want, but everyone gets something.

Perhaps armed with that knowledge, when our children grow up they won't spend too many years pretending to be somebody else, somebody more perfect, and somebody therefore more lovable. Perhaps as teenagers they will try on a few less costumes—as in, personalities and attitudes—that don't suit them. Perhaps as adults, they can understand what it takes to make a marriage work the first time around, instead of trying again, and again, to find that "perfect" partner with whom passion and romance will never fade. After all, a large part of a good marriage is figuring out who takes out the garbage when—literally *and* metaphorically!

Most child-rearing experts are sincere and offer advice that is well-meaning, informative, and valuable, at least to the reader with a vested interest, having bought the book. Sometimes it is even useful. "Sometimes" being the key word. If, as you read the book, you find yourself saying, "Oh yes, that does sound like me." Or, "Yep, that's just like my kid." Or, "Mmmm, I never thought of it that way but it does seem to ring true to our situation." If the book eases your anxiety somewhat and offers some alternatives you hadn't considered, it may be $24.95 well invested; if the parenting professional being interviewed illuminates a behavior you didn't previously understand, and offers a new way to understand it, listening is time well spent.

But one-size-fits-all advice? Use it to paper train your puppy.

Trying to act in ways that feel forced and unnatural to you will inevitably fall flat, and will make you feel like even more of a failure. Your most intimate relationship begins to feel alien. That was the experience one mother had when she read that the phrase "This is so *unlike* you" would be a good response to the willful misbehavior of a grade-school-age child, since it made the assumption that the child wanted to behave well and usually did. The problem was the behavior was not in the least unlike her child; it was absolutely characteristic, and both mother and child knew it. The issues went deeper—and they often do.

When the advice makes you feel like a total nincompoop, the likely culprit is the book—and the expert—not you. Even if your approach is less than optimal, any book that makes you feel like an anxious idiot will not make you a better parent. Anxiety brings out the worst in everyone—me, you, and Lord knows, our kids. It pushes you away from your child, not closer. What you need to do when you are confused is to relax and get comfortable enough to think about what to do next—because you are the one who is in the forever relationship with your child.

Let's return, for a moment, to the example of Dr. Richard Ferber's book, *Solve Your Child's Sleep Problems*, which offers some really good advice and details a specific crying-it-out technique. Many parents have tried this method of teaching a baby to soothe himself and go back to sleep with great success. Other parents couldn't make it work. "My son screamed till he vomited all over the crib," recalls one mother of three. "Then I realized, I didn't mind having him in my bed. So I never tried it again."

Her experience doesn't make Richard Ferber wrong and her right, or vice versa. Dr. Ferber's advice is sound and useful to many families. But as that particular mother applied it, it simply did not fit her style of parenting. In time, she was self-aware enough to recognize that to be the case. A generation ago, overanxious, obedient parents ignored every ounce of parental instinct they had when they let their infants bawl for hours on end because the doctor had told them to feed their infant only every four hours and never in between. Today, those who are less sure of themselves follow Ferber's—or some other expert's—instructions to the letter, leading to gut-wrenching scenarios where they hover at the door of a screaming infant at 3:00 A.M., feeling hopelessly inadequate. Does it really make sense for a grown-up to engage a seven-month-old child in a contest of wills to see who's the tough guy and who's the wimp? If the child's cry is a question that asks, "What do you do when I am panicky and desperate?" is the answer you want to give, "I stand helplessly by the door because I think that's what the doctor thinks I should do"?

Which neatly puts in a nutshell what is wrong with so many x-step, one-size-fits-all solutions to problems with kids. They seem to promise salvation but end up adding frustration and confusion to an already loaded situation. They do not recognize that each child-parent pair is unique and needs to work their relationship out in their own way to their own mutual satisfaction. They pay entirely too much heed to getting beyond the problem and too little to getting behind it. Numerous factors can lurk behind any parental issue—and numerous theoretical ways to look at what they mean and imply for a child's future— be it a baby's bedtime battles, a preschooler's temper tantrums, a grade schooler's social issues, or a teen's rebellious acting out.

But most of all, these solutions rob you, the parent, of the confidence you need to take all that you feel, read, and hear and to create your own personal way to be with your child. All children and parents have highly individualized needs and their own reasons for why their relationships evolve as they do, reasons that meet, on some level, their own psychological and cultural needs. Children master developmental tasks and stages in their own way and at their own pace, meshing them in some unique arrangement together with their parents' needs, and sometimes those of their baby-sitter. It becomes a tangled, interesting, intricate weave. There are no prefab solutions to behavioral problems because children are not now, nor will they ever be, simple, mass-produced products to be tinkered with and fine-tuned.

Every parent benefits from a support system of likeminded individuals familiar with you and your stage and state in life to vent to, lean on, turn to for advice and reassurance. It is wonderful to have a pediatrician you like and respect and can ask questions of. It can be enormously helpful to have access to a professional, such as a family therapist, social worker, psychologist, or psychiatrist you trust and respect to ask for child-rearing advice when necessary, most especially for people who themselves come from troubled and troubling families (and there is no shortage in that category). Friends and family may have surprisingly good advice. The active, involved, and assertive parent who sizes up advice she has sought, who questions it, tries to figure out whether she agrees or disagrees, tries it on for size before accepting or rejecting the suggestion, will likely not go wrong.

All of which is so very different than picking a book off a shelf, taking as gospel wisdom gleaned from a magazine article, or memorizing by rote seven steps to a solution parroted in a tight, four-minute segment on some morning news show. Those tidy little strategies make family problems simply a matter of finding the right tool or intervention to allow every single one of us to bypass any unseemly difference of opinion. All too often, we end up bypassing the real issue behind the behavior and the real opportunity it offers to have meaningful communication with our child and to thereby deepen our mutual understanding.

The toddler who balks at eating her beans is learning:

What she puts in her mouth is one of the few things she can control at this stage in her life, and the issue is autonomy and self-direction, not food intake or diet. If she won't eat it, it may be because that particular food does not taste, smell, or look good to her—true whether or not she was involved with the snapping and steaming of the beans. What is ultimately important in the interaction has less to do with appetite and good nutrition than with seeing how you react when she expresses her personal preferences, not to mention to your own frustration. One parent lamented that his six-year-old son liked no green foods. His sassy son corrected him: "Not true! I like green M&M's."

A smart-mouthed fourth grader *needs* to challenge your authority, and you need to get comfortable wielding it. Distraction and diversion may get you past some particular difficult moment, but the developmental learning will be sidetracked if you *always* avoid disagreement. The relationship will not grow, ethics will not evolve, and the issues will certainly surface again in new forms. And again. Ultimately and in total, they will set the direction for your relationship with your child.

Child-rearing experts are not an innovation of our generation. Our parents and their parents had access to books and articles on children and family life. Even Harriet Beecher Stowe, famous for *Uncle Tom's Cabin*, coauthored an 1869 book for American mothers that included advice on child rearing. There were trends in child rearing then as now: Schedules and physical punishment and affection and infant formulas have bobbed in and out of fashion much like hats and hemlines. Our own parents turned to *Dr. Spock's Baby and Child Care*, not only because he provided comforting reassurance, but also because they wanted specific

answers about rashes, fevers, and behaviors that have always flummoxed people who care for small children.

And that was as useful and valuable then as it continues
to be today. We parents need concrete information about,
say, which of the many analgesics and antipyretics are best
for relieving the fever of a child with an ear infection. We
may even benefit from knowing the biology of what is happening inside the painfully irritated ear. Understanding
has always diminished anxiety, which is part of why we find
science so helpful. It explains things logically, replacing
our angst with understanding. Learning about developmental stages is also useful and interesting—attachment to
a security object, for instance, or the normalcy of sexual
curiosity in preschoolers. Often excellent advice can be
had on the practical aspects of parenting, in books and articles on planning family vacations or deciding when to
start giving your child an allowance. Books, magazines,
and TV programs can offer sound, solid advice and we authors have authored plenty of recommendations ourselves.
We would never presume to denigrate the industry in a
general way and only partly because we don't want to bite
the hand that feeds us.

However as consumers, we need to be attuned to where
the information and advice comes from, to the particular
point of view being presented, because whether it is apparent or not, there always is one. Some people are
Democrats, others Republicans, and some just prefer remaining Independents. Some people like sushi; others
think raw fish is disgusting. Just matters of personal taste,
style, and outlook. There is no *one* right way to raise a child
nor one right child to be. It would be a pretty boring world
if we all turned out identical.

A while back, the media made much of a disagreement

on the subject of toilet training between two well-known, highly intelligent child-rearing experts. John Rosemond, the prolific and well-known family psychologist, syndicated columnist, lecturer, and author of numerous books on parenting, believes children should be using the toilet by the age of two. He recommends a straightforward, no-nonsense method for achieving that goal, one that uses a child's dismay and discomfort as tools to help him learn the fine art of toilet use. In general, Rosemond believes that kids—even babies and toddlers—are given too much power in today's families and that it is up to us parents to take control of our children and, indeed, our lives.

Some parents agree with Rosemond wholeheartedly, and quite likely those who do have great success with his potty-training method; others find it harsh, on themselves and their children. For those families, Dr. T. Berry Brazelton's "wait till he's ready" approach, which basically recommends waiting till your child tells you he or she wants to use the potty, seems a better fit. As is characteristic of his overall philosophy in child rearing, Dr. Brazelton believes parents should accustom themselves to pay close attention to what a child is trying to say—with or without words.

Both experts have crucial, intelligent things to say. There is validity to both points of view. But each has a particular philosophical—not scientific—outlook about parent-child relationships that speaks more directly to some parents than to others. The relevance of a particular professional opinion depends on the child, the parent, and the circumstances of their lives. Neither Brazelton nor Rosemond is right or wrong. It is up to us, as parents, to know what feels right *for us* and to find an expert who speaks to us. And to pay less attention to those who do not.

. . .

Most expert advice is far from neutral and simply scientific. But in many cases the professional's personal point of view is invisible to the consumer. Without question and usually without acknowledgment, the "expert's" preexisting beliefs carry a story in a particular direction. For instance, a journalist who delivered her two children by C-section may unwittingly write a story on how anesthesia affects a newborn rather differently than another who staunchly insisted on a natural delivery or one who has never even given birth. Because prejudice is exerted in ways readers—and often the writer—are completely unaware of, it may be hard to spot. It is woven into how a story is organized, which statistics and facts make it into print and which are tossed into the trash because the writer sincerely considers them to be beside the point, the tone of the concluding paragraph, the photographs that are used.

Even the publication itself has an editorial point of view that shapes its content. Sophisticated readers recognize the philosophical differences among seemingly similar publications like, say *Time, Newsweek,* and *U.S. News & World Report.* Among parenting publications or women's magazines, the differences may be subtler, but they exist nonetheless. Since most of *Working Mother*'s readers work and have children in child care, it may report a story on a research study concluding that kids who attend day care have more colds and ear infections somewhat differently than *Parents Magazine* for instance. Not only do magazines shape their stories in response to who they perceive their readers to be, but to who they want them to be—targeting affluent, educated readers who will be more attractive to advertisers, for instance, by slanting stories in their direction (which is perhaps one reason we've become convinced that a well-decorated nursery is crucial to good child rearing!).

Parents are more qualified than they likely give themselves credit for being, and it is in their interests to train themselves to view the advice, often unsought, that comes their way through critical eyes. They are the ones who have to decide what pertains to their family and what does not. For parents, this means that a trial-and-error method of learning the steps to a highly individual dance, which each relationship turns out to be, is very much a part of the process. The important point is that this very personal dance be loving, respectful, and passionately involving.

In our era of scientific precision, however, that old-fashioned learning process may seem anachronistic, not to mention inefficient. It takes such a long time to adjust to one another, so many mistakes get made along the way of getting to know one another's nuances, and we may justifiably wonder how a mistake can *ever* be a good thing.

So parents turn to the experts. The agglomeration of "latest" advisories and cautionary scientific tales on the news programs has seeped undetected into America's belief system. Parents now believe they need this information, every last bit of it, to raise kids right. They don't really understand how very fickle much of the "new" science is, particularly when served up by the media: The newest research study bumps the previous one very quickly. Often, the result of all the media attention to the absolutely newest research finding is that the simplest things get overthought, overanalyzed.

An example is the socialization literature that purports to study the effect of say, parenting style, on a child's moral development. While we authors take issue with Judith Rich Harris's strong statement that other than through genetics, parents have little impact on who a child turns out to be, we agree with some of her opinions on the failings of much of the child-rearing research. As Harris explains in her book *The Nurture Assumption:*

Socialization research is the scientific study of the effects of the environment—in particular, the effects of parents' child-rearing methods or their behavior toward their children—on the children's psychological development. It is a science because it uses some of the methods of science, but it is not, by and large, an experimental science.

She goes on to say that:

. . . since researchers have no control over what parents are doing in their own homes with their own children, for the most part, all researchers can do is observe and try to make correlations between their observations of parental behavior, and their interpretations of how it impacts the children.

There are numerous flaws within that model, according to Harris. First, it is virtually impossible to determine a causal link—even if a change of some sort is noted—since it is impossible to account for all variables. Some perceived effect might in fact exist—a parent's authoritarian style may seem to lead a child to rebel—but the link may not be the cause and effect. Who knows what else might contribute to that behavior? Harris thinks a child's friends are more influential, for instance. Second, the studies are designed in such a way that they are likely to yield some usable results. Scientists have bosses too, and it simply looks better if the research leads in some direction. And finally, it is impossible to measure for the influence of genetics, the other factor Harris believes is crucial to how a child turns out.

Much of what Harris says is inaccurate in our opinion, though this is another situation in which the media made a mountain range of a molehill. As Nobel Prize winner and former president of Rockefeller University Dr. Torsten Wiesel, whose research led to much of our appreciation of the importance of early stimulation on brain development, said, "To believe parents are not important shows a bankruptcy of common sense."

However, we do applaud Harris for throwing a bucket of cold water on the mania for hyper-parenting, for doing her best, as we are, to debunk the belief that every little thing we parents do has been scientifically proven to be crucial to child development. In contrast to Harris, however, we see committed, dedicated, involved parents as more fundamental to the shaping of a child's character than their peers. We want to give parenting back to parents and childhood back to children.

We are fighting powerful influences when we try to give every parent permission to stop holding their breath, to stop worrying about the impact of every minute event in their child's life. Because in trying to grab attention, the media promises that every latest finding will have a vital impact on children's lives. And they do so with a voice of real authority, aggressively using directive statements and action verbs. Reporters, few of whom are trained as scientists, skim right over the sections of the studies that speak cautiously in the measured cadence of scientific language, which detail exhaustively a study's methodology and limitations: Every serious scientist includes those. What the news reporters do is cut right to the conclusions in an attempt to provide service—"news you can use"—to readers. Which is how we have ended up with all these stories that tell us, "Here is how to make your infant smart," "Here is how to raise a drug-free kid."

Newsweek magazine, which seems to have targeted anxious baby boom parents as a major part of their market share, offers some prime examples. In 1998 alone, the publishers ran four cover stories on parenting topics: "Does Your Child Need a Tutor?" "How to Build a Better Boy," "Do Parents Matter?" (on the controversy surrounding publication of Harris's book), and "Tomorrow's Child: A Kid's Life in the 21st Century." Others in recent years have been "Your Child's Brain: How Kids Are Wired for Music, Math & Emotions" and a special issue, "Your Child from Birth to Three: What You Need to Know."

A close reading of these *Newsweek* issues reveals that while the tone remains consistent from piece to piece—definitive, certain, authoritative, and directive—the messages change dramatically. The story on brain development, for instance, included an engaging series of graphics that told us precisely when certain skills—logic, language, and music—are installed in the circuitry of the brain and provided very specific instructions on what parents can do to help things along. "Play counting games with your toddler. Have him set the table to learn one-to-one relationships—one plate, one fork per person. And, to hedge your bets, turn on a Mozart CD." It makes kids sound like PCs.

The 1997 special edition, "Your Child," told us parents to "engage . . . four-month-old(s) in face-to-face communication" and "try to phase out baby talk" by six months.

"How to Build a Better Boy" (1998) tells parents to teach their sons "It's OK to get mad."

Then, just a few months later, in "Do Parents Matter?" the author commended Judith Harris for . . . "acting as a corrective to the hectoring message of so many books on child rearing." Harris's book, she noted, "lands at a time when many parents are terrified that failing to lock eyes with their newborn [isn't that how you would define "face-to-face" communication?] or not playing Mozart in the nursery ["Your Child's Brain" recommended doing exactly that] or—God forbid—losing it when their kid misbehaves will ruin him for life" (though it is important to teach sons at least not to repress anger).

The inconsistencies in these stories are glaring. And while we single out *Newsweek* to demonstrate the point, it has excellent company. Other news outlets do exactly the same thing because they all are in the business of spinning engaging stories, not raising children. Furthermore, *Newsweek* generally does a very good job of reporting *facts* on health and family life and a wide range of other topics. But we doubt that news magazines should be shaping parents' child-rearing philosophy or trying to radically alter it on a regular basis. The child psychoanalyst Erik Erikson demonstrated, in his classic book *Childhood and Society*, that over time every society and set of parents slowly evolve child rearing to meet that society's needs. Either American society needs anxious neurotics who change their mind every few minutes, or magazines ought not tinker so casually with the process.

How parents raise children should be based on their own highly individual and well thought-out beliefs. Mothers and fathers would all do well to return to Dr. Spock's first premise and most useful advice: "Trust Yourself."

Go ahead. Read. Learn. Talk. Study. But in the final analysis, you need to know yourself in order to trust yourself. No matter what Judith Harris or any other expert says, in the end we will all *feel* responsible for how our kids turn out. So we all need to feel free and confident to choose from the vast cornucopia of available advice what suits us. See what fits, what deepens your understanding and emotional appreciation of the relationship you have with your child, what might further it. And then wrap up and tie the rest and take it out with the recycling. You don't need it. When it comes to your child, *you* are the expert.

5

Whose Life Is It?

Little Cara, a third grader, never has to worry about forget-ting her lunch, or her lunch money. Since the middle of first grade, her mother has made a practice of arriving at school every day just a few minutes before her daughter's class adjourns to the lunchroom. She meets Cara in the cafeteria to hand her a hot lunch—sometimes soup or pasta from home, often a Happy Meal from McDonald's or a slice of pizza from Pizza Hut. "Cara just won't eat sandwiches," confides her mom to a friend, insisting she doesn't consider it an imposition to organize each day around her daughter's midday repast. "And the food they serve in the cafeteria—I wouldn't eat it either!"

Al and Cindy are so frustrated. Their ten-year-old son Charlie is in the "High Achievers" program at school this year, which they know is an honor and a privilege. Charlie, however, is unimpressed and uninspired. He has put so little effort into his assignments that his continued participation is in question. Lately, his concerned parents have been working as hard as (ar-guably even harder than) Charlie on each assignment. Last week they even bowed out of a long-planned family reunion be-cause all three needed to spend Sunday afternoon planning and building an invention Charlie was supposed to have worked on for several weeks. "I'm afraid that if he gets dropped from the Achievers program he will get discouraged and put even less effort into his schoolwork," says Cindy. "But I don't feel right doing his work for him either."

Sam, the junior varsity soccer coach, picks up the ringing phone and isn't all that surprised to hear the voice of Angela Clark, mother of young Austin, a committed but somewhat lackluster player who spent most of the last game on the bench. It's the third time Mrs. Clark has called this season: First, she just wanted to introduce herself and offer assistance with managing the team, which Sam appreciated. Second, she wanted to suggest that perhaps Austin's talents might be better utilized in a midfielder position (Sam had slotted him as a sweeper). And now, Sam's pretty certain, she wants to find out why he didn't play more in yesterday's game. With a sigh, he settles in for what is certain to be a lengthy conversation.

Whose childhood is it, anyway?

No question, we parents should do our best to provide a good life for our children. But is it really in their best long-term interests (let alone ours) for us to behave as though we must personally edit every aspect of their lives to make them letter-perfect?

Let's start with a reality check: It can't be done. Since knowing that hasn't stopped us from trying, maybe we ought to ask a few other questions. For instance, what if working so hard to oversee our children's lives means that we end up intruding on what really ought to be their private space? What if in trying to get everything to go just so, we actually make life more difficult for ourselves and less enjoyable for them? What if our constant attention to productivity, learning, and creativity actually end up making our kids less competent, even in those areas?

Because those things can, and often do, happen when parents are unwilling, or unable, to allow children to live and, appropriately, as they mature, become responsible for their own lives. Yet it is hard to pull back. Giving up on hyper-parenting seems like a bold and ill-advised step in the wrong direction. We are utterly and completely convinced that good parents are fiercely attentive to every single detail of their children's lives. Anything less seems like negligence in the face of life's greatest challenge.

Isn't doing it ourselves the only way to make sure things happen in the right way? One mother was concerned about her twelve-year-old son's social life, or lack thereof. She supported him in every way she could think of, encouraging him to try new activities, inviting other families with kids of the same age over to their home. When at last the boy began to take a few tentative steps on his own, to make a phone call here and there and invite kids over from time to time, his mother was thrilled—but still concerned. Fretting that it still wasn't enough, she wondered whether she ought to step in and schedule a few more play dates and special events—just to be sure.

Our culture may worship the appearance of spontaneity (note the windblown hair, the rosy cheeks, and out-of-control laughter on the models on the billboards along the highway). But beneath the surface, the books and shows say that the best way to get there, to that place where life looks as fabulous and fun-filled as a Coca-Cola commercial, is by planning as carefully as possible along the way. We are told we can control it all—and we definitely want to do so, particularly when we feel so *out* of control by the demands of two, three, or four children! We accept that in reality the hair that looks so free in the photo is actually stiff with hairspray; we understand that the model's gorgeous smile has been enhanced with special whitening treatments and lots of special dental work. And that even after those ministrations, the whole picture has been airbrushed to make it all the more perfect. Every bit of it takes lots of time; hard, often painful, work; and airbrushing—the commitment to hiding our true, unedited selves from public view so everyone "out there" sees only the illusion of who we want them to believe we are.

Of course most parents don't go that far in their personal lives, but many are overly involved in trying to shape events to some prescribed vision of the way things ought to be. In our first several chapters, we discussed how parents begin being hyper about parenting even before they have children. Preconceived notions, materialism, and overreliance on expert advice lead them to try and control many variables in their infants' lives. That compulsion really takes hold as children grow up and go out into the world.

As the temptation to hyper-parent increases, so do the opportunities. In the school-age years—which typically start by a child's third birthday nowadays, if not sooner—parents feel they should immerse themselves in the details of children's academic, athletic, and social lives. All that, as they continue intensive efforts to enrich their child's free time with experiences to enhance their development.

What really should be beginning to happen as children get older is that they start to take over more responsibility for their own lives, and their parents start to let go. If the goal is for children to develop the skills they need to be independent and self-sufficient, they need *practice*. Little by little, as they mature and are ready, under a parent's "casual" supervision, even second, third, or fourth graders are old enough to *begin* juggling their responsibilities with their leisure activities. That's how they learn. They can decide when to do their homework (perhaps with the understanding that the TV is off-limits till it is complete and with someone around to remind when they forget), when to have a friend over, what clothing styles to wear, when to practice the trumpet, start the book report, or clean their room. Naturally, if they had fewer commitments to juggle, they might also do it better. That they will make some bad decisions, miss a deadline or two, and lose privileges as a penalty for a job not done on time is to be expected. Making mistakes is one of the best ways to learn.

Many of us parents today are, quite simply, too involved in our children's lives. We've become convinced that every single thing matters, every minute of every day. So we add and add and add activities and then have a hard time letting go of the smallest detail. To prevent even the tiniest mishap, misstep, or mistake, we believe we should act as stage managers responsible for all production details: casting, costumes, scenery, music, script changes, and making sure no one ever misses a cue or flubs a line.

And boy, does *that* keep us busy!

The compulsion to have our fingers in every mud pie our children make starts early and accelerates as they get older. If all the advice is followed, parental involvement knows no bounds. Not only do we need to know what's going on in our kids' lives, but we feel like it is our job to sprinkle our parental fairy dust to make it all happen in just the right way for them. Little, if possible nothing, ought to be left to chance.

Some parents feel they must specify every detail in their

child's life down to the microscopic level. It can get truly nuts! One mother, working with an agency to hire a nanny, asked that she be sent only applications for women taller than 5'8"—she believed that anyone shorter would not project the proper aura of authority to her preschooler! In the years to come, parents are told to feel personally responsible, not just for scheduling a preschooler's play date, but also for determining what he and his five-year-old friend do so they will be certain to have a good time. It is up to parents to provide insightful commentary and instruction so their fifth grader performs better on the tennis court; to instruct the football coach on what position a child is most suited to play. The quality of a ninth grader's English paper is absolutely within our realm of responsibility. And we ought to know exactly what our teenager is up to—despite our own memories of how clever kids can be at hiding those details from their parents and how annoyed and resentful we felt when our parents mistrusted us.

We believe it is our responsibility to regulate not only what our children have, in terms of food and shelter, but also the life they will experience and ultimately who they will grow up to be. We work overtime to make sure our kids feel good about themselves so that their emotional lives develop well. We see it as our responsibility, the goal we strive for, to craft for children the perfect childhood. It usually bears an uncanny resemblance to the one we wish we'd had ourselves, replete with smiles, successes, and a social life to beat the band. Parents are working to provide all the experiences that will make their children into the self-confident, successful people they themselves are working so hard to be, but secretly aren't all that sure they're pulling off.

· · ·

Micromanaging is a business term, but one that aptly describes what transpires in many American homes today. On paper, the concept makes perfect sense: If you want something done right, do it yourself. Plan it out, schedule each component, and if you have to delegate any aspect at all, check it—and then check it again. Leave nothing to chance, and no opportunities will be missed, no major mistakes will slip by. The buck has to stop somewhere, after all, and senior managers are often held responsible for all within their purview (even the tiniest details) since they get the credit, and megabuck bonuses, when all goes well. Depending on the outcome, micromanaging may or may not be a great way to run a business division, but it's never a good way to run a family.

Yet we do it, and for reasons that feel solid, unselfish, and true to us. We are intensely involved in our children's lives because we love them, we want what's best for them, and we believe that straight As, the starring role in the school play, or a sports scholarship to a top-notch college are the way to get there. Our kids may be too young to know the significance of each step along the ladder to success in later life—although we authors do know ten year olds who are conversant as to the characteristics of the ideal Ivy League applicant—but *we* parents know how good each of those achievements will look on a college application.

Our contemporary notions of child rearing have taken a philosophy that has given America great commercial success and applied it to our family lives. Parenting has become a "job" with supposedly good techniques and measurable outcomes. Corporate efficiency has been glamorized, productivity glorified. The scientific management principles and dehumanizing time-motion studies of Frederick Taylor, who early in the twentieth century worked to break down every manufacturing process to its most minute details, analyzing every worker's movements and redesigning them so no motion would be wasted or be without purpose, have come home with us, apparently to stay.

We cull through our Filofax schedules figuring out how to squeeze in every opportunity. If we can manage to reduce the amount of "wasted" time dramatically—assuming that time without a clear purpose is wasted—it makes perfect sense that we ought to use those salvaged minutes to stuff in just a little more that *is* constructive: another lesson, a family activity, tutoring, maybe even "quality time." But even family dinners, if scheduled and structured in such a way that they are constraining, can feel like a burden!

We've bought into the belief that everything in life can, and should, be rational, systematic, smooth, and highly efficient. Anything irrational seems unacceptable: We interpret our negative emotions, like annoyance and irritation, as dysfunction, and don't focus on the fact that our feelings are telling us something about our lives. We live for our lists, schedule every important activity (time for family, time for ourselves, time for sex), and convince ourselves that it's correct to live a life so crazed that we need a cute little pocket-sized computer to keep track of it. Time itself has become more precious—not really because we have less of it for ourselves. In fact, Americans likely have more potential leisure time than ever. But we have become convinced that we ought to pack ever more into every last moment of our discretionary and family time. We have been persuaded to slice every waking hour into thinner, sleeker, more precise segments, so that each might be filled with its own explicit purpose and clearly articulated goal.

All of the advice that encourages us, subtly or otherwise, to micromanage our kids' lives rests on the conviction that the human mind is stunningly powerful. Nothing evolves organically; nothing ought to be left to simple chance. It's a view of the world that at least gives us the illusion of having control. If we parents are the crucial variable in determining whether our kids do time at Duke or Leavenworth (Watson, the great American behaviorist, said that every child could be a criminal or a judge, given the right upbringing), we cannot relax for even a moment.

When you get right down to it, it is rather comforting to believe that good parents are able to construct a world that is safe and secure, in which everyone lives happily ever after. But if you listen carefully, you just might hear the theme music to *Mission Impossible*. Because that's what this vision, built on a platform of perfection that is not of this earth, turns out to be. No life can be a seamless success; human existence is the very definition of man-made and therefore flawed and imperfect.

Ancient artists would intentionally weave an imperfection into their textiles so as not to anger the gods by aspiring to an immortal's level of perfection. Even Persian rugs woven for the Shah were required to have an error in them because in Islam, perfection belongs to God alone. Our lives are often compared to such tapestries, and the metaphor is apt: There are mistakes, flaws, and imperfections to be found in everyone. The errors make the whole stronger. The slight imperfection enhances the beauty, for it marks things as being of the human world. Perfection is scary, a sign of hubris, for it might challenge the gods by suggesting that we covet their position.

Our children's lives will certainly be richer and more meaningful if we let them—gradually and appropriately— begin to take responsibility for themselves. And that includes, sometimes, letting them be flawed like the rest of us, to make mistakes, and to learn from them. Putting so much emphasis on success by, let's say, insisting on great grades (even if it means we must intervene to keep them high) makes it unlikely our children will learn about actions and their consequences.

One mother recounts how hard it was to not pick up the phone and call her seventh-grade son's science teacher when the child reported he'd been given a "D" for the quarter. Other parents had complained about this teacher and, by all accounts, they seemed to have some basis for their dissatisfaction. But the way this mother saw it, her son had not put out much effort in science—and however flawed the teacher might be, she didn't believe that her son had *earned* a good grade. In her mind, seventh grade was a better time to suffer such a consequence than, say, his junior year in high school when it might really have an impact on his future. Now that this boy is in the tenth grade, he has learned how to manage his academic life. He's not a straight-A student, but at any time during the school year, he can summarize exactly what he needs to do to get a "B"—the minimum grade he and his parents consider acceptable.

Kids need these experiences to learn how to manage their lives, but many of us are depriving children of the sort of childhood they really can learn from. We have truncated the freedoms and elevated the imperatives. The strive-for-the-best standard that is giving adults high blood pressure is now imposed on everything about our children's lives, even their play and games. A simple rec.-league hoop game becomes a testing ground that sifts out the worthy from the unworthy, that separates the men from the boys, those who will live the good life from those who are destined to fail.

No question it is generosity—spiced with dashes of guilt, anxiety, and ambition—that leads a parent to work so hard to shield a child from failure or disappointment. Love impels us to try and assure their success. (Frankly, though, it sometimes is also a wish to live vicariously through the child.) But as we strive so earnestly to smooth out their lives so that they can always be happy and so we don't have to weather the painful signs or symptoms of their unhappiness, we keep our kids from developing adaptability. We keep from them the gift of learning from their errors, a lesson that makes making mistakes easier to bear. We keep from them the skill set that ultimately will lead to self-sufficiency, which in the end is a more important predictor of survival and satisfaction in the adult world than a diploma from a highly competitive university. Most important, we deprive them of the sense that they are the authors of their own lives.

Consider the successful New York attorney who literally does not schedule evening activities for herself on weekdays, since her three sons, who range in age from sixth to eleventh grade, cannot seem to get their homework done—to her standards—unless she oversees it in person. Since the eldest boy began kindergarten, she has made a practice of sitting down next to him as he begins work on that day's assignment. He used to love having her there, and she loved sitting and working with him. It was a delightful time for both of them, but the dependence developed over the years was beneficial to neither of them—nor to the brothers who followed.

The fact that this mother didn't feel free to live a normal adult life was one problem; arguably a greater one is that her sons are not learning how to set and meet standards of their own nor to allot their time properly. The study skills her sons need can only be acquired through trial and error. Yes, that may mean that a child turns in a homework assignment that is not entirely correct or a paper that is not quite excellent. Even in anxious reality, no college we know of is particularly interested in a child's sixth-grade report card. Every day of a child's academic career—or any other aspect of his or her life—need not be scored with the intensity of an Olympic event.

Furthermore, all three of these boys have learned that school is so important to Mom that she can't trust them to manage it for themselves. Inadvertently, she has told them exactly where, and how, to act out if they feel angry at her and really want to get her goat.

Often our children surprise us when we let go of control for long enough to give them a chance. One mother, who works part time, recalls how she pushed herself week after week to come up with creative plans and play dates for the one afternoon her daughter was home alone with their sitter, since the child complained about being bored. One particularly stressful week, she forgot to schedule anything at all; her child, a second grader, coped (with the babysitter's blessing) by calling up a favorite friend and inviting her over. The same thing happened a few weeks later. Realizing that her daughter was now capable and very, very proud of figuring out how she wanted to spend her time, this mother stopped making all her plans for her. The little girl had shown her mother that she could do it for herself—and not insignificantly, the mother was willing to cede this small responsibility. One less thing for mom to do, one more thing for the child to feel good about.

That is exactly how the process of growing up is supposed to unfold. Bit by bit, our children begin taking responsibility for their own lives. A newborn infant is utterly helpless to feed him or herself, but by five or six months, is using both hands to bring food, and anything else the child can grab, to his or her mouth. At birth children cannot dress themselves; by eight months, they still can't, but they will have learned to raise their arms when a caretaker is trying to take off their shirt. By one year, they can pull off their own socks—within a few months, they'll try and work them *on*. A three year old is proud to master putting on his or her own jacket, and most preschoolers are completely capable of dressing themselves, provided we buy them the right kind of clothing.

But how many of us parents actually encourage them to do so—or even *let* them? Young children are so eager to display their new skills and talents—look at me, look at me, look at me now!—but so often we are too busy, too pressed for time, to allow them to take on responsibility when they want to—and that bodes ill for later on, when they really have to.

Many parents of kindergartners can rattle off entire lists of reasons—*good* ones, at that—why they *must* dress their children in the mornings. Because she's so sleepy; because we're running late; because she chooses wacky clothes; because she gets so frustrated with buttons and zippers. Valid reasons, perhaps. But the fact remains, a five year old can—and at least should be allowed to try to—be responsible for putting on his or her own clothing in the morning. And if a child's choices are somewhat offbeat, if your son sweeps his hair into a faux Mohawk one morning or your daughter arrays herself in three clashing prints, well, that needs to be okay too. (Okay, maybe not on the first day of school.) Children need to believe that their lives are theirs to live—even if we are hovering at the door to make sure their shoes are tied properly so they won't trip over the laces and to be certain they are wearing coats when it is twenty degrees outside.

Micromanaging every detail of a child's existence so that he or she doesn't miss a thing and striving to control every variable so the child doesn't mess up and have to experience frustration or failure gives children the unspoken sense that their parents suspect that without constant help they will never be able to take care of themselves. They are being told that their own tastes and preferences are invalid or inept. They must do it right, to their parents' standards or, they are told subliminally, they are just not good enough. Even if built upon the most hopeful of intentions, this is, ultimately, a hopeless vision. Children need to know that they will be loved, supported, and encouraged as they begin to take responsibility for their own lives, one tiny step at a time. They have a biological imperative to become independent.

That means that the parent needs to begin letting go, in ways that are safe and productive, as soon as possible and at a pace consistent with the child's natural growth. It will never be a precise process; everyone will make mistakes and readjustments. Attaining the correct balance between exerting enough control so that a child is safe and stimulated, and loosening up so they can separate and experiment, appropriately, with freedom is a process that we parents must fine-tune throughout our children's lives. Although we parents should provide enough supervision to assure that the playground is safe, we simultaneously need to let our children feel that they are completely free on the monkey bars, that they are brave, competent, well—amazing. It is certainly true that our children depend on us to *help* define who they are, but we parents have to allow our children to be the ones who author the description, who type it out laboriously, one letter at a time, and especially edit it, word by word, as they grow, learn, and evolve throughout the years of childhood.

We are not suggesting children should be ignored, or left entirely alone to figure out life for themselves. That could be termed neglect, or hypo-parenting, a form of child abuse that has been around forever in the lower, middle, and upper classes. We are just arguing that children need a little more breathing space than many are getting. Because in recent years, our children and their lives—in school, at home, on the playground and playing fields, and in their own social circles—have become much more interesting to us than is healthy for us or for them. As we adults have injected ourselves into every part of their lives because we have come to believe that is what good parents do, our children have stopped having aspects of their lives that are theirs alone, places where we understand it is not for us to intrude, oversee, arrange, and manage. Today the only place they can escape our well-intended intrusion is with GameBoy, PlayStation, and Nintendo, which may be one reason kids are so deeply entranced by and attached to these electronic games.

Children need to have some say as to what they do and who they want to be. They need to wear Halloween costumes more than once a year. They require the freedom to try on plenty of roles on their own, with no obligation to take them seriously. They must have room to maneuver, to experiment, and discard, when they choose, to explore and research and develop a unique and individual way of looking at life. Every child discovers the world anew; it is always fresh, and fascinating, as if it had never been there until they first spotted it. And from their point of view, it was not.

Often, with the very best of intentions, our earnest effort to be good parents deprives our children of this sense of joy and discovery. A five year old's obsession for learning everything she can about dinosaurs is exciting and thrilling to her. Part of her passion comes from the creatures themselves; they are intriguing, amazing, stupendously scaled—especially to a small person who may psychologically feel like she lives among giant adult dinosaurs—and more fantastical than anything some cartoon producer could come up with on his or her own. But some of the child's zeal also comes from pride, as she begins to master a new world, albeit one that is long gone. She learns to recognize the different species, memorizing their names and dining preferences. She may categorize them: Some are nice; others are mean. Some are cute; some are scary. Most of it is make-believe, but all these aspects are woven by the small dreamer into her imaginative life. It is, in fact, one way she tries to master her emotional world (a fact best left unconscious). For instance, she may think about adult and child dinosaurs as a safe way to figure out how to deal with Mom and Dad. Maybe it is her metaphorical way to investigate what the world was like before she was born and entered the family. These wonderful, extinct creatures may serve any one of hundreds of psychological purposes. Or they may just be fun for her. (After all, as Dr. Freud once said, sometimes a cigar is just a cigar!)

It's wonderful for a parent to support this very predictable phase of development by providing children with the tools and opportunities to learn. You can buy books, see movies, purchase toys and kits that give children a hands-on sense of how fossils are uncovered; you can visit museums. You can listen to them chatter on, engage them in conversation, and even encourage them to display their knowledge to their equally smitten grandparents.

But a parent's involvement ought to follow the child's pace and lead, not display a grown-up knowledge and skill at research. Some parents become so enthusiastically involved with dinosaurs, or other interests their children display, that their superior adult understanding of paleontology swamps, and ultimately devours, the child's passion. These earnest and well-intentioned parents buy themselves dinosaur T-shirts; decorate the child's room with posters, bed linens, new wallpaper; engage in laborious Internet searches; plan theme parties and even vacations, all in order to impart more information to the child. And then they are left with bewildered disappointment—not to mention a lot of stuff they don't know what to do with— when the child abruptly loses interest. That change is not entirely surprising. Because the whole point was that this was *his or her* world to play in, master, and leave behind when the time came to move on to something new and different.

In her wonderful memoir, *An American Childhood*, the writer Annie Dillard recounts a period of her childhood during which she played endlessly with a microscope she had been given. All alone in her room, she tried and tried to see that elusive microorganism she had read about, the amoeba—and failed, time and again. When one day she actually did see the creature in a sample of puddle water she'd "cultivated" by letting it stew in a jar in her room for weeks and weeks, she excitedly ran to tell her parents.

"Before I had watched him at all, I ran upstairs. My parents were still at the table drinking coffee. They, too, could see the famous amoeba. I told them, bursting, that he was all set up, that they should hurry before his water dried. It was the chance of a lifetime."

Being from a different era and of a mind-set almost alien to us, her parents chose to remain seated at the table. "Mother regarded me warmly. She gave me to understand that she was glad I had found what I had been looking for, but that she and Father were happy to sit with their coffee, and would not be coming down.

"She did not say, but I understood at once, that they had their pursuits (coffee?) and I had mine . . . but I began to understand then, that you do what you do out of your private passion for the thing itself.

"I had essentially been handed my own life. . . . My days and nights were my own, to plan and fill. . . . Anything was possible. The sky was the limit."

We all know how Dillard's parents likely would have reacted had she been a child of our era! Can't you just picture them rushing down the stairs, bumping into one another in their excitement to see what their very bright, very motivated child had done? Can't you imagine the unbounded praise, the positive reinforcement lavished on young Annie? Within twenty-four hours, she would probably have been the proud owner of not one but several children's books on microscopes, cell life, and scientific activities and experiments. She might soon begin spending her afternoons taking science classes at a local museum or be quickly enrolled in a sleep-away camp for aspiring scientists. Her parents would be searching out the nearest Little Scientist franchise, planning Intel science projects, plotting out a future for their intelligent young daughter that would certainly include Yale, Cornell, Woods Hole Oceanographic Institute, or the Salk Institute. Or maybe all of them.

Instead they left her to her own devices—and doing so dampened her enthusiasm not one little bit. It would not have killed them to show a little more interest—nor probably would it have diminished her enthusiasm markedly. But in their eyes, and hers too, the moment belonged to her. The discovery was hers and hers alone. Upon it she built a successful, and certainly rewarding, career—not as a scientist, but as a writer and observer of science and human interactions.

Well-meaning support and involvement in a child's life are welcome, but only to the point where the parent and child both enjoy it. One mother of three began taking private flute lessons with her eldest daughter; it was an enjoyable way for the two to spend time together and for both to try something new. A year later they were playing duets, enjoying the pieces each selected, laughing at one another's mistakes, high-fiving when one got some hard part right. They, these two students, were engaging, if not exactly as equals, at least as co-learners. The daughter often watches as Mom struggles to learn something, exactly the way the daughter struggles with both her music and her schoolwork. Another mom picks up two copies of the books on her middle schooler's reading list; she and her son read the books separately and enjoy talking about them together, comparing notes about what strikes each as relevant, significant, important.

In marked contrast, a man of forty and father of three recalls with distaste his weekly golfing outings with his own dad when he was a young boy. The son's role was to act as caddy, and on those occasions when he was allowed to join the game as a player, his performance was often dissected and critiqued so he would be a better player. Despite the gorgeous, privileged setting, despite the fact that these outings gave him valued one-on-one time with his busy dad, the games were no fun at all. He didn't enjoy golfing as a boy, and he doesn't enjoy it now.

Even "fun" has become a serious endeavor that we parents feel must be carefully planned for, that we understand we must work hard to achieve. Advertisers, marketers, and entrepreneurs capitalize on the fact that we are all so pressed for time by promising to provide pleasure in a package for the whole family to enjoy. They cater to the fantasy that, like a well-run business, we can all maximize profit by good planning ("guaranteed to manufacture good memories!").

The specialists have done such an excellent job of selling us on this "right" way for busy families to have foolproof fun today that it is no wonder the parents of toddlers want to take their kids to Disney World—even though small children will almost certainly be frightened of the spinning teacups, the grinning toothless witches, and the noisy, dark, haunted houses. Many families really enjoy Disney World, but for others it is a disappointment. The ads show parents delighting in their children's excitement. No mention is made, of course, of the crowds, the long lines (a joke, "What do Disney World and Viagra have in common? An hour wait for a two-minute ride"), the heat, the outrageous expense, the nagging for overpriced, fat-filled snacks, and—above all—the exhausting and overwhelming *sameness* of it all.

Similarly, toy stores and catalogues are filled with offerings that purport to expand a child's imagination, like brightly colored plastic trunks filled with ready-made dressups; kits for making very specific sorts of jewelry, pottery, craft projects, with photos of the perfectly finished product right there on the box. You can even buy a kit filled with the accessories for making a snowman—weather permitting. You can purchase science activity books complete with everything you need (string in three precise lengths, seven paper clips, two small magnets, and a tiny tube of food coloring) bound right into the book. A recent trend is the paint-your-own pottery and ceramic studios, where children can choose a ready-for-glaze flowerpot, mug, or pencil holder to decorate with their own designs.

It's not that anything is inherently wrong with products, craft projects, and promises like these. In fact, in some ways there is a great deal of good in the commitment to hands-on activities, to fun, to reducing stress by bringing together necessary items and making life easier for both parent and child. But many confuse interactivity with creativity, and even the projects that leave room for some artistic or mental originality restrict their form. They are so structured, so far from truly spontaneous, so contained within rigid boundaries that the activity has more to do with imitation than with imagination. It's almost against the rules for a child to think more than a centimeter or two outside the box.

A young artist may truly enjoy gluing colored sand in prearranged patterns to make a picture just like the one on the box, and there is no harm in learning to follow directions precisely (it's comforting, for instance, to know that the person driving behind you on the highway has that skill). But is the activity challenging a child in the same way as one where the child draws and paints his or her own picture, choosing the subject matter and colors and arranging the scenery in exactly the way he or she wants? When your child shows you some squiggles and says it is the Millennium Falcon from *Star Wars*, to him or her it really is and looks that way. And for the child that is true creativity. Would it be better if a child connected some prearranged dots so the final product looked more like a real starship? Does a child who constructs a basic electricity experiment from items preassembled in a kit that even includes the requisite double-A battery have the same understanding of the accessibility of science as the one who searches the house to find those same items in Dad's workbench, the tool closet, the kitchen, Mom's desk?

Not for a minute. It's a far more passive activity, one far less likely to give a child a true appreciation of the real process of scientific exploration, trial and error, and discovery. The experience is less vivid, less actual, sort of like visiting "Italy" at Epcot Center, instead of visiting Italy itself.

We provide for all these experiences—Disney World, store-bought snowmen, jewelry-making kits—because we want to enhance our children's development. We want their lives to be fun, and filled with growth-promoting experiences. Apparently we have forgotten that children can entertain themselves with the simplest of items, in fact, often with nothing at all.

A. A. Milne beautifully captured the way kids can spin a world from fantasy, using their inner lives, their imagination to make wonderful use of time we would now consider boring. In *Winnie the Pooh*, Milne describes a morning that Winnie and Piglet spent together. They went hunting, and believed they nearly caught a woozle. They see a set of tracks in the snow and go round and round a tree trunk for hours following paw marks in the white fluffy stuff. After a time, they realize that more, and different, paw marks have appeared (they never do guess whose), which must mean that there are even more animals to be hunted. As they continue to circle the tree, more paw prints appear; they fret that they might be in some danger from wild animals. Then they realize the tracks belong to those fantastic animals, the woozles, and perhaps some wizzles too. Finally Christopher Robin appears, they discuss the situation, and decide it is time for lunch.

All in all, it was a very good morning. They had fun, spent time together, imagined a hunt and great danger, and then went home for a good lunch in a safe harbor. Imagination had created the world, and the children had learned through actively amusing themselves and using their minds and their imaginations.

Many parents have trouble with this idea of leaving children alone to entertain themselves. How can we be sure they will do anything at all? We're uneasy with the idea of letting things happen spontaneously, so nervous that a child might just waste time. In laying it all out for the children, in making it all so easy and convenient and possible, parents may well be depriving children of what they really need to get the most from such experiences—namely, involvement in a creation all their own.

Crucial animal studies in the 1960s, which likely are applicable to humans, showed that a kitten that is *actively* involved in its perception had superior brain development to an animal that received the same stimulation *passively*. Prof. Richard Held of MIT raised two kittens in absolute darkness, except for periods when they were placed in an enclosed, lit carousel. Both were strapped to the arms of the central post: One walked, while the other rode in a gondola. Both "saw" the same sights, but the kitten who could walk had superior brain development to the one who simply was towed along behind. Beyond the fact that such a conclusion simply makes intuitive sense, experiments like these imply that for good brain development, a youngster needs to be personally and actively involved in creating his or her vision of the world—which is the reason good mathematics curriculums now include hands-on activities called "manipulatives."

When we take over—when we sort-of carry the kitten around—we inhibit that process. Interestingly, from a totally different point of view, child psychiatrists and psychologists have made the same argument. Many of them have spoken of the child's need to psychologically create his or her own picture of the world; a paint-by-numbers kit just doesn't get the job done. We ought to pay heed when different disciplines with very different assumptions, methods, and models come to near-identical conclusions.

Another problem is the implicitly very high standards such packaged play imposes on young children. Children's advocates have long lobbied for realism in children's advertising, understanding that young children witnessing a commercial in which a toy robot comes to life and cleans a messy bedroom will expect that robot to do exactly the same thing when they open the package in their own house. That is why the Children's Advertising Review Unit (CARU) of the Better Business Bureau insists that advertisers show children exactly how a toy actually can perform in their hands. In the same way, a child who is making jewelry from a kit will expect that her own earrings will look *exactly* like the ones in the picture—and might well end up bitterly disappointed. That disappointment may not be directed at the product but at herself—because, unlike that little girl in her perfect little ponytail on the box, she can't quite pull it off. A child who pinches a candy dish out of clay and paints it with hearts and flowers for Mothers' Day imbues the work with deep love and is thrilled with the result of his or her effort, particularly knowing the feelings that suffuse the work. But if children compare their creation with the pre-made cup and saucer that only had to be painted and then handed over to some adult for glazing and firing, the one that came out with no lumps at all, they feel like amateurs. An adult knows (one hopes) which project required the greater effort, demonstrates the larger mastery of skills, which tapped more deeply into creative and loving impulses. The child, though, is only disappointed by the lumpy creation.

We already impose so much form on our children's lives without all of these plans—after all, they must go to school, do drills at swim practice, and then come home and do their homework. Maybe we ought to think about freeing up some of that "free" time. Leaving some of it really and truly unstructured might be a good place to start. A little bit of boredom—not too much—is not a bad thing, since children have active minds that seek out interesting things and having nothing to do will impel them to create. A little boredom leads children to make discoveries: to "invent" new creations out of their K'Nex, to build forts from blankets and chairs, to make up stories and act out plays with their stuffed animals. It helps them explore and to become familiar with their inner worlds in fantasy play. We all need empty hours in our lives or we will have no time to create or dream. As messy, inconvenient, inefficient, and sometimes frustrating as it may be, our children need to have lives and time to have dreams of their own.

An eight year old in his room playing with Legos is not exactly idle. Peek in and you may see all sorts of adventure fantasies played out. Of course, as soon as he sees you he may stop playing because he does not want an adult intruding on his private life. But when you leave, the fantasy war will continue, complete with strategy, surprise attacks, heroes, and villains. He is creating that world, he is its master, creator of all the attack plans, of every defense, and of its final denouement. Given the stress of his day at school, that might well be a better way for him to unwind and lose himself than working all afternoon in a formal creative-writing class. On his own, he is truly creating. In an after-school writing class, he often ends up merely plugging his thoughts into an assignment someone else has given to him—and teachers may get annoyed when he insists on writing endlessly about the war of the Lego creatures.

In those quiet moments, the mind often works on its own, under the surface, to solve vexing personal problems. During sleep, the mind practices and refines motor activities—like swinging a baseball bat. So downtime may not be entirely down.

But real boredom and personal responsibility for your own free time also teach children other lessons. Like all human beings, children must experience frustration, dissatisfaction, unhappiness, and failure. We don't advocate them; they simply are unavoidable in virtually every life we've ever heard told of. Like us, children will learn from every kind of experience, bad and good, pleasant and unpleasant.

Children whose art projects are always picture-perfect

because their mother offers so much "help" will never know the true pride of individual accomplishment. (Not to mention that they will feel like a fraud.) The child who is never allowed to get the "C" that he or she deserves because Dad takes it upon himself to work things out with the teacher will certainly fail someday in the future, maybe in something that really matters. Because of past experiences, children may have a lot of difficulty figuring out how to solve their own problems, except through long-winded explanations of why it really isn't their fault, or worse, paying off someone else to make it go away.

Children whose every moment is scheduled and structured because their parents want them to have the benefit of everything the world has to offer may have difficulty learning how to be alone, and at peace, with themselves. And that may be the highest price we pay for micro-management. Because the parents are so uneasy being quiet with themselves, because they insist that they must always run faster on their child's behalf, because they are afraid to let themselves be reflective and hear what they actually think or enjoy their own fantasies, they guarantee that their children will also be racing like greyhounds, forever in pursuit of mechanical bunnies they get oh-so-close to but never catch. They imbibe that extroverted attitude from the atmosphere in the home. In the end, the one thing children can never learn in this way is how to know and be comfortable with themselves or their inner lives. Which, when you come right down to it, is one of the most important things parents can teach children—since they will be spending the rest of their lives with themselves.

Every life contains a multitude of human experiences, each in its unique proportions. Wonderful things happen, terrible tragedies occur—to everybody, even the most privileged. The lives of others may look perfect, but you don't really know all the details: How lucky is the man who has made two hundred to three hundred million dollars, and is the father to not one but two children with cystic fibrosis? As the expression says, into every life some rain must fall. Close friends spend wonderful sleepovers together; sometimes they fight. Sometimes they make up; others times they remain lifelong enemies. Good friends move away and there is nothing you can do about it. Some nights you have wonderful dreams; on others you have nightmares. Arms get broken; walls get scaled. Challenges are overcome; life defeats you temporarily. Santa gets you just what you want; Santa gets it all wrong. Toys give great pleasure; sometimes a treasured one breaks or gets lost. Pets run away and get run over. Dogs learn new tricks, are fun to sleep with, and have wonderful puppies that friends want for their own. Some dogs chew the furniture; some have puppies no one else wants so you have to take them to the pound. The new school is great and you make new friends even though you miss the old ones; the new school that you thought was going to be terrific actually is terrible. Teachers can be wonderful, inspiring; teachers can be unfair; some teachers simply ought to find another line of work.

No single event makes a life; it is the sum of all of them interacting with the temperament we brought with us into the world. We look forward to some experiences in life, while others are so awful no person would sign up to live through them. Some experiences that we dread in prospect end up being important and essential to our well-being, like seeing our pediatrician when we have strep throat. Some even change our lives, like the tutor who really taught us to love math and, more important, to stop being afraid to let others know that we really are very smart. Others we could have done very well without, thank you very much, like that time we were on a soccer team with a verbally abusive coach. Even those, though, can lead you to a conclusion that changes your life; perhaps you decide to teach or become a pediatrician when you grow up and swear to yourself you will *never* be mean to a kid like that coach was mean to you. The world will end up enriched.

Other experiences are unanticipated surprises: One child was put off by his new music teacher's appearance. The heavy man looked so odd and old and unlikely to forge any kind of connection with a ten year old who wanted to be a rock 'n' roll star. But the teacher turned out to be a wonderful, accomplished musician, who exposed the boy to a world he never suspected existed, and who inspired him to practice simply because he loved music and made making it such a delight. A father was agonizing over whether to take action against a soccer coach who wasn't playing his son very much at all—worries that were not simply misplaced ambition, but based on very solid and real concerns about the way the coach was treating the child. But the boy demonstrated an amazing maturity and, in his dad's words, bravery, by asking to, and succeeding in, handling the difficult man himself with real finesse. It is, no doubt, a lesson that will stick with the boy for his entire life.

Taken together, all these incidents make for a life that is yours, experiences from which you as an individual must make sense and create meaning in order to construct your own trajectory for your own life. We all create a picture of the world in which we live, etched from the sum of our existence thus far: the people in our lives, the experiences that shape us, the personality that fits the lens through which we interpret our time on this earth.

For children to feel at ease in their own skin, to feel that their life is their own, they ultimately must make the synthesis themselves. Otherwise, metaphorically speaking, they are likely to engage in a lifelong duel with their parents. Children who do not develop their own perspective will be in turmoil in adolescence and beyond, battling between trying to be good and to do what their parents want and think they should do and doing the opposite in some attempt to have freedom and a personality of their own. Neither position allows children to be their own person, since both are simply acceptance and rejection of the parents' wishes, both are orbits around Mom, Dad, both, or the conflicts between them. Children end up in constant turmoil, bouncing from one radical position to the other.

To grow into mentally healthy and happy adults, children need to learn, in the safe environment of a loving home, that reasonable amounts of pain and unhappiness can be endured. Pain should never be sought; inevitably it finds a way to us on its own horsepower. But children benefit by learning that good things can evolve from even the worst of experiences, not to mention the not-so-bad ones, like forgetting your homework.

We don't need to manufacture misery for our children; life will provide plenty. Nor do we need to shield them from every bit of it. First, it is impossible. Second, they're stronger than we think. We need to remember whose life it is after all and to let our children have the freedom they need to live their own and to learn from it.

6

Custom Kids

At ten, Nat is among the smallest kids in the fifth grade. Not that this should be a surprise, given that Nat's dad is just 5'7", a smidgen below average, a guy who has always wished he was taller. The news that smaller-than-average children might be helped by injections of human growth hormone (HGH) got Nat's dad thinking. Would it be a good idea for Nat to have HGH? After all, everyone knows that taller men tend to be more successful. Not to mention the fact that Nat would definitely be a better athlete if he were larger, which would please him immensely. Nat's dad decides to discuss the matter with the family pediatrician.

———

Elise's grandmother is puzzled. Why is it good news that Elise, an active child who has been having some trouble in school, has been diagnosed as learning disabled? The way she sees it, the label means something is wrong and Elise will have to work extra hard in school, maybe even always, to achieve what comes more easily to others. But the child's parents insist they are pleased with the news. Not only does it mean that Elise's mediocre grades are neither her fault nor theirs, but the official diagnosis means that, in a few years, when it is time to take the SATs, Elise will be among the kids who take the untimed version. "It *will definitely increase her scores, which will help her get into a more competitive school," they explain.*

———

A successful couple sits, somewhat uneasily, in a psychiatrist's well-appointed New Orleans office. They are discussing their thirteen-year-old son: They fear their sweet, studious seventh-grader lacks the drive, the "killer instinct" they know from personal experience he will need to make his way to the top in today's hard-driving business world. Can the doctor work with their child to help him toughen up, sharpen his ambition, hone his personality so he drives himself just a little harder . . . and thereby, perhaps, increase his chances of being successful in life?

———

With apologies to Mick Jagger, a lot of us parents today seem to believe that we *can* always get what we want if we are willing to work really, really hard to get it and maybe even consult a professional.

We come by this perspective honestly. To contemporary families of affluence, the possibilities seem endless, the old rules about our mortal limits old-fashioned. Accepting yourself is yesterday's news. Why bother, when we can change just about anything we don't like in ourselves and in our offspring? We can choose a new nose from a computer-assisted design program, inject playfulness into a ponderous personality, or take a pill that smoothes out edgy interpersonal relationships. From the most superficial concern to the most deeply rooted fear, passing disappointment to paralyzing anxiety, a quick and relatively painless fix can be found for pretty near everything.

Almost no problem is too complicated for a simple, logical solution. Look at all we've managed to pull off so far!

Human beings can now not only fly in the sky but also visit the Moon and gaze far beyond. Soon tourists like you and me may actually look at the Earth from outer space. Today we can replace a defective heart (the kind that pumps blood, that is) with a transplanted one that works better, and we are far along the road to developing a superior artificial one.

Even the biblical injunction that the "good" life will last three score and ten years and be awash in blood, sweat, and tears seems hopelessly out of date. Eighty year olds run marathons. Anti-aging, a new medical specialty, is working toward a scientific slowdown to the once-inevitable march of time. Once you earned bread by the sweat of your brow; nowadays sweat is a status symbol among the educated, evidence of time spent on a treadmill or training for a triathlon. Even tears and rage can be mitigated with Prozac. Sure suffering, sadness, and misfortune still exist, but with the right medication they don't have to feel so bad anymore, at least not for very long.

Given all we have managed to overcome, why on earth would any of us want to work on learning to love ourselves in any state more imperfect than absolutely necessary? Isn't it noble to strive to make ourselves even better? Isn't our ability to harness progress and to use it to our benefit what ultimately separates man from beast? For us, surgery, self-help books, and support groups offer the fastest route to getting where we would really rather be.

At first pass, ours seems like an optimistic, rational view of life, a victory of reason over limitations and magical thinking. By working hard, we have overcome many obstacles that still are part of the natural order in less developed parts of the world. But is it really in our best interests to fully embrace this new and improved vision of life? This chapter will explore the generation of custom kids we are creating—how we strive to make them into who we want them to be or think they ought to be rather than trying to get to know who they really are—and what our constant efforts toward improving these children really tell them.

A generation or two ago, childhood was merely a journey along the way to adulthood. Like time spent traveling in a car, everyone understood that being a child would sometimes be dull and boring—at least from the adult's perspective. But children could be counted on to figure out how to pass their time along the way . . . sleeping, daydreaming, playing games, or just watching the world go by outside the window. Kids had to be creative because it was up to them to entertain themselves.

In contrast, our children are experiencing a childhood that is no longer just a preparation for adulthood but a full performance in its own right. We parents act as the producers; our children are pushed onto the stage and scored on every single thing they do. It's too much pressure, on us and on them.

While babies and small children were certainly cuddled and tickled and played with a generation ago, no one worked to produce an endless parade of happy entertainment for them. No staff of enterprising and attentive parents was always at the ready to launch a scavenger hunt to fill the hour before a seven year old's dinner or to head out the door for a community safari on a holiday from school. Like a great deal of grown-up life, childhood was filled with drudgery and routine chores and the occasional "special" event like, say, a picnic at the park. As in the classic American childhood novel, *Tom Sawyer*, children had to manufacture their own adventures. Despite the fact that no one organized his play for him, Tom loved his happy, busy life and resented only two things: church and school. Our own kids might add early morning piano, after-school French classes, orchestra practice, math tutoring, ballet, and who knows what else.

Although childhood certainly wasn't as blissful and free as the adults wistfully believed it to be, from the child's point of view just having some freedom from school and chores was rich in and of itself. What else did they (that would be *we*, for it is our own upbringing we are describing) know? To a very young child, every unfamiliar experience is new. Small differences count as new experiences: "Oh, I never saw a *green* spider!" Life itself piqued curiosity. Watching as Mom hemmed a dress, helping as Dad hammered together a bookcase was remarkable, fascinating, and entertaining, as it still is to children. To the older child, exploring the neighborhood or surrounding fields and forests with friends was a true adventure into a land that might be filled with lions and tigers and bears (oh, my!). They might discover treasure or a dinosaur bone or a scrap of old cloth they were absolutely certain came from a dead Confederate soldier's uniform. The streets and stores, even the backyard, were filled with novelties and new experiences. Back then, it was believed that all a child needed was a small yard to explore, parents to make certain he was reasonably safe, and time and solitude for creating his own fantasies. The world children created and the play in it was theirs and theirs alone.

Ironically, in not having access to an endless stream of manufactured entertainment and planned peak experiences—each garnished with mementos, presented proudly on a silver platter, and recorded for posterity on a handheld camcorder—children were more likely to experience a sense of wonder. They had the notion they were discovering, almost creating, the world, all on their own. And their parents had the freedom to live their adult lives feeling no need to function as live-in camp counselors.

That's not to say childhood was a free ride, however. Just one hundred years ago, back when parents were truly too busy to pay close attention to every aspect of their offsprings' development, children in all but the wealthiest homes made real and meaningful contributions to the family's economic well-being. Their work *mattered:* The eggs needed to be gathered, the hearth needed to be swept, the stack of firewood needed to be replenished, the fence needed to be whitewashed (no matter how Tom Sawyer felt about having to do it!). It's a good bet that no one needed a sticker chart to be reminded of what had to be done! Children were considered cheap but essential labor, a family's greatest economic asset.

Today in our country children and even adolescents who could, theoretically, be helpful are seen purely as an economic liability. They are assumed to have no *practical* value whatsoever—not to the family, nor to society. Not only do we no longer need our children to contribute to the family coffers, but we now focus on what they cost us to *have*. It is a view so institutionalized in our culture that even our government tracks it: A recent report stated that, even adjusting for inflation, the cost of raising a child is 20 percent higher than it was in 1960. The accountants and actuaries who issue these reports not only add up such necessities as food and clothing, but also include a line item for "forgone wages"—the costs of providing parental care in lieu of earning an income.

Truly, very few of us look at our children in purely economic terms, but this way of thinking certainly has an impact. Since today's children are expensive and have no intrinsic economic value to adults, the entire family must get built upon the love, devotion, and shared experience that remains. Which, when you come right down to it, is a far more tenuous structure.

The challenge today's kids face is far more difficult because the expectations are so amorphous. We work so hard for them that we want concrete evidence it is worth the effort. Children feel a deep inner need to prove their value to their parents. Chores once served that purpose, among others. But in practical terms, in most of our homes, a child's help around the house is no longer a major requirement, or even all that relevant, in many dual-income and affluent families. If we have the means, we hire out whatever household chores we don't enjoy doing ourselves.

Now our children are expected to be "good kids" in ways that are hard to delineate precisely. We expect them to look, smell, sound, and do good—all for the camera, metaphorically speaking, since they have no real economic value to the family or society until they become functional adults. And since many of us have managed to be affluent enough to accumulate enough wealth in our IRAs and 401(k) plans to support us in old age, we may not need them even then. Rather, many children will be expecting an inheritance. The only way to pay back parents for their sacrifices and efforts—and make no mistake, children do feel an obligation to do just that—is through accomplishments, be they academic, athletic, artistic, or social.

What pressure to put on a child! Many crack under its weight: By the age of eighteen, 20 percent have suffered a major depression. Close to 9 percent of adolescents have been diagnosed with anxiety disorders. One fourteen year old broke down in tears, telling a family friend that he simply could not be the person his parents expected him to be. When the friend offered to speak to the child's parents, the boy said it wouldn't help. And he was right. The parents had no intention of lowering their standards. Is it surprising that some of these kids, out of anger and frustration, escape into drugs or alcohol-induced daydreams?

The purpose of our children, simply stated, has become to make us proud and happy. That's not all bad: They are welcome in our lives, and we feel blessed to have them. That's a great start for any child. But without even being aware of it, we put an inordinate amount of pressure on them to please us. At a time when so many people feel insignificant in a world dominated by transnational corporations, billionaires, and celebrities, we also look to our children to make us feel significant and fulfilled as human beings. This is no small challenge given the standards we set. It is not at all unusual among ambitious families to *require* their kids to get straight As; anything less is considered substandard performance and the resulting disappointment is clearly communicated to the kids in question. When milking the cows on time was the expected standard, you just had to get the job done, reasonably well. It was a pass-fail system, not something you had to do faster or more beautifully than any kid in the neighborhood. That was a lot easier than worrying about whether that B+ you got in biology was going to satisfy Dad's high standards.

Tremendous parental pleasure evolves quite naturally and joyfully: Nestling a new baby, soothing a distraught toddler, listening as your first grader reads a book aloud the first time, witnessing a young ballerina's debut performance on point . . . every parent treasures these moments. They are satisfying achievements, evidence that the child we have brought into the world, valued and cherished, is developing wonderfully. But as the years proceed, our ambitions need to remain at a developmentally appropriate level. And they need to defer to what the child wants for him- or herself. We have to be cautious not to load our children with baggage they should not have to carry: Our own unfulfilled dreams from childhood. Children need to learn and accomplish at their own slow and childish pace. They need the freedom to look like kids—messy, dirty, clothes unmatched—at least some, if not most, of the time. Ultimately they need to be who they want to be, not who we have always imagined our child would be.

One mother recounts how her nine-year-old son "forgot" to bring home the Little League registration forms from school. Frustrated, she told him it was going to take an awful lot of effort for her to get him back on his team; she was surprised when he said, "Well, you don't have to because I don't really want to play anyway." She knew he wasn't much of an athlete but thought he'd enjoyed the camaraderie on the team—and she was worried about his social status in a town that put a premium on athletic ability. But, "As it turned out, he's perfectly happy not playing any team sports at all!" says his surprised mom. "He is the scorekeeper when the kids play games at lunch, he plays violin in the string orchestra at his school, and our weeks are much less harried now. But it wasn't an easy thing for me to let go."

"Doing" childhood can be a full-time job nowadays. Every aspect of kids' lives gets tweaked. Five year olds work with summer tutors to get ready for the rigors of kindergarten.

We know nine year olds on diets; they and their parents recognize the importance of staying slim for gymnastics, no matter that biology has a different plan in mind. We know a twelve year old whose mother speaks frankly of her concern that her son doesn't yet have a girlfriend—never mind that he hasn't even started puberty! One Los Angeles mom visited a psychiatrist to discuss her concern that her sixteen-year-old daughter had refused to take birth-control pills, since Mom feared the girl might get pregnant. When the doctor met with the girl, she shyly confided that she felt too young to be having sex and had not, in fact, even "gotten to second base!"

One of the messages communicated in the media frenzy that surrounded golf whiz Tiger Woods a few years back was that his parents were people to emulate and admire, that they deserved some accolades of their own for acting as architects to their son's success. The book, *Training a Tiger*, was written to help the rest of us follow their inspiring lead, as though child rearing has become a competitive sport and we would all benefit from learning the secret formula so that we, too, could pull ahead of the pack. It sold well: Plenty of parents desperately want to raise a tiger (as the next chapter will discuss). Many play. Few win.

Most of us realize that pushing our kids so hard for success is unhealthy, but still we hope, on some level, that they will have what it takes to stand above the rest of the crowd. Bemoaning the toll it takes on the car, the family, and the kids themselves, some of us nonetheless feel we have to push them to achieve a little more, to set their own sights a little higher than they ever would on their own. That's what colleges are looking for—kids who truly excel at something. So we search for the best instructor, drive them three towns over if that's the program with the best reputation. We sign our children up for lessons with the "right" coaches, the ones who might make a difference—and all too often look the other way when they treat the kids less than ideally. One Boston-area preschool gymnastics program proudly advertised the fact that its coaches were Russian: Personally we know nothing about these particular coaches, they might well be loving, nurturing, nursery-school-teacher-types, but let's be frank here. What comes to mind when you think about a Russian gymnastics coach? Is that who you want teaching tumbling to your four year old?

We need to ask ourselves whether it is really in the interests of our families—let alone the kids themselves—to get involved with our children's lives in this way, to cultivate them to be world (or at least, citywide) champions by age thirteen? How much is for them? How much for us? Are our children doing the things they want to do, or are we fulfilling our own hopes and dreams through our kids?

Fred Waitzkin, father of a sports-minded chess prodigy named Josh, wrote a fascinating, and in our opinion horrifying, book titled *Searching for Bobby Fischer* (a far less troubling movie of the same name was made later). Interested in chess himself, motivated in particular by the success of Bobby Fischer—according to Waitzkin's description, a seriously disturbed individual who idolizes Adolf Hitler—Waitzkin decided to cultivate his son's apparent genius, even though the boy seemed to have less interest in beating opponents than hitting baseballs. Surprisingly aware that he was pushing too hard, Waitzkin nonetheless hired a coach for the reluctant player and kept pressing on, all the while worrying about his own overinvolvement. He had no trouble pointing a finger at the other chess parents:

If you ask these parents about their aspirations for their child, they answer swiftly, "Are you crazy? We don't want him to grow up to be a chess player." It is hard to believe them; why else are they devoting body and soul to his development? Yet their zealous support may ensure his choice of some other occupation. For some fathers and mothers, passion for their child's success has become so gargantuan that the kid's own predilections have been subsumed by their need. Some of the best young players go to tournaments with their wildly supportive parents to satisfy Mom and Dad rather than for love of the game, and as teenagers they will probably give it up when they discover other interests.

Sad! By definition, childhood is a state of transition. Children are works in progress, not masterpieces, a standard by which most of us adults would fall far short. To paraphrase from memory what the musician Paul Simon once said in an interview, "When someone tells me to grow up, I really feel like they are telling me to stop growing."

What children need from adults is experience, wisdom, perspective, and protection. By pushing our children to play and perform *today*, by scrutinizing every detail of how they look and act, by expecting them all to achieve at a notable level, we are setting them up for a fall—and ourselves for trouble down the road. By telling them that this peculiarly American vision of success is so important they need drugs, surgery, remediation, high-level coaching, and whatever else we can find to get there now, we are doing them a disservice. To succeed, children need values, ethics, and a goal to shoot for; a vision of what we consider to be a good person, and the ambition to make something out of their lives, whatever *they* decide that something ought to be. They do not need just a record that would look great on a college application.

We should consider an analogy from the insect world. Children are larvae, soft and tender and—most important—unfinished. In much the way we refer to an inexperienced person as being "wet behind the ears," the butterfly-to-be emerges damp from the chrysalis. They cannot use their gorgeous new wings until they have dried in the air. If they use them too early, they are crippled for life. Our children will someday be butterflies, most quite beautiful in their own ways, in their own time. They should not be pushed to preen, or to fly, before they are ready.

Our high hopes are very much a sign of our involvement and, often, devotion. Parents very naturally want the best from, and for, their children; most of us want more than anything to provide our offspring with a better life than the one we've had—not that it was so bad, either. Most of us, in fact, were raised by parents who had the same sorts of high hopes for us, who sometimes pushed and prodded us as we do our children, occasionally in ways that felt uncomfortable.

But it is worth pointing out that all those generations of parents who came before us were working with different expectations, usually a frankly lower and less ambitious set of standards. This sort of madness was reserved for stage mothers, like Judy Garland's and Mickey Rooney's. From the start, parents of our parents' generation understood and accepted that their children were simply human. Of course they wanted us to reach higher and to do better: That was a goal even before God called Moses to the top of Mount Sinai to record the Ten Commandments which, apparently, still proves to be one heck of a tough set of rules to live by. But even just one generation ago, the technological model of perfection, the bionic man, was still kind of a futuristic sci-fi concept—or the premise would never have made such a compelling TV show.

Back then, we all came into the world with a certain set of traits that were understood to be, for the most part, immutable. A lucky few individuals were born beautiful, brilliant, or athletically gifted; an unlucky few were the very antithesis of those things. Most of us, however, were average in most ways. Which was just fine, and besides, what could we do about it? Of course good parents worked to give their kids love, a good home, and an education, so the kids could make the most of themselves. Providing food, shelter, and ethical training have always been part of the parental package of responsibilities. There was an understanding, however, that most aspects of what we were, simply put, was the good Lord's will. A human being's basic endowment could not be tampered with, before *or* after birth. It was what you had to work with—or around.

Today we look at things rather differently. We have a clear view into a future in which a person's genetic make up can be altered and improved. As we discussed in chapter 2, while the bulk of the work in genetic research today focuses on solving serious medical problems, that industry is already becoming privatized and, increasingly as a result, profit oriented. It doesn't take a computer model to tell us where that will take us: Talk about a great investment in a growth industry! Is there any limit to what people would be willing to pay for perfection, or some close approximation of it in their children? Apparently not. Recently, an infertile couple made international news when they advertised that they were willing to pay the staggering sum of fifty thousand dollars to an egg donor who met their standards (which included a minimum height of 5'10" and combined SAT scores of at least 1,400) because, in the words of their own lawyer, "they can."

Short of having access to the technology that will enable us to engineer our own embryos, we've shown ourselves to be willing, in fact eager, to follow any prescription we can to stack the genetic deck in our offspring's favor. We are already screening for a vast number of hereditary diseases and genetic flaws. Can the day be far away when we parents come to believe that it is our fault, in some way, not only if our children are unhealthy, but just not excellent at some things we consider vital? We would argue that in many ways that day already is here.

While today's parents understand abilities to be part of our genetic endowment, we also firmly believe they reflect good parenting. We very definitely consider virtually every one of a child's deficiencies to be something we need to work on. We rarely see "problems" as an opportunity for a child to strengthen his or her character. Increasingly we are defining anything short of excellence as a "deficiency"—and treating them as though they must be some sort of a diagnosable deficit disorder.

How many of us can imagine ourselves admitting without rancor, as does one woman we know, that our child is a "late bloomer?" "He walked late, talked late, read late," she says with a loving smile. "He's such a good kid, so good-natured. I know he'll do fine. My mother tells me I was like this too, so I figure, why drive myself nuts over something I can't change?"

In our how-to, can-do culture, like the little engine that could, we tell ourselves over and over that we think we can, we think we can, we think we can ... change this, overcome that, improve just that one other thing. Good modern parents are expected to give their children every single advantage we can afford. Anything less shows a lack of commitment. So we sign our kids up for the right courses, hire the right tutors, enrich their lives with a busy schedule of movies, puppet shows, trips to the zoo, and every children's museum within a day's drive of our hometown. We feel compelled to do it all, as if actually deciding to forego something would be neglectful. Deeply uncertain as to what the future will look like, as one parent said, we are in a rat race for what *might* happen a decade or two from now.

But at what price do we parent in this way? How do ambition and uncertainty thusly expressed translate to our kids? By signing them on for a nonstop program in self-pimprovement, we are confirming that our expectations for them are high, maybe even out of sight. No price is too steep for success, our behavior shouts at them. It also says that although we want them to be really terrific, we doubt they can get there on their own two legs so we are willing to sacrifice ourselves and do whatever we must to make it happen for them. And nothing discourages a child more than the sense that a parent has little faith in his or her inherent abilities.

It says a lot about our culture that it is hard to figure out, at first analysis, why this isn't such a great setup for success. You've got good parents, reasonably successful and dearly loved kids, lots of fun and interesting stuff to do, the resources to support such a lifestyle. How could it not be a good thing for kids to have parents with high expectations, who stand ready to cheer and support their every little effort? What could possibly be wrong with this picture?

Plenty, when you look at it from the child's perspective.

By urging our children to fulfill every iota of their potential, as viewed from where we stand, we parents end up devoting an inordinate amount of attention to all the things that are wrong with them. Despite mechanically repeating how terrific they are—after all, we know that praise builds their self-esteem—our behavior shows that we take for granted all those things that are right with them. That's not what counts. We see ourselves as simply trying to do what is best for them; but from their angle, they feel criticized all the time, for if we are always trying to improve and enrich them, aren't we also saying that they are not good enough? As one ninth grader shouted at his parents, in frustration, "You never notice what I'm doing right! I really try, but you only notice the times I blow it!" All too often, when we look at our children, the glass is half-empty. We take careful note of what is missing and decry that the water level is down. In reality, in most of our homes, as regards most of our kids, the glass is not half but ⅞ths or even ¹⁵⁄₁₆ths full.

As often happens, our anxiety gets expressed in an effort to control every little thing. We work even to make our babies better! The parents of one newborn, apparently wanting him to have an edge on the competition among the stroller set, offered their nanny a five-hundred-dollar bonus for every developmental milestone the child beat: If the average age for sitting up is six months, and he beat that by even a single week . . . ching-ching! She would hit the jackpot. While that incentive clause certainly motivated the nanny to get the baby moving, and fast, it's doubtful whether her intensive efforts helped him in any way, other than, perhaps, to instill profound anxiety and insecurity. A mother of a nine month old signed her son up for Gymboree classes so he could socialize with peers and "not grow up to be painfully shy, like me." A dimple-kneed three year old is denied cookies in the afternoon; her dad, who regulates every detail of his own diet and watches what his wife eats pretty closely as well, is worried she will have a weight problem when she grows up. And he is increasing the odds that she will, thanks to his obsessive attention to every bite she puts in her mouth!

When we believe our smallest effort will help shape who our child will be, in matters large and small, it becomes difficult to accept that, like us, these kids will grow into adults who have strengths *and* weaknesses, qualities that enhance their lives and others that pose a challenge. For every single one of us, mastering our less-than-ideal inclinations ranks high among life's most difficult tasks. Intellectually we may understand that perfection is not *really* possible; but when it comes to helping our children, we are not all that sure we see the harm in trying to get as close as we humanly can.

Take, for example, the explosive growth in private tutoring centers like Sylvan Learning Systems, Kumon Math & Reading Centers, Huntington Learning Center, and, from the SAT folks at Stanley Kaplan, Score! Educational Centers. Tutor Time, which efficiently packages child care with educational enrichment, actually promises that "children ages 6 weeks and up will not only acquire skills, but grow as people."

Getting extra help for kids who need it is constructive: School does not come easily to everyone, after all. A 1998 poll in *Newsweek* found, in fact, that 42 percent of Americans think that children have a "great need" for private tutoring. It's not exactly a vote of confidence in our public schools—or is it perhaps that everyone thinks that almost half of all *kids* have problems? What's really fascinating though is that, of those children currently enrolled in programs at Sylvan Learning Systems, a full 40 percent are getting extra help in classes *above* their grade level. They are not children who need help to get by in school; these are children whose parents believe they need help to push ahead of everyone else.

In many communities, practical considerations force parents who want the best for their children to start planning early. When parents discuss getting into the "right" school, they may well be talking preschool admissions, not college: Like country club acceptances, nursery school admission has become a major practical concern for two year olds—still in diapers, remember—who are applying for one of the limited number of slots in one of the limited number of acceptable schools in major urban centers. Entrance exams winnow out unmotivated four year olds who might drag down or disturb the rest of the class in upper-crust private schools. Affluent, ambitious parents try to find out which psychological tests will be given to the applicants of these up-market academies so they can practice with the right games and puzzles. Some enroll their toddlers in preparatory programs, usually disguised as something else. One Westchester County, New York, mother was upset to hear, via the grapevine, that another mom had gotten hold of the WISC intelligence test so her child could practice ahead of time. Not only was it awful and unethical, in her eyes; but she was also, frankly, concerned that this other child had an unfair advantage over her own evidently, in her mind, perhaps insufficiently prepared pre-preschooler.

Increasingly, a goal among the middle class with available funds is to get their kids to where they feel they should be—and all too often that means to a better place than most other kids. It has even become commonplace to seek a diagnosis of a learning disability in order for a student to receive special supports not available to all within the school system. For instance, in Greenwich, Connecticut— for good reasons one of the most highly regarded school systems in the entire country and also one of the most competitive—fully one-third of the students enrolled in public schools are diagnosed as learning disabled. Understand, please, that Greenwich is not some toxic waste dump, where exposure to dangerous pollutants or other environmental factors has caused an increase in neurological problems. In Greenwich, the environmental risk factors are incredible affluence, remarkable opportunity, and, in some families, unbridled ambition. What such a diagnosis can translate into, in a well-funded public school system such as Greenwich has, is an invaluable boost for the lackluster student. "Learning Disabled" kids get one-on-one tutoring at school, exemption from specific requirements for course work, and—most attractively, when the time comes—the ability to take the untimed version of the SATs. Some kids need this extra help and benefit by this opportunity and succeed where they otherwise would have failed miserably. Maybe every kid in every school district ought to get just that.

One very bright and highly motivated student at an elite southern college described what the situation is like for kids like her today:

One of the major parental concerns these days seems to involve the enormous pressure placed on adolescents (I'm thinking particularly of high-school-aged students) in both the social and academic realms. Obviously peer pressure speaks for itself. However, I myself have noticed the ever-growing demands on students to strive to get into "THE" college. The résumés that kids these days need to have to get into a good school floors me—presidents of several clubs, valedictorians (etc.) of their classes, leadership conferences, community involvement . . . the list goes on. Undoubtedly, this must place an enormous strain on parents who want their children to succeed, as well as on the students, who are forced to deal with these pressures in the midst of a time of psychological struggle. Does it force an adolescent to grow up too early, or does it prevent him or her from dealing with the pressing issues of that stage of development, leading to difficulties later on?

While this thoughtful young woman described the dilemma with remarkable precision, she did understate it somewhat. She did not mention that many parents also seek an injection of desirable personality traits from therapists, tutors, or organizing and learning specialists for kids with no discernible problems but who just do not exhibit what they consider to be the "optimal" level of motivation. Or they may have personality traits, such as low frustration tolerance or lack of leadership skills, which seem, possibly, problematic. Many children in our world are disturbed and suffering, quietly; they could benefit from the help and care of a good therapist. But these so-called underachievers don't need that kind of help, they need some space. They need permission to find their own way in life. They need a chance to have a life that belongs to and is shaped by them, not by their parents' hopes and dreams.

Some parents are even willing to go so far as to seek performance-enhancing drugs for their kids to take tests—

and in our eyes, even more appalling, are even urged to do so by those in positions of power. One grandfather, a wealthy man and alumnus of an elite university, was invited to hear the admission director from his alma mater speak to a group of similarly well-heeled parents and grandparents. Among other recommendations made by this university official was that ambitious parents should consider getting their kids diagnosed with attention deficit disorder (ADD) in order that they might obtain a prescription for Ritalin. Not only would the medication boost their child's performance on the SATs, he told them, but also it might make it "politically" easier for the school to admit the student.

Some evidence suggests that Ritalin enhances mental concentration and performance in many areas. Vacuuming the house can become fascinating when you take this drug. The quantity of Ritalin manufactured every year in the U.S.A. has increased 500 percent just since 1990. Well over one million American schoolchildren (and by some estimates, up to 10 percent of all boys in this country) now take the drug several times a day. Many children really do have attention deficit disorder, a condition that impairs their ability to concentrate, pay attention, and learn. Ritalin is a remarkably effective tool for treating the problem, even a miracle of sorts, particularly when used in conjunction with other therapies. But many experts, and most especially those who do not live here in the United States, contend that in our country, the diagnosis of ADD is made far, far too frequently today.

Furthermore, as *The New York Times* stated about Ritalin recently: "No studies have studied the drug's effect on children who take them for more than 14 months." Not to mention the fact that accurate diagnosis remains elusive.

And, as the *Times* noted in a report on a National Institutes of Health panel's findings: "Although Ritalin and other therapies might correct classroom behavior problems, there was no evidence that such a correction improved a child's academic performance." Nonetheless, many children who squirm and disrupt their classrooms are automatically given the medication. Some need it; others don't. Some have ADD; others are anxious, depressed, or are just . . . boys.

As a culture, we are getting comfortable using what have come to be called "lifestyle" drugs for all kinds of previously unheard of reasons, even though scientists have been studying their efficacy and side effects for only a few years. In much the same way that size four is the only acceptable size for a woman to wear, even though the majority of women in this country wear something much closer to a fourteen, there seems to be only one acceptable way to *be*. A study published in the esteemed *American Journal of Psychiatry* reported on the fact that certain drugs (selective serotonin reuptake inhibitors or SSRIs) have been found to change basic aspects of personality and behavior—in subjects who are normal and healthy! Even the title of the study sounds futuristic and scary: "Selective Alteration of Personality and Social Behavior by Serotonergic Intervention." Remember the movie *The Stepford Wives*?

If a solution can be had, it simply does not seem fair to us that our kids should face any sort of challenge that others don't: Whether it is physical, mental, or emotional, we want a quick fix for every problem—and some want to go further than that. While pediatricians tend to be very cautious in actually prescribing human growth hormone (HGH) to boost height in children of short stature, stories in the media about newly available synthetic versions of the drug led to a notable increase of parents who wanted to discuss its use for their smaller-than-average children.

Anabolic steroids, which increase muscle mass and improve athletic performance, are another area of controversy. By some estimates, 10 percent of high school athletes and close to 3 percent of middle-school athletes take steroids, often with full knowledge of their coaches and parents. A recent study by the National Institutes of Drug Abuse estimates that 175,000 teenage girls have taken anabolic steroids at least once—a rise of 100 percent since 1991. Most well-meaning parents would still feel squeamish at the prospect of their children taking steroids. But when our most recent baseball legend Mark McGwire took a performance enhancer that was "legitimate" in baseball (but not in other sports), it is likely that some, at least, began to look at the matter a little differently. Much was made of how ethical McGwire is and what an excellent father and role model. If *he* does it, an aspiring ballplayer might ask, why shouldn't I? And if this drug is okay, why not that one?

According to the American Academy of Cosmetic Surgery, between 10 and 15 percent of all cosmetic surgery in the United States today is performed on kids in their teenage years. This figure, by the way, does not include body piercing and tattoos. Adolescents, intrinsic perfectionists, and tough critics, all who are notorious for believing that an ill timed, ill-placed pimple (and is there any other kind?) will ruin their lives, buy all too eagerly into the philosophy that no price is too high for success. A smoother nose, bigger or smaller breasts, ears that lie flatter on the skull—it is all worth the pain, not to mention the money. A recent report in *The New York Times* on the surge of requests for cosmetic procedures among teens, quoted several surgeons saying they now had in place policies to help them winnow out kids who really wanted the surgery from those whose parents thought they should have it. According to *Newsweek* magazine, 1,645 kids aged eighteen and younger had liposuction in 1998—and 1,840 had their breasts enlarged.

Extreme as these interventions may seem to the more temperate among us, in the minds of parents who seek them out or sanction them, they are quite honestly doing what they believe is best for their children. Even a naturally gifted swimmer has a difficult time competing with a peer who is pumped up on hormones. It is true that a fourteen-year-old girl with a lumpy nose and bumpy self-esteem—the latter being a description that fits virtually all fourteen year olds, at least some of the time—might feel better about herself, faster, with a nose job. Or she might be devastated and disappointed to discover that, after the surgery, she has the very same life and the very same problems and no nose to blame them on.

If money isn't an issue and an apparent solution is easily within reach, it may be quite difficult for a parent to rule out such measures on principle alone. Why not just wave a magic wand or, in our more contemporary version of the fairy tale, charge it on a credit card and make the problem disappear, just one time? If you can get the physician to label the cosmetic nose job a "deviated septum," it's even quite possible you can get your insurance company to foot the bill.

Antiquated as the concept may seem, it may be that sound and reasoned principles are the very best reason to steer clear of such interventions, unless they are truly medically indicated. Because that is what the issue ends up being all about. If the end justified the means one time, and one time only, that might be a valid road to take. Most of us have compromised in just such a way at least one time or another. But what about next time, when the stakes might seem even higher? Another problem always arises, once the one confronting you at the moment is solved. Parenthood is not only about solving problems, but also—maybe more important—about how you *model* solving problems and the ethics you teach in doing so. By following the "custom" kids approach to child rearing, we enlarge—perhaps irreparably—the chasm between our stated intentions and our actual practices.

We also widen the chasm between the kids who "have" and the kids who "have not." It is a little disconcerting to think that an integral part of wanting our own kids to succeed in life is hoping others will not, but our hopes for children today tend toward exclusivity. All too often, when our own schools let us down, rather than working to get at the real root of the problem, we either enroll our children in private school (a move that at least gives us the satisfaction of writing out a big check and believing we get what we pay for) or move to a more expensive suburb. And who can blame us? When it comes to our children, we are not willing to sacrifice them as guinea pigs to progress or principle, a stepping stone to a golden future that will find realization some twenty years from now when we sit rocking in comfortable chairs at the retirement community we've moved to, reading a blurb about it in USA TODAY. By then, it may be too late for our own children to benefit from widespread social change, if indeed we ever get there!

The ironic truth, though, is that our methodology often

turns out to be somewhat counterproductive to our hopes and dreams. By turning ourselves inside out to get for our kids the things they want, or that we want for them, we are actually damaging their inner sense of security and well-being and giving them access to exactly the sorts of tools we don't want them using as they go on to build their own lives. When we encourage our kids to do community service work "because colleges are looking for that" we are not teaching them real values. It doesn't impel them to be kind to their friend whose father has leukemia or to stand up against the bullies taunting the new kid at school; it doesn't encourage them to treat others who aren't as lucky as they with kindness and tolerance. Customizing our kids demonstrates that what is important is how you look and how you perform, not who you are.

The message the kids get is that they cannot ever, for a moment, take comfort and satisfaction in being who they are. They should take inspiration from the deep pain of inadequacy. They should learn to use every second of their day productively. They should learn that life is tough, and they should internalize that particular lesson as early as possible. They should know that nothing comes from nothing, even love and respect. That anything and everything takes hard work, that no one loves anyone just for who they are. That the aim is accomplishment, character comes in a rather distant second. The goal is admiration, not affection and community. As the insightful student noted, the kids had better be ridiculously good or they will never amount to anything at all.

Extreme? Of course it is. Most of us try hard to support our children's sincere efforts and we give them plenty of love and positive feedback. But, how do the lives we are constructing for our kids feel to *them* and what do our actions say? Our intensity tells them that everything they do matters, really counts for something. With the lessons we sign them up for, the leagues they play on, the competitions they enter, the attention we pay to every aspect of their performance in life—academic, athletic, social, physical—we are always and eternally telling them that they can, and should, do better. And that is all that counts in life. It is as though your boss, or your spouse, told you how great you are and how deeply appreciated—but just think, if you worked at it a little harder, practiced another forty-five minutes in the afternoon, how much better you could be! The underlying message isn't hard to read at all, in fact it is a no-brainer: It is, "You're not so great after all."

Which is exactly the message that a child, on an endless loop of activities and lessons and enrichment programs, receives. That, after all, is what our attempts to perfect our children turns out to be, no matter how well-intentioned they are. Is it any wonder so many kids burn out, drop out, or act out?

Why is this "custom kids" approach to child rearing so destructive? Because it gives the basic model kid-next-door—actually, the kid at your kitchen counter—the sense that he or she is fundamentally defective. Your everyday, imperfect, preadolescent individual—who chews her hair when she is nervous; really, really hates to practice the piano; and is having kind of a tough time with pre-algebra—gets, on a subliminal level, the deeply discouraging message that her parents have very little faith in her or her ability to navigate her world or succeed in her future. It sure is lucky that their parents are there because they could never manage for themselves without them. Unless the child finds a way to fix his or her many faults, what hope does he or she have? Kids end up believing exactly the opposite of what parents hope they will. The parents want their children to be well-rounded, self-confident, and able to just say "no" when they have to. They end up insecure, feeling inept and devoid of real value, and more apt to say "yes" when they ought to walk away, because what do they know?

The whole system is built on misperceptions and misinformation. A child's imperfections say little about who he really is or will be. Life and development are not linear processes. Success in academics, sports, or business is not really the measure of a person. Furthermore, test scores in fifth grade have little to do with performance in the adult world. We all know these things from our own experience, no matter what this week's most touted study seems to show or how brightly the teen celebrity of the week seems to shine. But we have a hard time trusting our instincts and living by that knowledge. Academic and social successes have some predictive relationship to success in life (whatever that term means specifically to the tester). Looking back, though, how many of us were anywhere near as good as we are asking our children to be? Could we really have predicted, even at the end of high school what we would be like or even what we would be doing as adults? It may be true, sadly, that to a child with few resources an early wrong turn really can ruin a life, but the American middle class usually gives its errant children plenty of second chances. Many such kids have taken those opportunities and built lives that are very satisfying and successful.

We act as though a small number of well-known colleges and universities offer the only avenue to success in life. We all know it is not really so (though it is probably true that certain decals do look better on the rear window of German high-performance cars). In fact, Harvard is less than ideal for most undergraduates. Most of the people who teach them are graduate students: Interaction with some of Harvard's famous professors is about as likely as spotting a whooping crane rowing a skiff on the Charles.

America offers so many other options. One extremely bright young man with a passion for airplanes looked around and decided that for him, Ohio State University would be a great choice. And it has been. Enrolled in the aeronautics program, he is racking up great grades and is well on the way to fulfilling his dream of becoming a test pilot. Though his parents wish he'd choose another career, since they are rightly concerned for his safety, they are proud of him. He has found his niche and is flourishing.

And he is not even a late-bloomer! Like this young pilot, most people do not turn out exactly as predicted in the senior-class prophecy. Seems like every twentieth high school reunion is abuzz with gossip about the gawky girl who became a well-known movie star; the squirt who grew up into a smart, successful, and yes, sexy millionaire; the class clown, who now holds a professorship at a major university. A near-criminal kid becomes a successful and honorable lawyer; the best hope in the whole neighborhood dies in a car crash during his freshman year at Claremont College.

Life holds no guarantees. Every one of us evolves, slowly, through the course of every day we live, making life decisions for very personal reasons, improving as we go along. Each of our lives includes plenty of missed opportunities, wrong turns, and some lucky swerves at the last minute. Human development follows a winding path. To borrow from philosopher Immanuel Kant (via Isaiah Berlin), nothing absolutely straight can be built from the crooked timber of humanity.

Our standards are way too high, for ourselves as parents and, equally important, for our children as children! Our misguided belief that we have the ability—or even the right, let alone the responsibility—to control events in our children's lives is erroneous and misbegotten. As a generation, we are taking their lives far too seriously, putting entirely too much importance on transitory traits in their personalities and transitional aspects of their lives. Remember, childhood is the preparation, not a performance. Our children's lives belong to them. We need to stop trying to live their lives for them.

We are not advising parents to ignore behavior in a child that is highly unusual, impulsive, immature, or anti-social. Such behavior certainly needs assessment and, sometimes, attention. But every little defect need not be remedied; every small curve in the road does not need to be straightened out. Some things are innate in our children; some efforts too large for us to undertake. Many stages of development are just a phase, as our own parents used to say, particularly in adolescence, when kids are actively engaged in trying on many different roles to see which ones really fit. If we can just let them be, trust that we are raising a good child who, with support, will figure it out for him/herself, if we stand ready to be available to our children when they need us, they will be far more likely to find a place in life that is comfortable for them. In their immaturity and insecurity (both natural states for children, remember), they need to have the sense that we, their parents, have an intrinsic confidence in them and an inherent respect for whom they are, and are becoming, as people.

If they see a positive reflection of their image when they look into our eyes, they will be strengthened and encouraged to grow further, to experiment with, we hope, safe forays into the unknown, and to grow into fine human beings. If all they see when they look to us for feedback is anxious uncertainty about their abilities, either they will rebel, often making a mess of their lives in the process, or they will accept a vision of themselves as hopeless failures.

The challenge is ours. We need to let go of our misguided belief that their personalities can and should be directed to some desired adult outcome, something that our own experience—as former children—ought to tell us is patently untrue. Better, perhaps, that we learn to apply the wisdom of the twelve-step groups to raising our children: "God grant me serenity to accept the things I cannot change, courage to change the things I can, and wisdom to know the difference."

7

Is Winning Everything?

The parents of the Winslow Whammies are one proud group. The soccer team, all first-time players in the second grade, has won the town championship for the beginners' league. It's an impressive feat, especially considering the team's lack of experience. The coach, who has two sons who star on the high school soccer team, knew what he was doing though. Despite the mandate to teach, not coach to win, he showed the little Whammies how to push, shove, and cut off the good players, just like the big kids do. Parents on the opposing teams, and even a few Whammie parents, groused. But as one dad put it, "If you want to be a winner, you have to play like one . . . and like we've learned at my office, that usually means pushing a little harder than everyone else!"

Dan, a fifth grader, has been arguing with his parents about his after-school activities. He takes piano (he's really good), belongs to a chess club (he won a trophy last year), starts as a pitcher for his Little League team, and does karate. They all agree Dan is doing too much, and needs to drop one activity. He wants to quit piano or chess; they want him to stop karate. "Piano and chess develop skills he'll use in life," says Dan's

mom. *"Karate is just for fun."* Her voice drops, *confidentially.*
"He's not really all that good at it anyway."

————

Gina, nineteen, has been swimming competitively since she was
six. She worked her way up through the local swim team circuit,
then the counties, and the states. She actually qualified for the
U.S. Olympic team in 1996. She came in fifteenth in her
event, the fifty-meter backstroke. But no one in her town, ex-
cept close friends and neighbors, even knew Gina had competed
in Atlanta. The local paper never bothered to cover the story,
since it was clear from the start that she never had a shot at win-
ning a medal.

————

We sure do love our winners here in America. We clap
hard for our sports heroes, our business moguls, and
our entertainment celebrities. In our own lives, we push
hard and place a high premium on success. It may be,
though, that our sky-high hopes and dreams pitch the path
to happiness too perilously steep; many of us cannot climb
it without great anxiety and distress. While some people
unquestionably thrive on the challenge of working hard to
get to the top, a larger percentage likely would find that, in
the end, a less pressured life is more meaningful and gratifying. It is true that great cultural rewards come with
reaching the summit. But striving for it full time—and
that's often what it takes—may throw our lives way out of
balance.

Which is why we parents need to think hard about what
our personal definition of success is. We need to weigh the
price of being a "winner," to determine whether devoting

our lives to wearing that label and getting our kids to display it early and prominently, is really worth the cost. We need to carefully consider whether our astronomical aspirations are really what's best for us and for our families.

We Americans have so much to be proud of. Our enterprising spirit enabled our forebears to build a new nation that has become the leader of the free world in just a couple of hundred years. A less determined country might not have won the race to be first to walk on the moon. In our land of vast opportunity, dreams really can come true if you work very hard at making them happen. But those who set high-level success as their primary goal in life, whatever the price, often pay dearly—and so do their children and spouses. Many superstars say they regret some choices they have had to make, particularly regarding their families. Not infrequently it is they themselves who end up alone and emotionally adrift—like the world-famous CEO we know who was not even invited to his daughter's wedding.

Even the very ambitious among us want to avoid that outcome, so we try to temper our desire for accomplishments with a commitment to good values and an ethical life. We parents work, more or less successfully, to balance professional or personal ambitions with a desire for close, connected relationships with our families. Yet it's easy to lose sight of the implicit messages our children pick up as they watch the way we live and look at the people we hold up as role models.

In words and deed we tell our kids that anything worth doing is worth doing 100 percent. We encourage them to strive to be all that they can be. Go for the gold. Never be satisfied. Aspire, achieve, and accomplish. Push the envelope. Be triumphant. But are those really the crucial values around which our children can build a good life? In real life they may conflict with our equally urgent exhortations as to the content of their character. Moreover, striving for that perfect score often puts satisfaction, maybe even solid self-respect, permanently out of reach for most mortals. This chapter will discuss how our obsession with competition and accomplishment often overwhelms our innate good sense. Then we offer some advice on how to get a better perspective.

Success is a drug in America, and many of us are hooked. As in the wildly successful "Rocky" movies, it feels terrific to accomplish a goal you have set, to stand triumphantly in the ring as the new champion, particularly when cash and a certain cachet come with the package. Like a cold beer after a long, hot day, the thrill of victory tastes great. However, if our whole identity is built upon the heady sense of accomplishment and the sweet sounds of other people's applause, the rewards often turn out to be, as they say in the ads, "lite and less filling." Reaching one peak is never sufficient. We will always need more kudos and more championships to feel content. As we continually move from one challenge to the next, hoping each time for more adulation, we can never sit still long enough to notice how much is right in our lives or to recognize that such perpetual striving comes from an inner neediness that never stops gnawing at us, a demon that demands to be fed. This way of life virtually guarantees that our souls will never be satisfied.

When it comes to alcohol or nicotine, even the toughest die-hard addicts usually try to keep their children from getting hooked. But in pushing to win, we have trouble holding ourselves, or our children, back, let alone taking the time to contemplate what being a winner really means to us.

Was Gandhi a winner? Was Mother Teresa one? How about someone who spends weekends working in a soup kitchen or playing music to the elderly in a nursing home? Is the gifted athlete who easily hits a couple of home runs every game a winner? How about the ten year old who shows up for practices every day and keeps at it despite a categorically disappointing batting average? Would you label as a winner the child who can always be counted on to invite the class misfit to join the game? Or the one whose good humor serves as the glue that holds the group together, but who never stands out and shines as a star? Is the goal to win the lottery, hit a home run in the bottom of the ninth in the World Series, or is life really about showing up and being involved every day, like Cal Ripkin who set the record for playing the most consecutive baseball games?

We hardworking, often successful parents instinctively feel proud when our children excel at something, be it painting a portrait, winning a blue ribbon in a horseback competition, or locating obscure municipalities in a geography bee. We enthusiastically cheer their efforts from the sidelines, and they usually love it when we do (although by adolescence, many discretely urge us to put a lid on it). No one can blame us for proudly recounting their successes to relatives, friends, and neighbors.

Many people complain that too many children are being unreasonably pressured today. But parents may find it really difficult to delineate where, exactly, lies the line between being enthused on their children's behalf and exerting overzealous pressure on them. We may cock a questioning eyebrow when we hear that the eighth grader down the street has been docked phone privileges because she got a "B" on her report card—in gym, no less. We feel pretty certain the line has been crossed when we learn that a kid on our child's hockey team is given financial incentives to improve his on-ice performance: three dollars for every goal, and a cool ten bucks for a hat trick. We are definitely appalled to hear that a teen we know has been caught hiring someone else to take his SATs for him because of the pressure he feels to get into a competitive college.

However, if it is our child who has a shot at winning big, we may feel far less certain about where the appropriate boundaries lie. In our celebrity culture, it's cool to be a hotshot. Nowadays everyone believes they have a shot at the big time. In his book *Searching for Bobby Fischer* mentioned in chapter 6, Fred Waitzkin recounts his own irritation when Bruce Pandolfini, chess coach to Waitzkin's talented son Josh, questions the validity of putting young kids in a situation of national competition where "one's self worth as a human being became linked to winning or losing." Waitzkin describes his annoyance at Pandolfini's "distaste and feigned neutrality." Why? In the words of the proud papa, "Like it or not, such an event has its bloody side. There cannot be ecstatic winners without miserable losers." At the time of this national tournament, little Josh Waitzkin was not yet nine years old.

It is easy to be repelled by Fred Waitzkin's self-account; *we'd* never put our third grader in such a situation after all. Would we? What if our child just seemed to want to give it a try and didn't care all that much about the tournament's outcome? What if his best friend was going to be there too? Or what if, like Josh, he had a really good shot at winning the national title? What if we had always wanted to play chess competitively but never had the chance? Would any of these reasons make this "bloody event" a valid way for such a young child—or anyone else—to spend a weekend? We often use exactly those sorts of rationalizations to involve our children in activities that we know, deep in our hearts, are not really in their best interests.

Somehow it is harder to pin down what pushiness is when we ourselves are the forces behind it. Nor can we always easily determine where encouragement ends and intensity begins, particularly for children who, on their own, aren't motivated to try new things or do much at all. The third grader who hates to read may benefit from a financial reward—commonly known as a bribe—to read more, particularly if the books are well-selected and help him or her overcome embarrassment at being a poor reader. He or she may even learn to love books. And the slightly clumsy kid who doesn't try hard at soccer may be helped with a little incentive for practicing.

But parents have to decide what to do case by case, not always an easy task. One father, a sports enthusiast himself, recalls when his son was six and wanted to quit swimming lessons. The little boy was a promising swimmer, with excellent natural form and unusual speed. But his prior lesson had frightened him—the instructor had him swim the length of the large pool, which seemed endless to the child. At first the dad tried to talk the boy into continuing, but caught himself: "Why am I doing this? He knows how to swim; he doesn't *have* to get any better." It was hard to let a child, who knows little about how the world works, quit a sport in which he might have had a future. As it turned out, the boy later became a standout baseball player, at his own pace; it's worth noting that without passion of his own, as he now has for playing center field, that "future" was likely questionable anyway. Despite all we know about how the world works, we must listen—really pay attention—to what our children say about what they want from their lives.

It is not a bad thing for a parent to have a vision for what they want their children to get from life; we all dream about what the future may hold, and indeed some of our kids will be happy enough to walk that path. It is laudable that we hold high expectations for them, that we want them to make something of their lives. Many adults we know understandably regret and resent the fact that their parents barely seemed to care who they were or what they became as long as they did not cause too much trouble. So they make sure to raise their kids differently. A surgeon we know takes her teenaged daughter on hospital rounds on weekend mornings and both enjoy the time together. A writer asks his preteen son's opinion of some of his work, and finds that the boy has some interesting insights to offer—and not incidentally, loves getting his dad's advice on some of his own papers as well. There isn't a child alive who wouldn't benefit from knowing, at their core, that Mom and Dad care what happens to them and want to be helpful and involved in getting them there.

Furthermore, in many aspects of life, competition is invigorating, energizing, inspiring, and even fun. If striving to achieve at a higher level, to score higher (or at golf, lower), run farther and faster, climb higher mountains, or earn more money, makes your blood run hot, that's terrific for you, especially if you are the one who chooses to compete—with others, or yourself. In some situations, competition can spur us to wonderful, richly rewarding achievements. That's true at any age. But when our children are engaged in intensely competitive activities, even if they seem to want to be, we proud parents must take care to make certain it is *their* passion at play and not ours.

Parents have probably always seen in their offspring an opportunity to fulfill certain elusive hopes; after all, children are our immortality, at least in the biological sense. At the very time in life when we are coming to terms with the realization that many of our most cherished dreams for ourselves may never come true, children seem to offer us one last round in the ring, one last chance to be a contender. For this very reason psychologists have given the pushy-parent phenomena its own name: "achievement-by-proxy." Of course a parent feels proud when a child chooses, of his own volition, to follow in the same footsteps. After all, imitation is the sincerest form of flattery. But if our hope for immortality is the main motivation, then we might do better to follow the lead of the Egyptians and commission a pyramid to that effect—freeing our children to live their own lives and to follow their own dreams.

Many parents push too hard. Bruno Bettelheim thought that this insistence on a child "performing" well was one source of psychopathology in American middle-class children. "Often, parents whose children are overloaded with activities display a disquieting indifference to their child as an individual combined with an insistence on very high performance." We need to remember that all children want to please their parents.

As we hope so desperately that our child will be the one called up to the stage, again and again, at the annual academic awards assembly, for it to be our own little quarterback who passes for the winning touchdown, we may have a tough time masking our dismay when they can't quite pull it off. So deeply immersed in coping with our own disappointment, we may not even notice our child's double dose—not only at not doing well, but also at letting us down. At those times, our children feel alone and abandoned, and we lose sight of how grateful we ought to be for the simple fact that our children are able to play! Both increase the distance between our children and ourselves.

Because just when we ought to be concentrating on their feelings about their lack of success, they realize that our real concern is for ourselves. One mother felt deeply embarrassed because for one quarter in middle school her daughter failed to make the honor roll—after all, students who do have their names published prominently in the local newspaper in the exclusive small town where the family lives.

To assure their success, we may overlook some dangers. Some parents let the fear that their child will be called a "loser" take precedence over good judgment. In one affluent community, some eighth graders were allowed to attend a party at which their parents knew alcohol would be far more abundant than supervision because the popular crowd might think their kids were "dorks" if they weren't allowed to go. One eighth grader told her dad that in their affluent community, being a member of the "in" group required giving at least one boy oral sex. Adolescents are known for going to extremes.

Confronting these sorts of issues honestly is hard to do; if we examine ourselves and our motives, most of us probably won't like at least some of what we see. Yes, we may want our child to win, to achieve, and to be cool and popular—just as we've always wanted those things ourselves. But no, it is probably not worth what it costs in every situation. It's one of the many reasons why we parents must figure out what being socially successful, being a winner, means to us. It is the necessary first step in communicating the concept to our kids—and they need to hear about it, clearly and consistently, as they grow into adulthood.

Many people yearn for stardom of one sort or another. Keeping up with the regular old Jones's may not seem good enough; they are, after all, a regular family no more special than we. Wouldn't we feel better about ourselves if *they* were huffing and puffing trying to keep up with us? If our child is one of those who sets the standards, and not one of the followers trying desperately to catch up, won't he or she be free of insecurity, discomfort, dissatisfaction, and unhappiness?

Not a chance! As so often happens in life, our actions inadvertently help bring about the very outcome we most fear. Having not yet tamed our own critical demons into submission, they remain alive, well, and far too powerful in our unconscious. It's a vicious cycle: The pressure we put on our children to succeed doesn't chase the demons from their lives at all. It propels the poor kids directly into the waiting arms.

We Americans have always worshipped winners, from Babe Ruth to Michael Jordan, but our generation has lowered the standards and amped up the volume. Anyone can be a superstar if they can just do one thing really well. Our cult of celebrity has become our culture. Individuals lucky enough to have one unique trait or special talent often are airbrushed and elevated to icon status, regardless of other aspects of their lives. Magazines like *People*, television programs that showcase stars like Madonna spouting off on social issues, and professional spin-doctors who, like the Wizard of Oz, manage the whole operation from behind the curtains, fortify this vision of stardom. Today's PR professionals know exactly what it takes to make even ordinary folks like you and me look like a cross between Albert Schweitzer, Albert Einstein, and Tom Cruise, a concerned parent, a genius, socially conscious, a pillar of the community—and utterly and totally cool. Just sweep your hair back like this and put on these Ray•Bans!

That vision colors how we view the world—not to mention how we look at our children and ourselves. Celebrities seem like gods, not people. We're amazed to hear that they get colds, pimples, and bad haircuts like the rest of us. *Daisy Head Mayzie*, a book published posthumously by the wise Dr. Seuss, tells the cautionary tale of a child who became world famous for growing a potted flower atop her head. She had fame, fortune, and people falling all over her—but she was miserably lonely because everyone forgot that under her spectacular headdress she was just a little girl who still needed to be taken care of. None of us really want that for our children, but when we train our parental microscope so intensely on a child's outstanding trait or talent, we risk doing exactly that. One particular aspect of who our child is becomes hypertrophied—and the heck with the rest.

It's a can't-miss recipe for insecurity: Whether we are gorgeous, academically gifted, athletically talented, musical, artistic, funny, or just really wonderful at baking bread, we all want to be loved for our whole selves. When a single trait gets magnified, that part becomes the whole person. What most of us want, in our hearts, is to be loved completely for who we are, not for that one thing we can do really, really well. No one wants to be a one-trick pony.

We Americans value competition and individual achievement more highly than many other nations. In a *New York Times* essay, author Nicholas Kristof recounted how, while living in Japan, he tried to introduce the classic American

party game Musical Chairs to a group of five year olds celebrating his son Gregory's fifth birthday. The game failed,
rather hilariously: The Japanese children kept politely
stepping aside, allowing others to sit in their chairs.
"American children are taught to be winners, to seize their
opportunities and maybe the next kid's as well," Kristof
wrote. "Japanese children are taught to be good citizens, to
be team players, to obey rules, to be content to be a mosaic
tile in some larger design."

While even very young American children have no difficulty with the concept of snatching the nearest chair from
another child the moment the music stops, such behavior
goes deeply against the grain of what Japanese children are
taught from the cradle. Respecting the feelings of others is
an integral part of their culture: Making another child feel
bad by being left without a chair is, quite simply, not done.

The Japanese are Japanese and have their way of doing
things; we Americans have ours. Each has its good and its
less appealing aspects. But it is fair to say that fitting neatly
and discreetly into some larger, more colorful mosaic is not
what most of us American parents want for our kids. We
aspire, secretly or openly, to the close-up photo, full-color,
front-page, the one that we can frame and display on the
family room wall. It's good if our children shine brightly—
better yet if they shine brightest. But the fact that we are so
very competitive about, and for, our children says a great
deal about how insecure we feel about their future and,
sadly, how unconcerned we are about the futures of those
other kids our child has bested. How exactly that attitude
of winning at all costs is supposed to fit in with other values we hold dear—like sharing and respecting the feelings
and rights of others—is anybody's guess.

Two boys we know, whose parents are Chinese immigrants, play Nintendo differently than most American kids. In contrast to the children who play, as most kids do, to beat one another, these two play together, as a team, to beat the machine. They have been raised in a family that emphasizes helping one another and obligations to the family. Competing against a brother seems alien.

Who's to say those boys will do better than their ultra-competitive American neighbors at the game of Life? Although they are high-achieving students (one received a full scholarship to Yale), no one can know for sure because none of us can see into the future clearly enough to predict what the world will need in ten, twenty, or thirty years. The best we can do for our children is to give them the tools for living a good life. We can teach them to take care of their physical, mental, and emotional lives so that they are healthy, able to think clearly, love and care for themselves and for others, and so they have sufficient self-worth to stick up for themselves when necessary. These vitally important interpersonal skills, the true keys to getting along in life, are unlikely to be dramatically different a century from now than they are today.

However, until we define what qualities we hope to stimulate in our children, they will be difficult to pass along—most especially true when we are urging them to push themselves hard, and harder still, which at the same time pushes others away. Forging a connection that instills the values and concepts that make for close relationships and satisfaction with one's life is challenging for parents. But it's the kind of challenge that makes child rearing such a complex and rewarding endeavor, one that makes life itself an adventure. As we discussed in chapter 4, it is part of creating that unique relationship that is yours and your child's forever.

There are many ways to win. Success of one individual,

especially a child, need not come at another's expense. Given how much children must master, how many missteps, accidents, and bumps we encounter in our lives, we parents need be able to take pride in children who are able to learn, explore, try new things, question, and figure out for themselves who they are and what they want to become. The rewards of living a good life aren't limited to a particular kind of blue ribbon, or a specified level of bank account. It is a very big world, with lots of jobs and niches to fill. Ultimately, most of us will find something that we are good at. Some of us like leading the charge; others prefer a supporting role. Both ways of being are valuable and essential. Finding a few things we enjoy and do well, and places in our lives where we can feel proud and successful, are what makes for a good and satisfying life—and, frankly, is the very best most of us can hope for.

So why then do we keep telling our kids that they have to do it all—and really well too?

Let's look more closely at the two arenas where we often define success as "doing better than everyone else"— school and sports. When a child enters preschool, parents who have devoted themselves to enriching the first three years may be eager to see whether their early efforts have paid off. How bright is Molly compared with others? A preschool teacher recounted a recent parent conference, which she started off by telling how beautifully the girl had adapted to school, how enjoyable and well-liked she was. The father's first question was, how was she doing academically? The curriculum for three year olds didn't really stress much in the way of academics, the teacher told him, but his daughter was definitely bright. The dad pressed on, eventually coming right out with the question foremost in his mind: "Is she the brightest in the class?"

The pressure to perform well academically is on right from the start. It never lets up. Increasingly kindergartners are expected to read fluently. Those who do not are urged to seek tutoring. Of course kids who need it should get extra help as early as is sensible and practical. But as one reading specialist notes, a few children are simply not ready to read until age seven or eight. It has little to do with intelligence. Early speakers and readers are not necessarily the most literate in college. Those who start later often just develop differently, processing words and letters fluently a bit later. Albert Einstein, for example, supposedly spoke quite late and never was a particularly good student. Pushing children who are not ready to read can lead to frustration and failure—and, not incidentally, to an aversion to reading later in life.

While every one of us wants our child to be "intelligent," that means many different things. Those who study intelligence believe that more *types* of intelligence exist than the fairly straightforward academic ability that has always been so highly prized. Harvard University psychologist Howard Gardner has identified at least seven different categories of talent, including verbal skills, visual aptitude, athletic or mechanical skills, musical talents, self-motivation, and social skills. These last two are the basis for emotional intelligence, the subject of several best-selling books by psychologist-journalist Daniel Goleman.

Many of us who did not exactly excel in traditional academics may be relieved to see that the world is at last recognizing that there are lots of different ways to be smart. We may feel less ready to think about multiple intelligences, however, when it comes to our own children. We still want them to top the charts academically. Intellect is where it's at. We feel true parental pride (a chip off the old block!) in a high standardized IQ score and a definite and undeniable disappointment in one that is closer to average—which, given the way statistics work, is what most of them turn out to be. Child and adolescent psychiatrist Stanley Turecki, author of *The Difficult Child*, recently said that on Manhattan's tony Upper East side where he practices, kids can be either gifted or learning disabled: No one can be average. Some parents even try to teach to IQ tests as though it were the score itself that mattered. What originally was a relatively objective measure of potential for school accomplishment for those raised in the dominant culture's middle class is being tricked through cleverly mastering testing techniques.

For many parents today, a score below 130—usually the cutoff for admission to gifted-and-talented programs at public schools—is a call to action. Likely the "problem" has more to do with the system of sorting kids than with the kids themselves, but that is another matter. An entire industry of toys, games, and puzzles are marketed as intelligence boosters; some, as we discussed in chapter 3, are aimed at infants! These parents are passing along their values so effectively that study guides are available aimed at the kids, such as "The 10- to 14-Year-Old's Guide to Boosting Your IQ Score." These workbooks improve neither native intelligence nor a child's ability to think clearly, creatively, or well. They don't give children anything that will help them find their way in life or help them think for themselves. All they do, theoretically, is boost their test scores and send children the message that learning isn't what is important; giving the impression of being smarter than the next person is.

Even though academic and industrial experts increasingly stress the need for cooperative effort and teamwork, we tend to raise our children as rugged individualists. This philosophy might have worked here in America, back in the days when you could move west and farm your own 640 acres. But that era is long gone; seems like most of those ranches are owned by movie stars or agribusiness today. Even if our children end up communicating by modem and cell phone, they will quite likely still need to work more closely with others than we do. By facing them off against one another at every conceivable opportunity, we may be making it harder for them to acquire the skills they will need in this new millennium.

The goal of school has become great grades for *my* kid and the places they can take him or her. All too often the learning process becomes incidental. We might learn something from the wisdom of the Proverbs: "If you lack knowledge, what do you have? If you have knowledge, what do you lack?"

One high-achieving fourth grader was discovered to have hired another child to do her homework; her parents actually knew about the arrangement but really didn't have a problem with it. She knew the material, they reasoned, and the entire family's schedule was so overloaded that they were relieved to take one chore off the list. Since no one in authority ever found out, and the parents didn't care, there were no consequences to her cheating. It may still be going on today: Think about what this experience is teaching her about how to get ahead!

True education, learning, scholarship, and erudition have become remarkably diminished in America. Whereas being a professor, a physician, a scientist, a classical musician, a writer—a really educated, cultured person—was once the highest achievement, today most of the smartest college students aim for the high-paying professions. Real learning has been devalued, a sad development that does not bode well for America's cultural future. That, however, is a story for another time.

Impossible as it may seem, our competitive intensity on the playing field may rival—even outpace—that in the class-room. Perhaps we are following the old English maxim that Waterloo was won on the playing fields of Eton and Harrow. In fact, many would argue that it is in the realm of kids' sports that one can observe the ugliest aspects of par-enting. In a hilarious piece written for *The New Yorker*, hu-morist Christopher Buckley satirized soccer parents in a "Memo from Coach." His "Game Schedule" read:

> Saturdays, 8 a.m. Important: Please be sure to have your daughter there *at least two hours before game time*. Note: As the girls will be biting the heads off live an-imals, we will need lots of guinea pigs, hamsters, para-keets, etc.
>
> Injuries: If your daughter has kept up with the summer-training program, there's no reason she shouldn't be able to finish out a game with minor injuries, such as hairline bone fractures or subdural hematomas. Remember the Grasshopper motto: That which does not kill me makes me a better midfielder!

We recognize prematurity to be a major problem for newborns, but we applaud it in our young athletes: The younger a child is able to do something, the harder we clap. One dad bought his eighteen-month-old daughter a set of plastic golf clubs: He proudly told her play group leader that he'd read that the colleges were literally searching for female golfers to shower with scholarship money. Two year olds strap on ice skates and learn to play hockey. They have to, parents in competitive communities claim, or they'll never catch up with the Canadians. Three year olds line up on tennis courts in ninety-degree heat and swipe at balls with rackets bigger than they are, while five-year-old gymnasts are already tracked by ability.

The problem is not the activities these kids are involved in, but the intent. "Fun" has nothing to do with it. Practically from the first time these children slide onto the ice or pick up a racket, parents are evaluating their pro potential. Unless the child is a superstar—and ultimately, relatively few are—he or she is certain to disappoint the parent. And in the process, him or herself as well.

In recent years, Little League has become as competitive as the Majors. Every year we read news stories about parents who are arrested for beating up coaches and umpires and shooting or even running down officials with whom they had disagreements. Reporting an average of two or three assaults on members each week, the National Association of Sports Officials, which represents game officials of all kinds, youth leagues to professional teams, now provides "assault insurance" as a membership benefit. One city has instituted a "No Yelling" rule for all spectators; another hands out a "Code of Conduct" for parents:

> I will place the emotional and physical well-being of all players and spectators ahead of my personal desire to win.

> I will *never* engage in threatening or confrontational behavior with players, managers, coaches, umpires or officials.

Most of us, who drive our kids to practices and weekend games, are distressed to learn that adults have to be handed such a rule book—but not surprised. Even if we manage to keep our own behavior within the realms of what is right and reasonable—not always an easy task—we've seen and heard other parents, often our own friends, behave appallingly in the realm of competitive kids' sports. What a sad development—especially when we consider the gentle origins of Little League, which was started by a man who wanted to give his eager nephews an opportunity to dress up in uniforms and pretend they were "real" ballplayers. As we understand it, Little League was conceptualized as an organization that would provide an opportunity for all kids to play in a fair, supervised environment, where every boy could pretend to be a big leaguer. Today, it has evolved into a complex system for developing superstars. Many communities even hold a player draft! The ostensible point is to even out the skill levels on teams, but somehow the coaches in the know always end up with an all-star roster of players.

We would never suggest that kids who want to should not play organized sports: Our own children do, with great enthusiasm, year-round. Some have won local and regional awards. While many decry the overstructuring of athletic programs, we find it difficult to aim broadside criticism at sports programs, given what they can do for the health and self-esteem of participants. Children who are involved in sports benefit in numerous ways: Sports help them to use their bodies well. Kids who exercise are healthier in virtually every way than those who do not. Sports offer another arena for excellence and achievement, since not all children do well in school. Sports teach commitment, teamwork, and social skills. They help kids learn about the difference between delayed and instant gratification; they teach that with effort and lots of practice, you can do better, and better yet.

Young athletes can learn sportsmanship and how to win and lose with grace. Sports can teach strategy, responsibility, organization, and discipline. Sometimes, like with a bad call by the referee, they teach the painful lesson that some things in life just aren't fair. Sports can even teach spatial skills, as in learning the angle at which to shoot a soccer ball or the proper arc for a basketball.

One family can pinpoint the exact moment when their young daughter, a third grader, began to think of herself as an athlete: She was playing softball in the last game of the season, her team was losing, and she hadn't had a hit in weeks. With two outs, she hit a line drive and made it to second base—where she stopped and grinned at all the parents who were standing and cheering her on. The next player popped a fly to the pitcher and the game was over—but it hardly mattered. Her confidence level touched the clouds. This little girl, now in high school, received lots of hugs and congratulations from everyone and has loved playing sports since.

That's an example of what sports can do for kids. But in contemporary life, much that organized sports programs can do to help children is eroded because the *adults* have trouble keeping their perspective. Most coaches start out their seasons with a little lecture to the effect of, "We play sports to have fun and to learn about teamwork, sportsmanship, and the game." But what do you do when the score is 2–2, with just minutes left on the clock? In an important match, one enlightened hockey coach gave the kids on his team the choice of whether to play to win, meaning that the less skilled players would sit the bench, or to play as they always did. No doubt following his excellent lead, the nine year olds chose the latter option.

Not every coach has the same priorities. For many, learning and having fun are far less critical than figuring out what needs to happen to snatch the game away from the other team. One could argue that even this is a good skill to acquire: learning how to try to do well, despite game pressures, and how to develop an internal mechanism to calm yourself when the stakes are high are important life skills.

But, as parents, we cannot lose sight of the fact that these are *children, at play*. If we decide that our kids will not get treated this way, they won't be. And they won't come to believe it is appropriate. Appalled at the intensity of two coaches, who'd even swatted girls for making mistakes, several parents in one community pulled their girls out of what was widely recognized as the best gymnastics program around. Perhaps surprisingly, the girls objected; they loved the coach and they loved winning. But the parents, who had a larger vision than the next first-place medal, felt it had gone too far. They insisted that this is a part of the kids' life that is supposed to be fun, to balance out the other, more serious aspects like school, where they have to sit still even if they feel like running around. And they were surprised a few weeks later when they noticed that their daughters, now out of this coaching situation, were loosening up, laughing, and enjoying their lives a lot more. Having grown accustomed to the situation, even these very attuned parents hadn't really taken note of how intense, whiny, and self-critical the girls had become under their overly ambitious coach.

Hockey is great fun—but perhaps not in a child's best interests when a team wants him to be a pro at thirteen. A typical schedule for an eighth-grade hockey player in one community is as follows:

6:30–7:30	Power skating
7:30–3	School
3–3:30	Study hall
4–5	Hockey practice (school team)
5:30–6:30	Karate
8:45–10	Hockey practice (town team)

This schedule leaves no downtime, no time for just playing around. No time to chat on the phone, to talk to your parents about what is happening in your life, to carp to friends about your parents. Heck, there's almost no time for sleep! There is no way this child could be in bed before eleven; at most he gets seven hours of sleep a night, assuming he lives virtually next door to the skating rink.

Saying no to such pressure isn't easy, but it's what we need to do. If we believe in kindness, we ought to refuse to treat a child who is not a star, or worse yet is not even so-so, cruelly, as so often happens. One town had a lacrosse league with a rule that anyone who wanted to play was welcome. Halfway through the season, one lackluster player suddenly found that he simply was not being informed of changes in the schedule. Unofficially he had been dropped from the team! Ethical parents concerned about their kids' development ought to assure that no eleven year old gets that treatment. It is too hard for kids to do this on their own.

In most cases, coaches—and even parents who do not object to these practices—have no idea that they are overstepping the boundaries and acting inappropriately and in a way that runs directly counter to the best long-term interests of their child. Pressuring children to perform early and often has become so accepted it is rarely challenged, let alone rejected outright. If our first and foremost hope is that our child will be blessed with the physical health and stamina he or she will need to live to the age of eighty or ninety, why are we subjecting them to physical abuse that will require a hip replacement at forty-five, the fate of one medal-winning gymnast we know?

If saying "no" to unreasonable pressures and schedule demands seems too difficult, we parents might need to take a serious look at what our motivations really are. Those of us who secretly hope that our children will be superstars without really grasping what that would mean—to our kids or to us—had better reconsider our aspiration. The real-life superstar arena is sadly littered with cautionary tales of child athletes who can't win, in the end, even at the game they are so good at. Tennis star Jennifer Capriati, coached on the court at age three, was a millionaire at age thirteen, an Olympic champ at fifteen, and a shoplifter with a police record at age sixteen. Profootball player Todd Marinovich, raised by his dad to be a football superhero, fell into drug addiction and bottomed out before his career ever really even began. Gymnast Dominique Moceanu, who, if some press reports are true, was hung by her arms from a clothes-line at six months by parents who were determined to carve a career as a gymnast for their daughter, recently en-gaged her parents in an ugly public battle. At age seven-teen, claiming they had mishandled her earnings and that her father had hit her for such transgressions as gaining a few pounds, she was granted legal status as an adult, so she could be free of him. Her future in gymnastics is uncer-tain—as are her emotional health and well-being.

And those are the kids who have "made it!" For every

one of them there are a thousand kids who made the sacrifices, practiced six hours a day, gave up friends and other interests, neglected the other aspects of their lives—and never made it to the top. Furthermore, many marriages break up around the pressures of raising a supercompetitor. Is that really what you want for the child you love so dearly or for yourself?

Maybe this kind of intensity isn't surprising in the culture that has given us *Teen People* magazine and *Sports Illustrated for Kids*. They persuade us that the sacrifices just may be worth it, that stardom for its own sake is a valid pursuit. Until, perhaps, we reflect on little, too-cute-for-words Jessica Dubroff, the seven-year-old who was to be the youngest child to "fly" across the country. Everyone loved the wacky story of the little girl who asked for flying lessons and was given them. Loved it until she nose-dived from the sky and died, that is. Then it became clear how really inappropriate the whole adventure was.

Culturally we are abrogating our adult sense of what is truly important by buying into a dream of fame and fortune for the kiddy set. We are selling our ethics to buy an illusion, a terrifying one if you examine it closely. We adults have a responsibility to protect our children, and ourselves, from ridiculous expectations. We need to recognize that children simply do not have the tools to perform to adult standards, let alone Olympic-level ones. *Childhood is the preparation, not the full-dress performance.* As the saying goes, We need to let our kids be kids.

Clearly, kids' sports are about something other than having fun. The point has become winning—if not the game itself, then winning approval, winning an invitation to the next level of play, or perhaps winning that all-important athletic scholarship to a great college. Most parents will answer, almost reflexively, that of course life is about more than simply winning; but as the saying goes, you vote with your feet. It is what you *do* that counts most. Very few children have the self-awareness of one young soccer player we know who, when invited to play on his town's travel soccer team, opted not to. He loved the game, liked playing and winning, but felt that three practices and one game each week was just too much for him. His parents supported that decision, knowing it was right for him and for their family.

Many adults would also have a hard time making such a decision in our own lives. It can be so exhilarating to succeed at a goal that is important to you. It is natural to want our share of attention for the things that we are quite justifiably proud of accomplishing. Many of us would find a life without challenges unbearably dull.

It's out of hand, though, when the pride of accomplishment we feel from within is not sufficient, when we come to depend completely on adulation from others to feel good about ourselves. Local stuff seems little, often even pointless: Helping an elderly neighbor, being active in the church or synagogue, or volunteering as a candy striper in the hospital doesn't seem very significant. Few feel content to shimmer as one among a thousand points of light; we want a bright spotlight trained on us or on our children.

Today love of the lifestyle rather than love of the game fuels the dreams of many aspiring athletes (though probably not the ones who will end up making it). Prima ballerina Cynthia Gregory, famous for her starring role in *Swan Lake* with the American Ballet Theatre in New York City, loved ballet more than anything as a young girl. She cared so much that on the rare occasions her mother needed to discipline her, she would get her quickly back in line by threatening to keep her away from ballet lessons for a few days. When Gregory's young son Lloyd heard her speak of this punishment, he laughed and said, "So Grandma took away *your* Nintendo!"

The prima ballerina sort of passion must evolve on its own, as kids are encouraged and allowed to discover, for themselves, the inherent rewards in mastering a skill or sport. In today's world, though, endorsements have become the endorphins: Kids who cultivate dreams of playing professional sports, as they always have and likely always will, are quickly sold a vision of fast cars and fancy parties. Many end up craving fame purely for fame's sake; fortune for now, not later. Raised in the cult of celebrity, they want to enter the circle of the gods rather than remaining simply idol worshippers. Their parents support this vision of success, racing their pro-athlete-wannabes from private coach to practice to tryout, hoping for that one big break. Most sincerely want success and happiness for their kids.

But this is not the easiest avenue for arriving at that destination. A desperate need to achieve and the single-mindedness it takes not infrequently goes hand in hand with self-centeredness. People who focus on winning—running fastest or farthest, climbing highest or longest—look terrific in the newspaper articles that extol their accomplishments. They make those of us with more average lives feel wistful, wondering whether we might not be somehow squandering our time here on earth.

In real life, most such superachievers are difficult to live with. They are frequently fanatics. Often a neglected family is behind the scenes and an unhappy one: Those who structure their lives around the stricture that winning matters most are constantly assessing where they stand relative to everyone else, rather than trying to connect and live comfortably with themselves and their families. The models are often anorexics; they are paid not to be who they are but the world's fantasy of what a human could be. Many celebrities are narcissistic, spending more time attending to their washboard abs than their kids' adolescent angst. Their primary commitment is to looking great and winning. Three or four hours a day of mirror time does not leave much time for caring about anyone else. Not every celebrity is that way, it's true, but many are. Rather than accepting the compromises that go along with getting along, rather than working to sustain intimacy with the people already in their lives, many of these "winners" trade in and trade up. Hence the successful middle-aged man's trophy wife.

In most of our lives, though, from grade school on, there are and always will be others who seem to have a little more than we can ever hope to get: cooler shoes, a hotter mountain bike, higher grades, a better-looking spouse, a pricier house, a more powerful car, or lots more money. If your self-worth is always measured in relation to what others have, the odds are that it will never amount to much. There can only be one "richest" person, after all, and he or she usually doesn't stay on top for very long: It's the reason *Forbes Magazine* issues a new list of the four hundred richest people every year.

Rather than comparing our own standing relative to theirs, those of us who will never make that "A" list—and maybe even many people who do—would do better to make a practice of regularly examining our lives and relationships. We ought to ask ourselves whether the rewards we are seeking are worth the sacrifices we are making. To what end are we doing all that we do? A parent may believe she is only following her child's wishes. But when a seven year old's enjoyment of swimming gets translated into teams, daily practices, and weekly meets, and then she starts working with a private coach, it may just be that more is at stake than her fondness for water play. A parent who will only accept As on a child's report card has lost sight of the fact that school is the place to learn—and that one can only do that by making some mistakes along the way.

We desperately need to figure out what we really believe about winning, for that has an enormous impact on how we raise our children. If first place is the only one that counts, we ought to reconsider those pedantic parental lectures on sportsmanship, sharing, and cooperation because we are being hypocritical, and our kids ferret that out even faster than they do the latest fad or fashion. Do we really believe that good guys finish last? Being a good person does not necessarily mean getting to the top. However, it usually does lead to greater satisfaction in life, to pleasure in human relationships, to a community that counts you as a member and that appreciates your contributions.

Remaining unimpressed by power, wealth, accomplishment, and success—even if the prizes were attained by questionable means—is very difficult. But it is important to remember that external success often has another, less attractive side to it. A world-renowned Harvard Medical School professor could be found at the hospital, most anytime, day or night. He was a genius in his field. When a young student shared an 11:00 P.M. snack with the esteemed doctor and casually asked when he saw his wife, the professor replied, "Oh, she knows that every Tuesday, from

6:00–6:30 A.M., we breakfast together—no matter what."
Clearly relationships ranked low on his list of priorities.

We do not have to buy into this view of success, nor do
we have to live our lives by its dictates. What do you really
value? Take this little test.

1. Would you rather your child became a highly paid
   CEO or a good parent?
2. Would you wish that your daughter or son grew up
   to be fabulously wealthy or someone who loves life
   and cherishes the children he or she brings into
   the world?
3. Would you want your child to reach the pinnacle
   of corporate success if that corporation knowingly
   poisons people or addicts them to harmful sub-
   stances?
4. Would you hope your child grew up to be number
   one in some important corporate position or had
   friends and relatives who really adored him or her
   as a person?

These questions help pin down what life is really about,
for us and for our families. The traits may not be mutually
exclusive, but we must take the time to figure out what we
really value, what aspects of life are simply nonnegotiable.
Souls are for sale today, usually at a remarkable low price.
Even if you've made your own questionable trade-offs, do
you want to raise your child to join that auction?

Behind the media portraits, celebrities are not gods: they
are humans, with all the foibles, needs and failings that the
rest of us have. Sadly, they have no privacy. Their choice is
to work out their problems in full view of the interested

public or to pretend they don't have them—only to be caught soliciting prostitutes or getting into fistfights. Many celebrities can't find friends who will treat them as people, who talk to them, rather than at them. If you are rich and/or famous, or both, lots of people will want things from you and will flatter you to get them. Psychiatrists have learned that one of the major problems of the rich and famous is that they never truly know who their friends are or whom they can trust—and that often includes their therapist. Many are afraid to get the psychiatric help they ultimately sense they need because they fear their anxiety and depression will be exposed to the public, that it will ruin them. It's awful to realize that what everyone cares about is your persona, not you as a person.

When the focus is on the goal, the reward, the fame and fortune that one assumes will follow, instead of the process and the life you live along the way, the payoff is illusory. Accomplishment is but a moment; most of life is spent on the journey. Adventurers who climb Mount Everest do so for the experience and the challenge, not the view. After working months, sometimes years to achieve this goal, many never even get to the summit; those who do spend less than an hour atop the mountain they've worked so hard to climb. One can only wonder what inspires such a quest, risking life and limb to briefly reach the summit, whatever the danger, whatever the cost.

Ernest Hemingway, who spent his life chasing one adventure after another in search of ever-higher highs, and who died unsatisfied and by his own hand, expressed this idea beautifully in a lovely metaphor we would do well to ponder. It begins his short story "The Snows of Kilimanjaro":

Kilimanjaro is a snow covered mountain, 19,710 feet high, and is said to be the highest mountain in Africa. Its western summit is called by the Masai "Ngaje Ngai," The House of God. Close to the western summit there is the dried and frozen carcass of a leopard. No one has explained what the leopard was seeking at that altitude.

8

What About Us?

*P*auline's "To Do" list is daunting. Up before her three children, she lays out the school uniforms, cooks a hot breakfast, packs the lunches, and organizes the backpacks. She drives the kids to three different schools (lower, middle, and high) each morning, picks them up for afternoon sports practices, tutors, and music lessons. Last year Pauline decided to limit each child to two activities (logistical considerations made even that a near-impossible schedule). It was hard to make that decision, but she felt she had to. Even though she recognizes that she simply cannot have done any more, she still feels guilty. "It seems unfair to limit what a child can do, simply because she is one of three kids," she says, obviously uneasy with her line of reasoning. "No question I was frazzled, but I still should have been able to do it. Other moms do." Then she gets back to making dinner—always a sit-down affair with candles (though her husband rarely makes it home to eat with the family) because she has heard that dining together as a family is an important predictor of academic success.

Celia and Larry count themselves among the few who know how lucky they are. Both successful in their careers—she is an architect; he is an executive at a regional airline—they have three children, two dogs, a cat, and enough money to afford cleaning help, a live-in nanny, and a lovely house (designed by Celia) that is large enough to hold all of them. What they don't have, however, is time alone together. The last time they went out for dinner as a couple was to celebrate Larry's forty-fifth birthday—six months ago! They're too tired, and their work schedules are too unpredictable, to go out during the week; and they'd never dream of leaving the kids with a sitter on the week-end—it is the only time they are together as a family!

———

Terri feels like a failure for making an appointment to see a therapist. There is no disputing the need: She has gained fifteen pounds, lies awake in a state of near panic at night trying to organize the day ahead at home and at the office. She is always exhausted. Her marriage is rocky: She and her husband, John, argue constantly over who is doing more, and—needless to say—their sex life is virtually nonexistent. Terri finally knew she had to do something when all she could think about was the entire holiday season was getting to New Year's Day so she could take the damn tree down. "I have so much," she says to a friend on the phone, canceling lunch because she can't take time away from her desk. "How can someone with a life so full feel so empty?"

———

Overextended, overworked, overwhelmed, and over the top!

What a shame that these adjectives now describe our lives at home as well as at work. When we moms and dads try to be everything to everyone, everywhere at one time, we too often find ourselves saying a resentful "yes" when the answer really ought to be a rueful, but reasoned "no."

Instead, over and over, against our better judgment, we give in: I'll take you here, pick you up from there, buy you this, or arrange for that. I will plan for it, pay for it, schedule it, and do it. All for you, all because I love you.

All for you—even if it means little or nothing for me. Most of us honestly consider raising our children a sacred trust, our life's truest, most important work. We sincerely want to be the best moms and dads the world has ever seen. Yet as we've discussed in previous chapters, our contemporary approach has transformed child rearing into one more job to do efficiently and expeditiously, one more performance on which we will be judged, by our children, by other parents, by our own parents—and most severely, by ourselves.

Working to be the best parents we can be, we run and run, and then get up just a little earlier so we can run some more—still feeling guilty that we are not doing just that one more thing (Chores to teach values? Viola, to give a child a special and unique talent? Quality time?). We are drowning in car pools and crowded calendars, trapped by high expectations and ever-escalating standards. We end up ignoring, sometimes even sacrificing, our interests, friendships, and often marriage—not to mention our sense of what is sensible. Many of us end up teetering on the edge for a while. Eventually some of us lose balance altogether, falling into anxiety, alcohol abuse, despondency, depression, dysfunction, and sometimes even divorce. All because we've lost sight of the fact that everyone in the family, even the grown-ups, is entitled to a life.

Usually, when we lose our balance it is because we have lost our perspective. Not only have we taken on the responsibility to provide our children with everything they need, we also have come to believe that if we are to be the great parents we aspire to be, we should give them any-thing and everything that might possibly make their lives—in the present or future tense—happier, easier, or more successful. No matter the cost. As our society has be-come postmodern and even more insufferably materialis-tic, we have also bought into the consumerist view that the next generation is entitled to have, if not all, at least al-most everything they want. And not just materially. What our kids deserve is happiness, nothing less, 24–7. We will willingly twist ourselves into pretzels—no fat, no salt please—to make that happen for them.

A grown-up weekend away? Not a chance. What baby-sitter could ever manage that complicated weekend sched-ule of swimming lessons, basketball, and birthday parties? Time for a daily three-mile run? Not likely, not if the kids are going to get to the places they need to go. A romantic dinner by candlelight with your spouse? Not when ice time is 9:00 P.M. Saturday. It's not frivolous, but a real dilemma, because if your child isn't there for that practice, the coach will bench him for Sunday's game. Is that fair to him? So the romantic dinner out gets put off for another week. Eventually it becomes easier to just forget it; there wouldn't be anything but the kids to talk about anyway.

Balance, limits, compromise: These are anachronistic terms, about as relevant to our times as spats and crino-lines. Few among us can give endlessly without eventually bottoming out however. Even if we think it a good idea to pour for our children an endless stream of the milk of hu-man kindness, sooner or later we will find ourselves coming up dry. And we wonder whether these lucky, "spoiled" kids will ever truly appreciate the enormity of the sacrifices we make daily on their behalf.

The odds are, they won't. Tempting as it turns out to be

later, when they aren't always so cute and cuddly, we can't really blame our kids for this. From their perspective, from day one we have acted as if they were entitled to everything. In the beginning, they didn't even have to ask for it; now they certainly shouldn't have to work for it. They may end up feeling guilty, or they may expect that that is just the way life is. As one besotted couple used to sing to their two month old, "You make the poop and pee, we clean it up, that's the way life is, boom, boom, boom."

And that *is* how life is, and has to be, for a new baby. That, and plenty more, is what parents must do for a tiny, helpless infant. But infancy comes to an end, at least biologically. A family is not a fiefdom, after all. Babies are supposed to grow up, pull away bit by bit, and develop their own identity and autonomy. They are hard wired to do that so the species can go on. Parents are supposed to encourage and applaud that. Children are supposed to develop the ability to do things for themselves, to help out, and to eventually accept that they can't always have what they want. If they don't learn those things, resentment festers on both sides of the equation. Ours, because while we outwardly insist that we want nothing but to give our offspring the good life, the way *we* have to live to make *their* lives so categorically wonderful feels anything but good. Theirs, because they know no other way to live and can't do it all for themselves. What choice have they had in the matter? They resent how irritable we get when they want more and more from us. "Why are you so mean to me?" they wail, at the same time they apologize for *needing* the ride across town that has you so annoyed, since getting to tennis lessons means you won't have time for your own evening bike ride, the one you gave up last night, and the night before too.

Doesn't this seem like a skewed vision of what a "good" family life is? Do families who structure their lives in this lopsided way have any hope of living comfortably and happily together? It's a good bet that almost all of us who practice this sort of martyr management of our children's lives will end up feeling inadequate and somewhat resentful of the fact that we feel that way.

We need to change the way we are organizing our lives—and we can, but not until we put serious thought into what kind of child we really wish to raise and what way of life is right for all of us, including the adults, who also have rights and needs.

In endeavoring to be good parents to our children, many of us have misplaced our selves, the person at the core of who each of us is. Not only do we sacrifice too much in our own lives to make our children's lives good, but we also are trying to squeeze ourselves and our circumstances into someone else's notion of correctness. It feels about as comfortable as jamming ourselves into a smaller person's favorite jeans. Like the tired cliché about trying to fit square pegs into round holes, no matter how you work at it, parenting in a way that feels inauthentic can't be done well, unless you are willing to saw off a few vital parts.

Many of us know parents so extreme they are proud of how much they give up on their children's behalf! But it is not healthy for any adult—or child for that matter—to derive satisfaction from putting his or her own needs last. Not only does that virtually guarantee that those needs will never be met, but it also bodes ill for any and all relationships in your life. It has been said that the definition of a saint is someone who has to live with a martyr: Martyrs are notoriously unpleasant to be around. We'd guess that *being* one isn't exactly a picnic in the park either.

We want to be commended for taking on the daunting task of trying to parent "right," but in actuality no single right way to parent exists. Each choice, each step of the way, is primarily ours alone. It is true that social mores are reflected in many of our choices—for example, most parents no longer subscribe to the belief that children should be seen and not heard and some even slap bumper stickers on their cars to that effect! And the Japanese good child is very different from the American one. Yet our daily choices are highly individual. And they should be.

Each of us has a different "right" way in mind. We also likely have very different "right" outcomes in mind. Most important, we have different, also highly individual children at home, each with a unique temperament, aspirations, desires, hopes, and abilities. All these must be woven together as we try to find a better, more rational way to live our family lives.

We suggest that a good goal might be to parent well enough—and to accept that doing so might mean doing less and setting a different set of standards for ourselves and our families. That is the essence of compromise. It's something to talk about with the kids as they mature—*they* know what it is like to have wants and needs, Lord knows, and they are also more than passingly familiar with the concept of fairness, having paid close attention to such matters as who has to take the first bath and whose cupcake has more sprinkles on it practically since the day they were born. At least, that's how it goes in our houses!

One single mother reports being utterly amazed at how cooperative her eighth-grade daughter became when she made an effort to change her style of communicating. Where previously she had made the rules, set the schedule, and more or less neglected her own needs and desires in order that she might be the wonderful mom she believed she had to be to make up for her divorce, she began to approach each day as an opportunity for compromise. "You have dance and I know you want to go to the library," she would say to her thirteen year old. "But I really want to fit in a swim. We'll do your stuff in the afternoon, but how about you watch your brother for a couple of hours after dinner so I can go to the Y?" The daughter, whose needs had previously seemed limitless, caught on quickly. Not only is the mother less harassed and cranky, but, probably not incidentally, the two now enjoy a relationship better than it has ever been.

Parenting well enough, in this way, ought to have a payoff: Everyone in the family should get something. Kids deserve to be loved and cared for, well provided for, and well-raised. Those are things we should do for the children we bring into the world. However, the term "family" doesn't just refer to the kids: Every one of its members is part of the family and is entitled to a good life. In fact, the archaic definition of "family" even included the servants who worked in the house.

Each of us deserves time for ourselves, for doing the things that are meaningful to us. Every family member has to sacrifice and compromise. Our own adult friendships are important. And a bad marriage has never been beneficial to anyone: Just ask the kids whose parents have divorced. Sacrificing a marital relationship to make life good for the children will have the opposite effect; it's an equation in which everyone ends up a loser.

We all, as individuals, need to chart a course that feels right to us, and then work to fit it in with the very individual needs of everyone else in the family. The process is neither simple nor exceedingly complex, but it does require respect, time, and a willingness to communicate openly. A family weighs and works with the different personalities and wishes of children and of each parent. The equation will look different at different times in life, and it will unquestionably differ from the one others we know, and even admire, work out for themselves. We must each figure out our own way to live our lives.

Getting to a balanced position today seems harder to do for several good reasons. Somehow we have come to see parenting as an "all or nothing" proposition, as though only two options are open. Either we are entirely immersed in doing everything for our kids (often, in addition to our full-time professions, another source of gut-wrenching guilt), or we are self-centered, self-indulgent, narcissistic hedonists. So of course we, a generation concerned with doing the right thing, make the noble choice: We devote ourselves to making life good for our children. In many ways that feels good and right—and, in fact, *is*. But we don't have to be so black-and-white about it.

Though doing it all, all the time, doesn't always feel so great to us, we soothe our uncertainty by telling ourselves that our selflessness must be at least beneficial to our children. We take some comfort from knowing that at least we aren't like those selfish types who never see their kids because they are too busy enjoying their own lives. Sadly and paradoxically, though, those of us who try hardest to do a good job may unwittingly weight the odds in the opposite direction. Most parents who try to make their children's lives not just good but stupendously great end up so ridiculously stressed out and exhausted that they have little energy left for living their own lives. The morning smiles are forced; the hugs rote and rigid. The bathroom becomes the only refuge where a parent can be alone—and many mothers of young children know that even their time there is not sacrosanct!

Despite our extensive, and for many of us expensive, educations, despite years spent building our own careers, we forget what it is like to discuss something intelligently with other adults. Many of us have no idea what's going on right here in America, let alone halfway around the world in Eastern Europe, the Middle East, Africa, or Asia. Aside from the logical answers that are easy to frame in a moment, like a personal or knee-jerk reaction to a local political scandal, we have few opinions to offer on current affairs. Try a little experiment. See if you can spend an hour with a few parents from your kid's soccer team and talk about anything *other* than children. Do you have anything to say to one another? What has happened to those once-fine minds we cultivated? Not only do we have no "life," but unless you count the daunting task of trying to figure out how to get each of the kids from here to there, on time and without getting a speeding ticket, we may have little mental life left either. There's no time or energy for pursuing one.

Working parents wrestle with real conflicts about the time they devote to their jobs, and feel additionally guilty if they take more time just for themselves. Quite often, parents who are at home full time today had demanding jobs before they devoted themselves to homemaking and caretaking, a consuming endeavor in its own right. In trying to reassure themselves that they are still really useful, many apply their high-achievement principles to child rearing, trying to make each moment "productive." Because society so often devalues the work we do in our homes, it is in some ways even more difficult for stay-at-home moms and dads to believe they are doing something important and stressful and that they, too, deserve a break. As one full-time mother said, somewhat grimly, "I know this is supposed to be fun and fulfilling, especially after all that time confined to an office, but it just doesn't feel that way because I can't even finish a sentence, let alone a book or a project! Someone always wants something from me. Even, it seems, in the middle of the night."

When highly intelligent people attempt to fill their heads only with the things going on in their kids' lives—their clothing, interests, activities, schoolwork, and social affairs—they end up paying far too much attention to small matters and too little to their own lives. Truly, Kids Я Us. How did it come to be that personal deprivation is a measure of commitment? Why are we so very proud of crazy schedules that allow almost no time for our own interests? Why do we accept that no "good" parent has time for pleasure reading beyond the monthly book group selection—and many claim not to be able to find time for that? How about time for thinking? We rarely make a point of scheduling time for the things we want to do.

The thought of taking back our own lives seems selfish: We unquestioningly accept that this is just the way life is, that this is what is means to raise children in today's world. No wonder we get so cranky and played out as we find ourselves wondering how everyone else manages to get their entire families to smile, at least once a year, for that smashing holiday photo.

For many contemporary parents, family life all too often feels like a series of lockstep, must-do chores. But even those who acknowledge that they are moving too fast, or at least so they say at dinner parties, feel anxious about the cost of slowing down and doing less. Extremists that we are, we argue that doing everything possible for our families, and doing it well too, has got to be the right way. It's an ascetic formula to aspire to, rather like eating only uncooked food and vegetables—which according to *The New York Times Magazine,* is the ultimate high-status diet.

Being active, making the most of every single moment, has to work; how could doing less be better? It's against our ethos. Some of us even feel anxious that our level of fatigue will interfere with our goals: What's wrong with us that we can't do it all—and maybe even more? Maybe we need some ginkgo or St. John's Wort to get us back to speed. It doesn't even occur to us that our exhaustion is a message we need to pay attention to. So we push ourselves harder. Giving our all to giving our kids the good life becomes a badge of honor, an embossed emblem that goes in the back window of the family car, right alongside the "My kid's an honor student at . . ." decals and team-booster bumper stickers.

This life of pressure and perpetual motion—the very essence of hyper-parenting—is giving us a generation-wide headache. It makes us feel tired and inadequate because no matter how much we have already done we could always be doing more. Guilt and anxiety become our constant companion. It's too demanding a way to live. And it doesn't make our kids, the ones we are doing it all *for,* feel so great either. They feel anxious about needing so much, annoyed that we resent them for needing it, and perplexed about how to make us happy—which, when you come right down to it, really ought not to be their job.

One thirteen-year-old girl confided in an adult friend that she felt sad and lonely, that her mother never had any time for her. The friend was surprised to hear this: The child's mother was one of the most involved parents he knew. She attended every school function, every sport practice, every game—he'd even seen her at the garden center, helping each of her four children pick out the flowers, fruits, and vegetables for the individual gardens she was helping them to plant in early spring. Yes, her mom did lots of things with the children, the girl conceded. But she was always frazzled and crabby, irritated at one or another of the kids for doing something they shouldn't have. What she really wanted, she told him, was just some time alone with her mom, just some conversation and cuddling that would mean that she, herself, was especially loved. But there was never time for that.

The way we organize our entire lives around our children's schedules and requirements may be unselfish, but it is not really good—for them or for us. Oddly but inevitably, the more we try to control, the more slips out of our hands. You can hold two balls easily, maybe even three. But try and keep a grip on four or five and every one of them will surely end up on the floor. And if they are fragile and break, they may never be able to be glued together in quite the same way again.

The popular movie *Honey, I Shrunk the Kids* comically portrays the events that follow a father's mistake when he has shrunk his kids to miniature versions of themselves. It's an interesting psychological idea—it's what kids often *feel* like—but, of course, in the movies he is eventually able to get them back to the proper size and ends up not only enlightened but a hero of sorts. Life, however, has no such "undo" option. (Or screenwriter, as we've pointed out previously). If we really diminish our children to nothing, or conversely blow them up into giants, they will definitely have a hard time getting themselves, or their self-image, back to human proportions.

So often the harshest words, the ugliest situations in our families, the times we say the things that *do* make our children feel about two inches tall arise when we are stressed beyond our ability to cope. And yet from our own past we know that a parent's single cruel comment can echo for an entire lifetime; those feel like the times they are being most honest. So many of us are spending too much time rushing around, too little time nurturing ourselves and our relationships. What does total self-abnegation teach a child about the most important adults in their lives? What does it say about a parent's sense of self-worth and, by identification, a child's obligation to respect his or her own self-interest, particularly when he or she becomes an adult? Can you really love someone else if you do not love and respect yourself first?

We have accepted without question the notion that a full and happy life has to be a busy, almost frantic one. All the chattering, beeping, vibrating, talking, and clicking devices we buy to help us keep track of our many commitments add to our sense that everything—most especially time—ought to move quickly. Slow reflection is a dated concept—though one might surmise, from the new interest in meditation, that at least some people crave a more contemplative existence, sensing that something crucial has been lost in our age of efficiency.

In his wonderful book *The Age of Missing Information,* author Bill McKibben contrasted two experiences—1,700 hours watching cable television and the for-real experience of spending a weekend in the woods. The book demonstrated how television has grossly distorted our sense of time and reality. One surprising example of how it has done so is with heavily edited nature programs that create the illusion that life in the jungle (let alone on the streets of New York City, Los Angeles, Chicago, or Dallas) is filled with excitement and constant motion. McKibben noted that even the very best nature programs, the ones most of us laud as beautiful and educational—what television really ought to be—portray lions as active, energetic hunters, frequently on the prowl for gazelle and antelopes, when in reality they sleep more than teenage boys, sometimes for twenty-three hours a day!

In the TV view of life, everything is calculated to move the plot forward, written into the script for a clear and comprehensible reason. Everything means something. The rest of us, the people who prowl around in the real world, have internalized that vision of life as a constant challenge and adventure; indeed anything less has come to seem like time misspent. We no longer accept the fact (and it is a fact) that a well-lived life must include rest, relaxation, reflection, boredom, along with instinct and intuition, as opposed to clear, rational deduction. After all, a Chinese *curse* says, "May you live in interesting times!"

We have to come to feel—and to model for our children—that everything we do in our daily lives must have a point. If life just goes well, smoothly, without a hitch, if we don't feel a little stretched and stressed, we call it a real yawner. If life lacks excitement and pizzazz, it's boring and dissatisfying. And then, of course, we are dismayed when our kids are unable to find some low-tech way to entertain themselves for more than a few minutes without complaining to us that they have nothing to do.

This image of constant motion and adventure has invaded our sensibilities. We are so proud of our ability to multitask. We end up truly believing that it is a good thing to be able to, say, juggle talking to an important client on the telephone, while sending a stream of faxes from the stove-side computer, while stirring the spaghetti sauce for dinner, while burping the baby who dangles over our shoulder—safely away from the stove, of course. And as we live our lives this way—undeniably getting lots and lots done, but never enough, it seems—we wonder why none of it feels all that satisfying.

Why doesn't accomplishing three things at one time feel anywhere near as good as doing one thing with your heart and soul—like playing a hard game of squash, reading a long story to a wet-haired child fresh from the bath, staying up too late and losing yourself in a novel, really listening to Oscar Peterson play piano? Those things feel great in ways time-saving multitasking never can—because attention that is divided is not directed. Because it is hard to care about something you are, by definition, only doing with half your mind. Perhaps it is efficient to live your life doing three things at once, although we have our doubts, since in our experience you end up making an awful lot of mistakes. But it is neither satisfying nor fulfilling.

By the same token, it is doubtful whether our children feel as good about finally getting that piano piece right when the practice session is squeezed between after-school drawing lessons and a 7:00 P.M. diving practice. One very hard-working parent shushed his child, who complained that he wanted a little time to relax on a given day, by saying, "That's how life is, and you had better get used to it." But is that really the way we want our kids to live? Is it really the way *we* want to live?

Not too long ago, in fact, mental fragmentation was considered a sign of psychiatric illness. Now meditation programs teach the concept of "mindfulness" and mental health professionals work to instruct stressed out, dissatisfied people on what it means to live "in the moment"—both of which mean to fully experience what you are doing in a way that the present tense is all that matters, and so you are not distracted by what you should have done, should be doing, or will soon be doing, once you get this chore finished. The idea is that being fully and passionately involved in your life, even in the daily minutiae, is the key to happiness and satisfaction. It may leave you feeling somewhat vulnerable, it's a little risky to commit to such immersion, but it is deeply fulfilling. As a wonderful, experienced, accomplished, jazz music instructor said to his hurried, overprogrammed, perfectionistic student, "Girl! You have to relaxxx!"

What an alien concept for many of us today. To open yourself to honestly feeling those notes as they course through your veins and insinuate themselves into your soul? To really concentrate on the warmth and comfort and sweet slurpy sounds of a nursing infant? To focus on and *enjoy* the process of washing and drying and brushing out your small daughter's hair? To work up a real sweat playing one-on-one with your fifteen-year-old? To really and truly live in the moment, as if time past or to come didn't matter at all? Can't fit it in. We are working too hard at trying to schedule and squeeze as many "moments" into our lives as we possibly can. And it doesn't feel the same, not at all.

As we parents have placed our children at the center of our existence, we have created a double-edged sword. What do our children owe us for this endless self-sacrifice to their supposed benefit? In a way we have inadvertently handed to them the responsibility for giving meaning to our lives. It is a heavy, long-term burden they did not ask for. And quite frankly, it shouldn't be a part of their job description.

In making our children our raison d'être, we are missing the point. Finding meaning in life is hard, yet it is something we each, individually, must struggle to do. Signing that important job over to our kids is certainly a convenient shortcut. It's nothing if not efficient, making their lives ours, so we can, we believe, share in the satisfaction. But it burdens them with a huge and unfair weight. Parental fulfillment is not a child's job. Children need to be free to live their own lives, when the time comes, albeit to do so with the obligations to us they feel a good upbringing requires—like calling every Sunday evening, and showing up, preferably with a couple of pies in hand, for Thanksgiving dinner. Of course we want to remain deeply connected to them, to be a "family" forever. It should go without saying that we want them to be good people, the sort who do unto others as they would have others do unto them. But we must remember that to do so, they must have their own lives, not exist primarily as a set of supports for ours.

In entwining ourselves so intensely, we are actually robbing our children of some of the most important experiences they can have while growing up. For instance, we overlook the fact that one thing every child really needs is to observe their parents living adult lives, up close and personal sometimes and at others from a bit of a distance. Our children need to emulate us—not playing math games with them, or driving them to skating lessons, but us doing the things that grown-ups do: running our homes, working at our jobs, engaging in meaningful relationships with our spouses and friends, taking care of ourselves, enjoying our own lives. For families to be happy and healthy, the adults' obligations and needs must be satisfied as well.

Children are meant, particularly in their earlier years, to stay close to the grown-ups in charge of their lives. In millennia past, if they strayed far some predator would certainly eat them—talk about an unsafe neighborhood! Our contemporary kids need to be with us to see—and to internalize—how adults act in an adult world. Observing us is one important way they will figure out for themselves how to act like grown-ups when the time arrives and the world belongs to them.

This used to happen more naturally in a world where the children orbited around the grown-ups, rather than the flip-flopped way we live today. It still is the case in most of the world, where subsistence and survival are so pressing that people don't have the time and energy to spend on power parenting. In times past, and in poorer parts of the world, providing food and shelter were evidence of love and care: Almost all of a parent's energy had to go into eking out an existence or the family would starve. As it has gotten easier to provide for basic needs in the developed world, we keep refining and adding to the definition of what it means to show parental love. Now we not only have to feed them, keep them safe and warm, provide them with an education and emotional nurturing, but we feel we must raise funds citywide so they'll have a really nice playground to enjoy! Not that there's anything wrong with playgrounds, but they are hardly a necessity along the same lines as food and shelter. It is very much a measure of our quality of life that these are the issues that parents are stressing out about.

Historically, it has only been in the past century or two that childhood has been so set apart as a totally separate kind of existence. In prior centuries, though it was recognized that youngsters needed adult protection and nurturing, children were basically expected to assimilate into adult life as best they could. Until children could help out with the very hard work of subsistence, which they started doing in basic ways at an age when many of our kids aren't even dressing themselves yet, they simply played on the sidelines. They were more like their parents' servants, rather than the other way around. By the early teens, children were working and living adult lives. They were often married a few years later, ready to start families of their own. In Shakespeare's *Romeo and Juliet*, the father says of Juliet that it is high time the wench got married; she was all of fourteen years old!

Today's fourteen year olds are just starting high school. Not only do many of us consider them not old enough to do their own laundry, let alone work for pay, but they have only the vaguest idea of what their parents do for a living. Our jobs are often too arcane to be easily understood, and other than an annual visit on the sometimes wonderful but unnecessarily sexist "Take Your Daughter to Work Day" (many of which are such large-scale, PR-managed productions that the young visitors spend virtually no time with their working parents), our kids don't spend any time at all watching us work. How do you explain the daily activities of an inventory control specialist, a bond trader, even a neuropsychologist to a grade schooler?

These are our business lives, which is where we end up feeling most ourselves and most appreciated. That likely is one reason why people work long hours, according to author Arlie Hochschild, whose book *The Time Bind* made the compelling case that many contemporary parents prefer being at work rather than at home. We have more control there. We get more positive feedback and appreciation there. We know what is expected there. Home is far less predictable.

This may be true, but it is not a road to mental health—or family happiness. In times past, work and home lives were not this separate. Despite the psychological distance that was then an accepted mode of interaction, children in centuries past may actually have had a more intimate relationship with their parents—even though the term "quality time" had yet to be coined. They knew exactly what work their parents did, since, more often than not, they were right there to see it being done. Children expected to do the same sort of work when they grew up: Boys and girls watched their fathers and mothers, helping, serving what became a preapprenticeship. Before labor-saving devices degraded housework, a wife and mother's role at home was complicated and valued. A house that did not have a person who could cook, make candles, gather food, sew, clean, and take care of all household matters, often including financial management, was in deep trouble. Women may have been second-class citizens, but they were a vital part of every family's economic survival. It was clear what it meant to be a homemaker, a farmer, a blacksmith, a midwife, or a baker, butcher, or candle maker. In working closely together, parents got a sense of what kind of person and worker their child was, and children knew who their parents were and learned from their skills.

Hard as we work today, many children have little or no appreciation of what we do, aside from parenting. One five year old's interpretation of how his two working parents spend their time "making money" is that they were literally responsible for the manufacturing of our country's legal tender (they are not). A twelve year old reports that his dad, a senior manager in marketing and a guy who is no slouch in the parenting department, "fills out forms for Kraft-General Foods." What's to aspire to?

As we have grown affluent, industrially successful, and more recently, technologically advanced in a service economy, an enormous chasm has opened between childhood and adult life. Today, adult life is compartmentalized; at work, we work—and feel guilty about the time we are not spending with our children and even guiltier about how much we may like being at work; at home, we parent, while worrying about all we didn't get done at the office. Furthermore, few of us have any idea of what our children will be doing for a living. So how exactly should we prepare them, what skills ought we try to impart, what really is "good" parenting?

Our zero tolerance for error makes us feel like we are disappointing everyone, everywhere. Our employers, because we can never work long or hard enough, not with all this new technology and information that we could be making great use of, if only we didn't have to eat, sleep, and raise our children. Our children, because it is hard to give to them everything we believe we should. But perhaps most of all, we disappoint ourselves. Because our own expectations are unrealistic and there is no time left over for doing the things that make us feel happy and whole. And it's awful to feel that we have no hope of ever becoming the type of person we always told ourselves we would be.

Many of us have lost touch with the joy we could feel in this phase in our lives, the pleasure of connection that helps us feel recharged and replenished, the sense of how wonderful and real what we are doing is. Once the long and difficult child-rearing years are behind them, most parents feel that the nest is terribly empty. But living life in the regretful "it might have been" mode is nowhere near as fulfilling as living right in the here and now.

As we rush around trying to get out the door, we may miss completely, for instance, the sweetness behind the three year old's effort to take upon herself the task of feeding the family cat. Feeling so perpetually put upon, all we end up noticing is the mess she has made all over the floor. If we weren't so distracted by some phone call and the long list of places we need to get to, by the chores we have to do for the older children's school projects or plays, practices that must be attended, purchases and repairs we need to make, we might be free enough to cherish this as a wonderful moment in a (long—for let's be frank and admit that it is not all pleasure) day with a small child. Every family must hurry sometimes, but many of us are always on the run, rarely relaxed even at home. We are diminishing the notion of home as a safe harbor and depriving ourselves and our children of having even one place where you can always be just the way you are.

A parent needs to be there and relaxed to really listen. Children don't tend to ask the big and important questions on the evenings we've scheduled "family time"; in fact, those tend to be the occasions they'd rather hole up in their bedrooms, use the computer or play Nintendo, and chat on the phone. This kind of interaction came about much more naturally when there was at least one day a week—the traditional Sabbath—for attending religious services, sitting beside Mom and Dad, and doing no work at all. Many families today are pleasantly surprised by how wonderful it feels to stay home a weekend day and just do nothing—but few, including our own, are willing to give up weekend soccer for a traditional day of rest. How many of us are willing to schedule that sort of day on a regular basis?

So what happens is that many parents report that the most important conversations they have with their children—you know, where do babies come from and do you miss your dad since he died and I met this really cool girl at the pool last week—actually come up sideways, in the car, in the kitchen, as the two of you are cleaning up after dinner together, or as you are tucking a sleepy and relaxed child into bed at night ("Dad, I have a question . . ."). And those are the lucky parents. Many sadly say that their kids hardly talk to them at all.

The important and meaningful connections that make relationships rewarding, and not just hard work, defy scheduling. They cannot be put on, or crossed off, a list, or squeezed into an hour at the end of the day, twice a week. They arise when a child feels he or she is being focused on, unhurried, safe from interruption, and free to wander and wonder in a conversational way. They happen because you are there with nothing particular to accomplish. They most decidedly do *not* happen when we are following Frederick Taylor's mandate to use every moment efficiently.

The real stuff of life is inefficient and messy. We need to accept that and allow for it in our lives. A good life cannot be planned and scheduled three months in advance, even with the most expensive, sophisticated personal organizing systems or the fanciest exotic vacations. Important conversations and connections come about when you are open and receptive, when you feel relaxed, fed, and have nothing you are trying to accomplish. We all need more such unplanned—and, most important, unplannable—moments in our lives, even if they must come at the expense of karate or piano lessons.

It is true that each of us has only twenty-four hours a day to work with. Certain requirements must be met: We must do our jobs, provide for the most basic needs of our families, eat and sleep. If all that is left goes toward maximizing the children's quality of life, what's left for us? How much energy remains for our own lives, our own relationships? The psychologist John Rosemond is fond of saying that too many women today are married to their children. It's a sentiment worth thinking about. For some families, his comment is unfortunately a masterpiece of understatement, even if somewhat sexist. Because in them, parents and children are joined at the hip, Siamese twins and triplets who can never keep track of whose life it is, anyway.

If couples, both men and women, ignore doing little things that help keep their marriage solid and renewed and themselves warmly connected as a couple, their children will have lots of parent time but will not experience a good male-female relationship. What good is all that Mommy or Daddy time, in the long run, if in the end your parents have nothing in common and want little to do with one another? That's not a scenario any child with the wisdom to see the future, which of course they do not always have, would choose.

A fulfilling adult life has many facets, some of which do not include children. Every couple needs time to be a couple—time alone, to cherish being together, to talk about the things that are going on in their lives (and not only about their children), to hope and dream and plan for the future, to enjoy the things about one another that brought them together in the first place, to make love. Few marriages can endure long periods of time without some major investment and involvement in the relationship.

And married or not, every adult should have some aspects of life that are his or hers alone. Whether you work outside the home or not, whether your spouse shares the same passions or not, if you have always enjoyed going to the theater, or painting, or working in a garden, you should be able to construct a life that has some room for doing just that, so you can feel replenished. So you can feel like a person who matters. Dreams should not die entirely just because you are a parent.

It has to be okay to let go of the reins sometimes. Sanity requires it, and children benefit in numerous ways. They certainly do better in a home where the parents are satisfied with their lot in life. Fulfilled, happy, loving, and occasionally spontaneous parents are better parents—but it is hard to be fulfilled and/or happy if you have no time to yourself.

Children will also grow up with more trust and less anxiety if they are allowed, even encouraged, to experience the world as a relatively safe place, filled with plenty of people who love and care deeply for them. Parents are supposed to have a life apart from their children. Investing in your marriage, and in yourself, is not selfish, although it does feel great. Time with your spouse, seeing a movie, having a romantic dinner, playing tennis, or whatever helps you feel close, is a gift to the *entire* family.

There is an important symbolic irony, however, to the fact that many of us need to be reassured that taking time to enjoy an adult life, to cherish a marital relationship, and to fulfill our own highly individual needs as people and adults must be justified as being "good for the entire family." Shouldn't it be enough for it to be good for us too?

We need to get back to some real notions, like a full life needs some boundaries so we do not feel terrified that we will fall off the earth's edge. Like compromise is an art. Like telling our spouse, "I really love you and am not afraid to say it, so we have to work this out so we don't grow apart." Like we love our kids and aim to do this parenting job well. Which means that they grow up to be whole human beings who will leave us. And while we cry over being left behind, we can still smile together at a job well done. It is hoped that as that particular chapter in our life closes, we can look at our partner in the process, our spouse, and feel the deep joy that comes from raising kids well. It will never win us a medal, but it surely makes life rich.

9

What Really Matters

What really matters in life?
What do I really believe in?
Who am I, really?

Are you kidding? When, exactly, are we busy parents supposed to find time to ponder deep philosophical questions like these—between kindergarten drop-off and a grocery store run? No one we know has an afternoon free to devote to contemplating Kierkegaard. Most of us cannot imagine ourselves—or anyone else who is both a parent and a homeowner, not to mention a professional, son or daughter, coach, friend, or any of those other roles we work so hard to juggle in our lives—making time to wrestle with questions like these. Earning money to pay the bills, putting food on the table, taking care of household chores, and organizing a schedule that allows everyone to get where they need to be does not exactly leave much time for contemplating the cosmos. The meaning of life? Most of us would rather have the mortgage paid off, thank you very much.

It seems possible, even reasonable, today to live a full life without ever facing an existential question bigger than, "What's really better, buying or leasing a Ford Explorer?" When confronted with life's big questions, many of us are inclined to give a reflexive, Cliff Notes kind of answer: "I'm on this earth to make a good life for myself and my family." But this rote reply fails to specify what, exactly, that "good life" means to us, let alone what ingredients go into creating one that will best suit the unique needs of our own family. As our media culture endlessly dribbles out values, priorities, and standards, we—like some sort of superabsorbent paper towels—just soak them up. It is easier to pick up what's lying around than to take the time to figure out what it is *we* consider worth caring about.

But life's "big" questions aren't big because some celebrated philosopher wrote a book and a publishing company hired a publicist to get a buzz going. They are important because, even without conscious thought on our part, the answers to them define what our lives are about, and direct the decisions we make every single day. Whether we've consciously thought them through or not, our answers to these questions shape our core values. They italicize what's important and delete what is irrelevant in our daily lives and to our family's future.

Perhaps predictably, we are not going to provide those answers in this book—in part because we authors are still very much engaged in the process of searching them out and solving them in our own lives (it is the work of a lifetime, after all) and in—perhaps larger—part because doing so is antithetical to our purpose in writing. There is no ten-point program we can outline for families to follow in this process, because ultimately, as we've said in other parts of this book, there are many right answers. The challenge is not in circling the correct response on a multiple-choice test, but in writing an essay—living a life—that supports your beliefs.

The fact is, we broadcast our answers to these complicated questions every time we take an action or make a de-cision. Whether we intend it that way or not, the things we do and say, as well as those we choose not to do or say, make clear to our children what we value and what we do not. Do we believe pleasure has a place in our lives? Is love a risk worth taking, even if being open and vulnerable means you might get hurt? Do we believe in charity, even if it requires sacrificing something important—like free time? Do we believe every person is truly created equal—or do we see those of higher status, lighter skin, greater wealth, or a particular religion as somehow more equal than others?

We parents simply cannot be neutral about values. By acting in a certain way, by saying we approve of this, ap-plaud that, find this idea weird and that one reprehensible, by saying yes to this play date or activity and no to that one, we pass our values, beliefs, and culture on to our chil-dren. Not a child alive really listens to what his parents say; they watch what we do and come to their own con-clusions, accepting or rejecting them based on how well, from the child's perspective, that way of life seems to be working. Based on their conclusions, they will choose a self that is most clearly a reflection of what we have valued or a reaction against it.

Far from being merely intellectual or incidental to daily life, ethics—the basis on which we decide whether to do something or not, to say this or hold our tongue, to affiliate with a particular person, position, or party, or to keep a safe distance—are the foundation for almost every decision we make in our lives, from the most mundane matters of our daily existence to those involving major life changes. "What do I believe in?" is not a hypothetical question. It is the foundation for how we raise our children and what we teach them about life.

Every one of our children needs to know how the world is organized; each needs principles to guide his or her actions. They need to know what is right and what is wrong, what makes the good guys good and the bad ones bad. They need stars to steer by. And those are the ethics we impart and the messages we give about what matters in life. In the end, those lessons will enrich their lives far more than gymnastics, piano, or the very latest computer. In this, our final chapter, we will explore some ways that our existential angst—to put a grand label on what really turns out to be a pragmatic question that impacts every facet of our daily lives—fuels and feeds our hyper-parenting.

Staying busy makes it easy for us to evade introspection—not to mention difficult for us to connect with our children in the ways that will turn out to be most meaningful. During pregnancy we rush around, trying to get ready. When our babies are born, we run around trying to get the things we think we need to raise them right, to give them the food and shelter and activities we believe they need in their lives. As our children grow, we work hard to nurture and enrich their brains and bodies. We oversee the details of their complicated schedules, work to smooth out their rough edges, and push them to push themselves just that much harder, all in the hope that our attentive parenting will make our children's lives work out well for them. When it comes to those big and important questions about values and ethics, we just assume they will get answered somehow, somewhere along the way.

In the long run, though, the way we adults live our lives

in front of our children matters far more than anything we can tell them about how they ought to live theirs. Like it or not, children are splendid observers: They watch us and see for themselves, by the choices we make and the principles we live by, what we believe is truly important.

One man we know recently made a conscious decision to become very serious about teaching values to his children, believing it to be something that he and his wife should make a higher priority than they had done previously. The very first dilemma he confronted was difficult: A family friend died, suddenly and unusually tragically, leaving behind a wife and three young children. Knowing how uncomfortable it would be for his kids but still believing it to be important, the father insisted that his two children, ages seven and nine, accompany him to the funeral to offer comfort to the bereaved children, their friends. He told them, "I know you don't want to come. Nobody wants to go to a funeral! But doing the hard thing, the thing you really don't want to do but know you should, is what being a good person sometimes means."

The family also invited the widow and her children to their home—even though the first few visits after the death were uncomfortable, teary, and filled with sad reminiscences. These occasions were unquestionably awkward for the children, but they offered an opportunity for the family to talk about how people feel when someone they love dies. These parents assured their occasionally worried kids that their own health was excellent, that they believed they would be alive for a long time yet. And they also reassured them that their friends' mom would recover, as she eventually did, more or less. Doing something you know you should, saying something when there really is no right thing to say, confronting feelings of awkward discomfort and moving beyond them—sometimes these are the things that being ethical boils down to. The essence of ethical behavior is *doing* what you believe, not just saying what you believe or taking credit for meaning to do it, if only you could find the time.

This father also felt that he was giving his children a dry run for the inevitable. He was right there beside them, showing them how people grieve and how they get beyond it, at a time when their connection to the deceased was not a particularly intimate one. He believed that seeing that death and grief were real also made his children less willing to think of gratuitous violence as acceptable. And a few months later, he was deeply moved when his young son insisted that a few other students in his class stop taunting a handicapped child. It certainly wasn't that his son had never been cruel to a child, even to this one, but rather that the father saw that the lesson was beginning to take root. For it to flower though, for the child to be fully convinced that life is richer and easier if you treat others the way you want them to treat you, will take years and years and numerous such experiences.

Values are everyday matters. Do you give back the dollar of extra change the waitress mistakenly gave you, even if no one has noticed? Do you apologize for yelling at your child? Do you let Daniel have that sleepover, even though he just called his younger brother a sphincter hole? Do you remonstrate your own dad for yelling at your daughter, or do you ask *her* to forgive and forget because, right or wrong, we all must respect our elders? Actions always speak louder than words.

That's not to suggest life is a deadly serious business, that both adults and children must be ever on the watch and are never allowed to have some fun. We can no more live our lives as saints than we can ask our children to be angels! Who wants a conscience so severe there is no room for fun? Our children will benefit enormously from seeing a real picture of what a good, balanced life looks like—and joy and pleasure are certainly key components. One woman we know, who had a grim upbringing, needed a professional to teach her that life wasn't supposed to be an endless turn on the treadmill, that her whole family would benefit if she started taking time out for herself. Aware of the irony in having to "learn to have fun"—sort of like the oxymoron of "just *act* naturally"—she reports that her life feels transformed by this revelation, and her children are happier too. Not that they exactly cheer when she heads out the door without them, but they definitely like the more relaxed mom who knows how to laugh and doesn't care so much about the mess.

It used to be that deep questions often seemed to translate into advice on how to avoid spending eternity in hell or how to minimize the time you had to spend doing penance in purgatory. That old-fashioned, punishing mentality seems dated now. Yet in a surprising and ironic twist, doesn't it seem that the way we live today translates into a living purgatory of sorts? We organize our lives as though there is no limit to what we can or ought to do to improve ourselves and have a shot at the brass ring, as though we must produce an endless stream of efforts and nonstop, ever-more-impressive accomplishments to escape the hell of disappointment and our fatal fear of failure.

One New York–area mother structures her life around auditions and rehearsals for her talented ten-year-old son, whose modeling and acting career is ever on the edge of that big break. He has appeared in two national TV commercials, came close to getting a minor role in a movie, and regularly lands small parts in off-Broadway productions. It's a hassle for both of them. The child is losing interest in his "career," and his mom complains endlessly about the insanity of it all. But still, she urges his agent to keep looking and encourages her son to keep trying, just one more time. "It'll be worth it," she promises him and herself. Maybe it will. But more likely, it won't.

If all we do is work and act as though life is a serious business indeed, our children will never believe that we see family as a priority. And they may not realize that we consider joy an important component of a good life. If our most intense efforts go toward manicuring reality so that the world sees only our life's deceptively highly polished surface, they won't grow up believing we think truth and honesty are important. If we push them to be better than everyone else, they won't absorb cooperation and caring as values. If we aim always for achievement and act as though acing that diving competition was the most important goal in sight, they will not consider balance an important human trait.

As we parents race our families from activity to activity, we should ask ourselves whether we are really doing what our heart tells us is right or best. By doing all these things, are we really providing our children with the sort of childhood we want them to have? Do our actions teach them what we actually want them to know? What are they learning as they watch us run so fast? Are we grown-ups really so rushed, do we really have to do all the things we've jotted on our calendars, or are we running so we won't have to look at our lives to see that they have become so devoid of meaning that we look to our children to fill them?

One highly successful businessman became severely depressed in his late fifties and went into therapy. It didn't take long for him to realize that his entire life had been organized around escaping from the tragedy of a painful childhood—but in so doing, he had structured and scheduled himself out of the sorts of meaningful relationships that he yearned for and which might have really helped him to heal. His long list of achievements meant little to him. If we—like him—spend too much of our time on a rush of activities that do nothing to create intimacy and feed our real emotional needs, we will miss out on the things that make our lives unique and meaningful, that make them feel truly *lived*, rather than just lived through. It's important to make such a commitment earlier in our lives because, in the end, time is the only irreplaceable commodity.

Right now there is a spiritual hunger in America, evident in the popular embrace of soul-soothing New Age topics like crystals and meditation. We're into discussing values, ethics, beliefs, and meaning. It can get a little "out-there," even amusing—particularly when people contemplate taking up residence in pyramids to tap their power, when public figures, like Ronald and Nancy Reagan, admit to consulting astrologers for advice on scheduling events of national importance, or when the slick ad guys try to convince us that buying a certain kind of car will add meaning to our previously empty lives. Books tell us how to nurture our souls with chicken soup or parables. Others offer instructions on how the rest of us can emulate the author's quest for meaning. But few can tell us how to be better people. That's one we have to figure out for ourselves.

Robert Coles has spent most of his career wondering about what makes for a moral, ethical human being, and whether traditional religious beliefs contribute to a child's moral development. In his book *The Moral Intelligence of Children*, he relates a day in his pediatric training when a distinguished pediatrician, Rustin McIntosh, raised an important question: What makes children "good?"

All the time we comment about "smart" children or "emotionally troubled" children, but we're not so quick to speak of good-hearted children, or the ones who upset us because we think they're *not* very good at all—they may, in fact, have traveled, already, a long way toward badness.

How often do we count "goodness" as one of our children's most important traits or focus on the lack thereof as a significant deficiency? Is it more important to be good or to look good? These goals need not be mutually exclusive, but we parents should know which choice we would make—and we should make sure our children know too.

Happiness and satisfaction and the ability to form close, connected relationships are not automatically compatible with the way we, as a society, are living our lives. Many of us lack a sense of community. We bend over backward not to ask favors of others; partly we don't want to impose, partly we don't want to be asked favors *of*. One of us authors admits to knowing life was out of balance when, listening to a friend's story of helping out a widowed neighbor on the day his wife died, she realized she'd never have been able to carve such time from her own life, even for someone who really needed help—although she'd always wanted to be that kind of person. Given what she wanted from her life, it immediately became clear that changes needed to be made, that extraneous commitments needed to be shoveled out of her family's life to make room for the things that really do matter, to her.

A friend, a successful attorney who lives with all the trappings of material success in an affluent southwestern suburb, told us that his life felt much happier when he was growing up in Burma as the poor child of missionaries. Although his current community is quite social, people are very materialistic and competitive about all aspects of their lives—activities, schools, possessions, even careers. All that competition pulls them away from one another. Most specifically, he feels the lack of caring and connection he was accustomed to in his youth when, as he recalls, "every man was your uncle, every woman your aunt." "As a child I felt embraced and not confined," he recalled. "With that confidence and security, you could be much more *there* as a person, because you didn't have to worry about what others thought of you."

Can a country like contemporary America, that so values competition, build communities that truly care? We think so. But working so hard to be better than our neighbors, to best the Jones's, makes it much more difficult. We must make some small but important changes in our lives. We need more time to contemplate the things that matter, less structured schedules to free ourselves up to focus on the things that really are important. It's not necessarily an efficient way to live, that's for sure. It is much richer and more fulfilling however.

Many adults decry the loss of values in America's youth, taking a doomsday position that we need to take decisive action right now, to impart real values. Just read the papers for the latest horrible accounts of children gone wrong—killing classmates; building bombs to bring to school; attacking teachers; abusing drugs, sex, alcohol, themselves, and their classmates. All evidence that little hope remains for America after we are gone. But there are two problems with that position.

First, it ignores history. A publication on adolescence from the Group for the Advancement of Psychiatry (GAP) quoted an author, who lamented:

> I see no hope for the future of our people if they are dependent on the frivolous youth of today for certainly all youth are reckless beyond words. When I was a boy, we were taught to be discreet and respectful of elders, but the present youth are exceedingly wise and impatient of restraint.

That author was Hesiod, writing in the eighth century B.C. As the GAP report points out, despite the dire predictions of social collapse and sweeping generalizations about youth that have been with us since ancient times, "each successive adult generation and society somehow survive the presumed threat posed by adolescents." We suspect that contemporary America will do so as well, that the next generation will teach us something about our foibles and ourselves, and will do many things better than we do—even if, in the process, they listen to the dark music of Marilyn Manson.

The other problem is that the exhortations to get our kids back on the ethical track may well be pointing the finger of blame in the wrong direction. It's easy to believe the kids are the problem, that they ought to be the focus of our busy efforts. Doing so absolves us adults implicitly—but maybe we don't deserve such an easy absolution.

The fact is that children do not learn values by hearing

Barney sing about sharing and being nice to animals or listening to our clumsy efforts to read them morality tales disguised as bedtime stories. Sure, these are good reinforcements: *Aesop's Fables* have had quite a shelf life. In reality though, children have always gotten their real education in ethics from watching how the adults in their lives behave. They do as we do, not as we say. As one psychologist described the process, they swallow us whole and take us inside.

And that's especially so nowadays when the unfortunate truth is the messages put forth by the popular culture—at least after they leave Barney behind—do not impart the kind of values we would openly want to pass along. A child who gets no ethical education from his parents may well believe that the world works like it does on TV and at the movies; that young people do meet, fall in love, and fall in bed together in one fell swoop; that such occurrences can constitute true love; that even if things don't work out, they have no lasting consequences more serious than the embarrassment of seeing each other in the halls at school. They may internalize a vision that vile language and violence are normal ways to resolve conflict; that no one can be trusted; that the business world portrayed on television dramas is a valid model for how to lead a good life. Programming executives state, for the record, that they produce what people *want* to watch, not what people *should* watch. Ethical education is the parents' job, they say—and so, apparently, it must be. We authors believe they are ducking responsibility, but this is not the place to go into that.

Man does not live by bread alone. In order to find satisfaction, we humans need to find meaning in our existence, to sense that we have some purpose to our lives higher than our most basic biological functions. Cultures vary on what that purpose is, but most deeply believe there is one, be it a goal or a cherished inner state that people strive to attain. We each must find a purpose for our life, a reason for being on this earth, a mission that transcends both the good and bad days, that sustains us in the verdant spring times of our lives as well as in the bleak, dark winters.

Some people say that they just want to be happy—and ours is certainly a culture that believes we are entitled to that. Just look at the commercials on any popular TV program: "Don't you deserve this car?" "Aren't you entitled to experience this kind of vacation?" "Shouldn't a person like you have clothes that look like these?" But many philosophers make the point that happiness is in the process, not the product. Striving for happiness will only lead to disappointment because true happiness almost always sneaks up when you are engaged in other meaningful pursuits and are looking the other way. As the late, preeminent psychiatrist and concentration camp survivor Victor Frankl said, in his best-selling book, *Man's Search for Meaning*:

> For success, like happiness, cannot be pursued; it must ensue, and it only does so as the unintended side-effect of one's personal dedication to a cause greater than oneself, or as the by-product of one's surrender to a person other than oneself. Happiness must happen, and the same holds for success; you have to let it happen by not caring about it.

Because religion has let so many of us down, our search for the symbols we can use to interpret and make sense of life and to give purpose to our mortal existence increasingly leads us to science and technology. The rational pursuit to understand and manage objective reality has brought us to previously unimagined heights. We can take photographs from a vehicle we've sent to Mars. Our computers can instantly translate one language into another. We can conceive a child outside the womb, using sperm from a man who is already dead.

These modern "miracles" are powerful and persuasive. But while they are dazzling, they cannot answer the fundamental questions and mysteries of life. Those relate to feelings, not to objective reality. We can find scientific answers to all sorts of questions in books and magazines and newspapers—but we will never find, in those places, an answer for the child who asks, as every child eventually will, "Why do you and Mom have to die?" (A question that has launched more than one family on a quest for a house of worship!) Argon has the same atomic mass no matter where scientists weigh it; the "right" way to grieve and to honor the dead differs from one community to the next. Science will never come up with the universal right answer for psychic pain because it offers so little in the way of comfort when you must face the betrayal of someone you love and trusted. Rationality does nothing to dispel anguish, to repair a broken heart, to fill a questioning soul. Science and objective medicine, in the end, offer a very thin gruel for our very hungry souls.

Religion no longer gives meaning to many people's lives, though for others it still does. In many ways, they are fortunate: The faithful accept that religion's path is the road to a good life. And that "good life" is reflected (ideally, that is), in every personal decision and action. It is not just about what you believe but about how you behave. As times have changed and religions have lost their persuasiveness for many people, some of us are left feeling lost and without direction, without our spiritual road maps. Our pride in being human, created in the image of God, has eroded. We have lost the sense of being God's favorite species. At a time when we are disconnecting from the idea of local community, we are also disconnecting from the bonds of family life. Who will we be able to count upon? How will we know what to value, other than the next purchase?

Our consumerist culture doesn't fill our needs. Material goods are like a sugar high, a quick boost with no real sustenance at all. As one man, a thrice-divorced member of a phenomenally wealthy midwestern family, puts it: "Without the right relationships, all money does is allow you to be miserable in nicer surroundings."

Many people worry that we are beginning to construct a virtual world, in which relationships between people—not to mention with a higher being—are replaced by the notion that everyone can be a self-actualizing individual. It is your own fault if you don't look out for number one. Television continues to mesmerize our children, as it mesmerized us two, three, or four decades ago. But the total electronic world may be leading us down a somewhat different path today, buying for our families a self-contained world, one which seems to promise that we will have no need for actual contact with another human being. If our children resent being dragged from activity to appointment to lesson, they can listen to their Walkman, play on their GameBoy, or find other ways to tune out the human beings in their daily lives. They can play chess with a machine, race a Mario Kart against a computer-generated opponent, or "play" on the Internet with an actual person a world away, with whom they will not speak a word or exchange a glance.

If we do not take steps to prevent it, we can now have a

world in which a family does not really interact with its other members. You need have no problematic friends who want to do something that you don't and no reason to bother working to harmonize your requests with the interests of another person. Talk about creating a situation that promotes an "autistic" way of interacting with others. Talk about a way of life that tells humans, the ultimate social animal, that we do not need other people in our lives. It is horrifying. The problem with our materialistic lifestyle is that it feeds only our most superficial needs and leaves our deepest longings neglected. In the end it doesn't take us where we want to go or get us intimate in a way that makes the darkest nights seem a little bit warmer. All that technologically designed "company" leaves people alone ultimately, and lonelier than ever. And because we feel so hungry spiritually, empty materialism leaves us vulnerable to every guru, huckster, and nut who confidently asserts that he has the answer to our existential angst.

We are good people, most of us. We try to be decent, kind, and try hard to do what is right. We sacrifice a great deal for our families, as this book has shown, and are willing to give more if it will make life better for our children. We pay close attention to what is required to bring our children up to be, not only healthy and successful in life, but emotionally well, something our grandparents did not typically see as part of their responsibility or as a factor in their family goals. However, despite our best intentions and great sacrifices, sometimes the things we do in the short run are not the things we, and our children, need in the long run. After all, if recent reports on the "aging gene" are to be believed, our children's life expectancies may be 150 years! As parents we need to find an ethical road map for our families that our children can follow in that very long run, whether we choose the generic "higher power" of the twelve-step programs, the God of Abraham, or a self-designed system of ethics. And we need stronger pathways that lead our families to more intimate sharing and more comfortable togetherness.

To become independent and successful parents, to give our children the real tools they need to go through life well, to teach them to think for themselves, we have to think *for ourselves*, to decide what life *means for us*. It is not an easy task. Nor is it one that everyone consciously chooses to take on. But like it or not, we do it every day of our lives in the way we act.

As parents, we have to ask what is the right way for us. What values do we want to impart? How firmly do we want our children to have faith in *something* they can believe in and value? What are we doing to make the right choices happen? The goal is not heaven nor endless activities to avoid a long stay in purgatory. The goal is to be living a life we are involved in passionately, one in which we feel active and alive. It is to feel fully involved with our lives so we make the deep connections with our children that they, and we, need. And out of that, if we are lucky, happiness may emerge.

It may be much easier to try and avoid this issue entirely, to bury ourselves in our work, the children's academic life, Little League, piano lessons, the American Heart Association. We can feel we have covered all the bases, including charity. But if we have not ourselves faced the question of what gives our adult lives meaning, we will not be equipping our children to face it either. And they do need a guidebook to help them with the hard questions of life, which start out as, "What do I do when my one favorite friend is saying mean things about my other favorite friend," and end up far more serious than that.

It is not difficult, really, to learn to tune in to what we, and our families, are hungriest for. But usually it is not what we are working so hard to serve up. Only rarely do epiphanies occur on moonlit mountaintops at midnight. In fact, when they involve how we are living our daily lives, they are as likely to hit us over the head in the kitchen, as the kids are bickering, the phone is beeping, and the frozen macaroni-and-cheese casserole bubbling in the microwave has just exploded—and you're already running late for basketball practice, the PTA meeting, or homework. Yes, a major personal crisis—like diagnosis of a serious illness, dissolution of a marriage, loss of a loved one—can give you cause to reevaluate how you are living. But so can the gradual realization that happiness has eroded, bit by bit, while you have been so busy chasing the American Dream.

Let's face it. Many, if not most of us, who can afford the lifestyle that allows us to hyper-parent are living lives that are truly charmed. We have everything we really need and much of what we want. Our children are doing well in their lives: They may fall far short of perfect, but few are in serious trouble. Most are performing well enough in school, are involved in activities, have plenty of friends and much to be happy about. America is at peace, something we take for granted but which parents in many parts of the world would trade almost anything for. On a given day we have our complaints, and our lives are certainly not perfect; but when we think about what matters, most of us already have more than enough of what we need to live a good life. If you can awaken in the morning in a warm and comfortable bed, with a healthy child (or several) asleep a few rooms away, if you have people who love you and a life that sustains you, aren't you blessed? In our quest to polish and perfect it all, we lose sight of that essential truth.

Our lives are rich and full. Overfull, in fact. Not satisfied with having 95 percent of what it takes to be happy, we are pushing to get to 110 percent. And it's often that last 15 percent that pushes us over the edge. Being realistic about what a good life is makes all the difference.

In every chapter in this book, we have urged readers to look more closely at the choices we are making every day in our lives, and what the decisions we make tell our children implicitly. We are so lucky. We have so much. We have *too* much. We need to learn to cull through our many choices, and identify the few that are really important—to *us*. The plans, the goods, the advice, the activities, the lessons—choose which ones enrich our lives, and which merely add stress.

If we really learn to know ourselves, we will also know when it is time to slow down and where we can safely cut back. We will know what we need, what our children need, and what we can all do without. If our relationships are sound and solid, we will also know when the scales are well-balanced and when they are tipping too far in one direction. We will know if everyone is getting a fair share of what they want, need, and deserve; we'll see when someone is not getting enough. We will know how much space we need in our own lives, how much our children need in theirs—and how much space we can afford before the mortgage becomes too large to leave time for the things that matter more. We will figure out a way that lets everyone in the family live more comfortably with one another—not perfectly, mind you, but more easily.

Then, perhaps, we will also learn to live more comfortably with ourselves.

And in accomplishing those goals, in knowing our-selves, we will also come to know our children. There is no greater gift, nor any better parenting advice. In putting a stop to our hyper-parenting, in measuring what we value, in making sure that everyone gets enough of what we need, the resentment we "parent" with can dissipate. And what a good life that can be—not only for our very lucky, much loved children, but also for us.

10

How to Stop Hyper-Parenting Now

Advice from the "anti-advice" parenting book? We weighed the question long and hard, and indeed the first edition of our book steered clear of parenting suggestions for one simple reason: We believe there is no single right way to raise a family. Every one of us needs to find our own path. Yet, since our book was first published we have been asked, repeatedly, "But what can we do?" So we developed some fundamental principles to help you make decisions about what might work best for your family.

Limit Activities. Think long and hard before signing up for new activities. Some families make firm rules (such as, one sport per child per season) while others make decisions on a case-by-case basis. But if you say yes to too many enrichment opportunities, the whole family will pay the price. Weigh the benefits of participation against the cost—time, energy, logistical effort, stress, and expense—to you, your child, and the rest of the family.

Develop Healthy Skepticism. Be discriminating about the advice you pay attention to. Experts should help alleviate stress, not add unnecessary anxiety to an already overloaded life. It makes sense to follow time-tested advice on how to childproof your home, say; it makes less sense to alter your family's diet dramatically in response to the latest study that promises some purported benefit, but will likely be contradicted and replaced by other findings in the near future. There are trends and styles in science, health, nutrition, and education, just as there are fads in fashion and home design. One year we are encouraged to limit fat in a child's diet, the next we are warned that doing so may be harmful; two years later, studies come out announcing that, in fact, it is okay to restrict fat intake in small children. Who knows the truth? In most cases, moderation and good judgment are the best standards.

Give Yourself a Break. Your family life is meant to be your own creation, an ever-changing dance between you, your children, your spouse, your family and friends, and the community at large. Do it your way. You only get one chance. The next time you experience it, you will be watching your children being parents. So embrace the uncertainty, enjoy the new dance steps, and know that because you are trying hard, because you are an individual, and this has never been done quite this way before, you will feel awkward at times. That's the human condition—it's normal, and it is fine.

Family Is a Priority. Relationships matter, maybe more than anything else. Our children are with us for a short time before they head out into their own lives, busy with friends, college, jobs and eventually their own families. We ought to enjoy them, and the brief flicker of time we have with them. Family life should not be overloaded with chores and commitments that add unnecessary resentment to daily life. If your family is too busy to hang out together, if you and your spouse hardly ever spend time alone together as a couple, adjustments need to be made. Family time should be as important as education, athletics, social activities, and other outside commitments.

Buyer Beware. We live in a market-driven society, where just about everyone is selling something, directly or indirectly. Go into the world with that awareness, and ask yourself whether a particular product or service will enrich your life—or merely distract you, appease your child, or add further complications. Do not spend your hard earned money on unnecessary products—despite how hard advertisers work to persuade you that life will be smoother, happier, and far closer to perfection if you buy just this one additional item.

Character Counts. A lot! Know that how you live your life in front of your child matters more than how you tell him he ought to be living his. Character lasts a lifetime. Live the values that are important to you, because your children will emulate your daily conduct when they grow up and go out into the world.

Be Unproductive. A life that consists of endless activities demonstrates to our children that we expect them to be hyper-active workaholics who run from 6 A.M. to 9 P.M. with no rest. It tells them they need to work hard at polishing and perfecting themselves, and says implicitly that we don't believe they are "good enough" as they are. It is good for families to spend unproductive time together—shooting hoops, taking walks, playing games, sitting and talking, reading. The fact that you, the parent, enjoy spending time with your child with no apparent goal lets her know you find her more interesting than just about anything else in the world—there is nothing that will bolster her self-esteem more effectively.

Childhood Is a Preparation, Not a Performance. No one ought to be on stage all the time, not adults and certainly not children! Kids should not be judged on every aspect of their performance in life—it puts too much pressure on them, and too much pressure on us. By definition, children are immature and should not be expected to perform to adult standards. Resist the pressure from coaches, and the media, that tells you how to push your child to excel early.

Pleasure Has a Place in Parents' Lives. Our brief time on earth is meant to be enjoyed, at least sometimes. Our closest relationships should be a source of pleasure, not constant pressure and tension. If we aren't having much fun with our children, spouses, friends—and even ourselves— we need to consider making some changes in our lives. Make time for a romantic dinner with your partner; every child we have ever known has done better if he knows his parents are happy, and are getting pleasure from life and their relationships.

Pleasure Has a Place in Kids' Lives Too! Childhood needn't be an endless treadmill of productivity and self-improvement. Kids deserve to have fun, down time, and empty spaces in their lives to fill any way they choose to. Many supposedly "fun" scheduled activities are anything but fun; they are tense, pressured times when a child is expected to perform. Remember, if your child enjoys his time with you now, it will stay with him forever. And emotionally at least, the relationship that has meant so much to him as a child will stay with him and bolster him as an adult.

Leave Empty Spaces on Your Calendar. Parents worry about kids' boredom, so they schedule their lives to keep them busy. But empty hours teach children how to create their own happiness—and that is an important skill we would all benefit from developing. *Unscheduled time* encourages children to create, imagine, see new possibilities that no one before has thought of, certainly no one designing scheduled or pre-packaged play. It teaches children to fill their own empty time enjoyably.

There Is No Single, Right Way to Parent. Every family is unique and must find its own way in the world—its own values and priorities, its own strengths, its own interests. So disregard the experts who believe they have the one right answer. With some caveats, we should all feel free to raise our children our own way—but in order to figure out what that is, each of us needs to invest some time and energy into learning what our lives are about, what we believe in, and what we value. Rush a little less; reflect a little more.

Trust Yourself. Don't believe the experts who tell you they know how you ought to raise *your* child. When it comes to your family, you are the expert. You are the best parent your child could ever have. In the words of the good Dr. Benjamin Spock, who said it first and said it best, "Trust Yourself. You know more than you think you do."

Endnotes

Chapter 1

Melvin Kohn, "Social Class and the Exercise of Parental Authority," *American Sociological Review* (1959):352–66.

Chapter 2

Vern L. Katz, "Two Trends in Middle Class Birth in the United States," University of North Carolina, *Human Nature* 4, no. 4 (1993): 367–82.

Alice Dreger, "Guilt Trips, and the Art of Blaming Mom for Everything," *The New York Times*, Tuesday, November 3, 1998, F4.

Lillian Bressman, "Tales of Mama: Doing What Comes Naturally," August 1976, *The Jewish News*, Newark, New Jersey, now *The New Jersey Jewish News*.

Arlene Eisenberg, Heidi Eisenberg Murkoff, and Sandee Eisenberg Hathaway, R.N., B.S.N., "The Best-Odds Diet," chap. 4, p. 81, in *What to Expect When You Are Expecting* (Workman Publishing, 1984).

Chapter 3

Clyde Hertzman, "The Lifelong Impact of Childhood Experiences." *Daedelus: Journal of the American Academy of Arts & Sciences*, vol. 123, pp. 167–80.

Cathy Lynn Grossman, "Chicken Pox Vaccine Slows Rash of Outbreaks" *USA TODAY* (January 18, 1999).

Matthew Fordahl, "Studies: Listening to Mozart Won't Make You Smart," *The Stamford Advocate*, August 29, 1999, 23.

Chapter 4

Erica Goode, "Mozart For Baby? Some Say Not," *The New York Times*, Tuesday, August 3, 1999, F1.

Jean Rich Harris, *The Nurture Assumption: Why Children Turn Out the Way They Do* (The Free Press, 1998): 15.

Sharon Begley, "Your Child's Brain," *Newsweek* (February 19, 1996): 55–61.

"Your Child from Birth to Three," "Cultivating the Mind," *Newsweek*: 38–39. Spring/Summer 1997.

Jerry Adler, "Does Your Child Need a Tutor?" *Newsweek* (March 31, 1998).

Barbara Kantrowitz and Claudia Kalb, "How to Build a Better Boy," *Newsweek* (May 11, 1998).

Sharon Begley, "Do Parents Matter?" *Newsweek* (September 7, 1998).

Chapter 5

Annie Dillard, *An American Childhood* (HarperCollins, 1998).

A. A. Milne, *Winnie-the-Pooh*, chap. 3, In Which Pooh and Piglet Go Hunting and Nearly Catch a Woozle (E. P. Dutton, 1926).

Held, R., "Plasticity in Sensory-Motor Systems," *Scientific American*, 213:89–94, 1965.

Chapter 6

Phillip J. Longman, "The Cost of Children" *U.S. News & World Report* (March 30, 1998).

Fred Waitzkin, *Searching for Bobby Fischer*, (Penguin Books, 1989).

Jerry Adler, "Does Your Child Need a Tutor?" *Newsweek* (March 31, 1998).

Rick Green, "For Many, Special Ed Is a Tough Label to Shake," *The Stamford Advocate*, March 16, 1998.

Gina Kolata, "Boom in Ritalin Sales Raises Ethical Issues," *The New York Times*, May 15, 1996.

LynNell Hancock, "Mother's Little Helper" *Newsweek* (March 18, 1996).

"Attention Disorder in Children Still Eludes Treatment Method," *The New York Times*, November 19, 1998.

Brian Knutson, Ph.D., et al., "Selective Alteration of Personality and Social Behavior by Serotonergic Intervention," *American Journal of Psychiatry* (March 1998): 373–78.

Diane Elliot and Linn Goldberg, "Intervention and Prevention of Steroid Use in Adolescents," *The American Journal of Sports Medicine* (November 1996).

Avery D. Faigenbaum, Ed. D., et al., "Anabolic Steroid Use by Male and Female Middle School Students," *Pediatrics* (May 1998).

Jane Gross, "In Quest for the Perfect Look, More Girls Choose the Scalpel," *The New York Times*, November 29, 1998.

Holcomb B. Noble, "Steroid Use by Teenage Girls Is Rising," *The New York Times*, Tuesday, June 1, 1999, F8.

"Our Quest to Be Perfect," *Newsweek*, August 9, 1999, 52–59.

Chapter 7

Nicholas D. Kristof, "Correspondence/Uncompetitive in Tokyo: In Japan, Nice Guys (and Girls) Finish Together," *The New York Times*, April 12, 1998.

Christopher Buckley, "Shouts & Murmurs—Memo from Coach," *The New Yorker* (October 1997).

B. Bettelheim and A. A. Rosenfeld, *The Art of the Obvious: Developing Insight for Psychotherapy and Everyday Life* (Alfred Knopf, Inc., 1993).

Ian R. Tofler, M.B., P.S., Penelope Knapp, M.D., and Martin J. Drell, M.D., "The 'Achievement by Proxy' Spectrum: Recognition and Clinical Response to Pressured and High-Achieving Children and Adolescents," *The Journal of the American Academy of Child and Adolescent Psychiatry* (February 1999).

Ernest Hemingway, *The Snows of Kilimanjaro and Other Stories*, (Charles Scribner's Sons, 1927).

Chapter 8
Bill McKibbon, *The Age of Missing Information* (Plume, 1993).

Arlie Russell Hochschild, "There's No Place Like Work" *The New York Times Magazine*, April 20, 1997.

Arlie Russell Hochschild, *The Time Bind: When Work Becomes Home and Home Becomes Work* (Henry Holt & Co., 1997).

Chapter 9
Robert Coles, *The Moral Intelligence of Children: How to Raise a Moral Child* (Plume, 1998).

Viktor E. Frankl, *Man's Search for Meaning* (Insights Books, 1997).

Index